W9-CTD-081

Twelve Original Essays on Great English Novels

TWELVE ORIGINAL ESSAYS

on
great
english
novels

edited by *CHARLES SHAPIRO*

WAYNE STATE UNIVERSITY PRESS   DETROIT   1960

823.09
S529t

Library of Congress
Catalog Card Number 60-6374
Copyright © 1960
Wayne State University Press
Detroit 2, Michigan
All rights reserved

ACKNOWLEDGMENTS

To the literary trustees of Walter de la Mare and the Society of Authors, London, for permission to quote from Walter de la Mare, *Desert Islands and Robinson Crusoe* (1930).

To Random House, Inc., New York, for permission to quote from Karl Shapiro's poem, "Crusoe." This poem appears in Karl Shapiro, *V-Letter and Other Poems* (1944).

To J. B. Lippincott Co., Philadelphia and New York, for permission to quote from James Sutherland, *Defoe* (1938).

To Martin Secker and Warburg, Ltd., London, for permission to quote from Brian Fitzgerald, *Defoe, a Study in Conflict* (1954).

To Schocken Books, Inc., New York, for permission to quote from Franz Kafka, *Diaries* (2 vols., 1948–49) and *Dearest Father* (1954).

To George W. Stewart, Inc., New York, for permission to quote from F. R. Leavis, *The Great Tradition* (1948).

To Viking Press, New York, for permission to quote from D. H. Lawrence, *Sons and Lovers,* Compass edition (1958). (First published in 1913)

To J. M. Dent and Sons, Ltd., London, and the trustees of the estate of Joseph Conrad for permission to quote from Joseph Conrad, *Victory*. (First published in 1915)

To Random House, Inc., New York, for permission to quote from James Joyce, *Ulysses* (Modern Library edition, 1942). (First published in 1922)

To Brandt and Brandt, New York, for permission to quote from Frank Budgen, *James Joyce and the Making of "Ulysses"* (New York: Harrison Smith and Robert Haas, Inc., 1934).

To Harcourt, Brace and Co., Inc., New York, for permission to quote from E. M. Forster, *A Passage to India* (Copyright 1924, by Harcourt, Brace and Co., Inc.; renewed, 1952, by E. M. Forster).

CONTENTS

v

INTRODUCTION

The English Novel in America

As Americans approaching the English novel, we feel somewhat handicapped. The language, while often strange, is recognizable, but the tradition is alien. Many attempts have been made to show just how and why the English novel differs from ours. William Dean Howells, for example, made much of an English critic who described the English novel as working from within outwardly, and the American novel as working from without inwardly. And Henry James, who tasted the best offered by both worlds, insisted that it took an old civilization "to set a novelist in motion"; yet it was also James who once observed that "the house of fiction has . . . not one window, but a million."

By reading English novels we become, in a sense, tourists, viewing a foreign country through its literature, unaware, quite often, of the special pleadings of our guides. But because we are reading novels we are getting more than a chair-side glimpse at other places and other customs. We are increasing our awareness of how people act and interact, and if the novelist is especially adept we are learning about ourselves and our potentialities.

Lionel Trilling has called the novel the "most effective agent of the moral imagination" of the last two hundred years, and certainly, from its very beginnings, the English novel has concerned itself with moral problems. From *Robinson Crusoe* (1719), studying the effects of human loneliness, to *A Passage to India* (1924), concerned with seeing how diverse human groups can seek unity, we have ample evidence of how ideas basic to modern civilization can be brought alive through fiction. Harvey Swados, in the opening essay in this book, shows how Defoe re-imagined the story of an actual neurotic castaway and came up with one of the great tales of all times, producing a novel which, by normalizing the abnormal, reaches us today, bothered as we must be with our contemporary doubts, isolation, and ever present loneliness. Most novelists, however, deal with group problems as these react on various characters. *A Passage to India*, as Richard M. Kain points out, expresses, above its comic and adventure levels, the constant concern of Forster's, "that of the attainment of harmonious union, whether between personalities, social groups, or contrasting ideas and attitudes." We are alone, we do seek unity, and certainly these feelings are far from being the exclusive condition of the English.

Similarly, two Victorian novels, *Great Expectations* (1860–61) and *Middlemarch* (1871–72), deal with matters of interest to the twentieth-century American reader. As Mark Spilka demonstrates, Dickens, like Kafka, was an astute observer of childhood problems, specifically with "the violation of childhood peace which defines existence." The Dickensian heroes never escape that experience, repeating it in their later lives under the dominance of harsh parental figures. By studying Dickens through Kafkan eyes, as it were, Spilka reveals the depth and subtlety of *Great Expectations* and demonstrates the belovedly misunderstood English writer's basic kinship with our modern world. But unlike Kafka, Dickens does include the possibility of faith in others, a faith necessary to combat a world of pain and isolation, thus giving his work an added dimension which makes it seem "considerably richer, warmer, and more true to our own experience."

A current American problem is that of when and how to conform or rebel, at heart a question of deciding at what point the individual must break away from the group if he is to be true to himself. George Eliot deals with this dilemma in *Middlemarch*, for, as Newton P. Stallknecht shows us, she has judged her characters in such a meaningful fashion that her modern readers are reminded "that human morality is a fascinating subject." *Middlemarch*, in exploring Dorothea's decision to remarry, also explores her ideals, ideals which are explainable in terms of the lives of the people of *Middlemarch*. As a result we have an exhaustive study of human motivation, of the interdependence of people and their mutual influence upon one another, certainly a theme pertinent to all countries.

In his essay on *Victory*, R. W. B. Lewis cites Conrad's definition of art as the effort "to render the highest justice to the visible universe, by bringing to light the truth, manifold and one, underlying its every aspect." In *Victory*, perhaps his best novel, Conrad presented all the themes that interested him by refracting them through the closely observed conduct of a tiny group of isolated people. He produced "a tale of violence that oscillates richly between the fundamental mysteries of being and nothing." His characters, Lewis feels, do not really grow, but grow more visible as fundamental questions are brought out. "They come from opposite ends of the universe, and they meet where opposites are made to meet: in a world of art."

The world of art often perplexes the reader of a novel, who promptly reads into any work of fiction his own preconceptions of right and wrong. Richard Ellmann, in his study of *Ulysses*, shows how dangerous this can be as he destroys the contention that Joyce's masterpiece is, in essence, a defense of organized religion. Joyce "searches the epic past, as he searches the present, for its humanity, not its supernaturalism," and he picked Ulysses as the model for Leopold Bloom because he believed Ulysses to be the only complete, all-around character in literature. Bloom, becoming the modern personification of Ulysses, acts out a simple, universal theme—the triumph of kindness and decency over cruelty and barbarity. Ellmann believes Joyce is one of the last secular writers to use the word *soul*, "and in his work the soul carries off the victory."

Too often we lazily allow our opinions of novels to be dictated by conventional categories, and one of the purposes of fresh criticism is to break through stereotyped conclusions and reappreciate good works of fiction. Joseph Prescott does this in his discussion of *Jane Eyre*, a work usually dismissed as "romantic." Admitting that there are large gestures of romance in Charlotte Brontë's love story, Prescott goes on to show the erotic strain "which grows more and more pronounced as the narrative unfolds."

Another unconventional study of a well loved but not too well understood work is made by Leo Kirschbaum, who sees Jane Austen as an active critic of her British society. In *Pride and Prejudice* she is steadily conscious of the role money plays in guiding her characters, for the novel "represents Jane Austen's attempt to see the real currents be-

neath a world she chose to regard as frozen into immobility."
Unfortunately, as Kirschbaum documents, "she sees, and
yet she does not see."

Novels, of course, are much more than frameworks for
ideas. They are carefully constructed works of art. Irvin
Ehrenpreis, for example, in a close study of an early novel,
Fielding's *Joseph Andrews*, demonstrates how the novel
progresses by shuttling. "For instead of an organic or cumulative plot of suspense, the structure of this story depends
upon small oscillations of emotion which gather, as the large
design, into massive waves of reversal." To the modern
reader, the changes seem like an inward conflict, but to
Fielding and his readers it was a process of "unmasking."
Fielding produced a symbolic comedy, without regard to
the principles or to the consistency many contemporary
critics demand of a novelist.

Similarly, as Gerald Weales shows us in his humorous
and loving defense of *Tristram Shandy*, Sterne forms an intricate book with the aid of a grab-bag of digressions, tricks,
and mechanical surprises. There is a consistency to the
novel, but it is one of attitude, not plan or order. The attitude is one of defiance, and *Tristram Shandy*, in essence,
becomes "an anti-book." Much of the Shandian defiance has
meaning for us today, whether the attack is on professional
jargoneers or our other assorted brands of hypocrites with
headquarters in Washington, Madison Avenue, Wall Street,
or the academies.

Close readings, concerned with literary devices as well
as construction, will discover inherent weaknesses in novels
as well as giving us an understanding of what makes them
so important. Charles C. Walcutt, a student of the naturalistic novel, turns his attention to *The Return of the Native*
and shows how Hardy uses the device of coincidence to

remove blame from his characters, with the result that "the flaws in the universe do not remove the flaws in the characters, and so the tension in the novel is sometimes painful rather than tragic." Louis Fraiberg, concerned with the inter-relationships between psychology and literature, studies D. H. Lawrence's *Sons and Lovers* and decides that the author's vision exceeded his means. The character and the ideology of *Sons and Lovers* do not always work together. Paul Morel, the central figure, never changes, and his failures simply repeat themselves.

We can learn, then, from the English novel, about how a novel works, and more important, about the human condition and the problems of man and men. Each essayist in this volume (as in the preceding volume on the American novel) had complete freedom to discuss his chosen novel in any way he felt necessary. The essays, therefore, vary from close textual readings to studies of structure, from Freudian analyses to discussions of existential themes. If there is any unity in this volume it is in the belief in the lasting importance of the novel as perhaps the best artistic vehicle for studying our lives. In this sense the English novel, in common with all other good works of fiction, becomes a part of our American experience.

* * *

I would like to thank Dr. Harold A. Basilius, Professor Alexander Brede, and especially Mrs. Barbara C. Woodward of the Wayne State University Press for their kind help in preparing this book for publication.

Charles Shapiro

ROBINSON CRUSOE: THE MAN ALONE

DEFOE, 1719

by Harvey Swados

.

Gladly he gives this tale to all mankind
To tread the hills and shores with countless feet.
Henceforth the globe itself swims in his mind,
The last unknown and insular retreat.
    —from KARL SHAPIRO, "Crusoe"

Tough minded journalist that he was, Daniel Defoe would have blanched if he had known that future generations would classify him snugly as the father of the novel. Indeed it was precisely in his greatest works of fiction that he was at pains—because the temper of his time demanded it—to claim that he was only setting down the unvarnished facts and that he had no intention of concocting romances or other questionable works of the imagination. But if this is a historical oddity it is hardly the most remarkable paradox psychologically of this complicated man: one must be particularly struck by the disparity between the materials he sought out so methodically and the literary uses to which he put them. This disparity is most intriguing in *Robinson Crusoe;* an examination of it may perhaps reveal to us a little more not just about the personality of Defoe, but about the vaster problem of human loneliness, which spreads like a stain as more and more of us are pressed closer and closer together. Since the pages which follow are merely reflections on this question, I hope that exception will not be taken to their lack of systematic organization or closely-knit argument, that they will be accepted, instead, in the very tentative spirit in which they are set down.

In the spring of 1944 I was cycling along the North Sea coast with several companions, equipped with neither map nor guidebooks, with only a turkey and other picnic necessities borrowed from the merchant ship on which we were employed. One of the most pleasant occurrences of that delightful day in peaceful County Fife was our sudden discovery of a statue about the size of a cigar store Indian standing forthrightly on the front lawn of a modest row house in the town of Largo. There was barely room for the statue; and when we saw that it had been erected in memory of Alexander Selkirk, we nodded wisely, exchanged some comments about *Robinson Crusoe*, and continued on our way.

But that statue remained in a corner of my mind, obstinately, as such things will. The world is full of statues of all sorts, and I have stared at my share: statues of authors and statues of their creations, statues of Montaigne and Balzac in Paris and of Tom Sawyer and Huck Finn in Hannibal. But I am not aware of many statues erected to the memory of those who have inspired the authors of great works, or who have served as the models for their characters. Is there a statue of Gogarty in Dublin, of Mrs. Wolfe in Asheville, of Thalberg in Hollywood, or of that little piece of *madeleine* in Paris?

I knew rather vaguely, I suppose, that Alexander Selkirk had been a seafaring man, that he had been shipwrecked for a time, and that Defoe had somehow made use of his adventure, but it was not until, browsing through Walter Wilson's rambling three-volume *Life and Times of Defoe* (1830), I came upon a hair-raising footnote that I began to sense what kind of fellow Selkirk had been. After he was rescued from his desert island, he returned in 1712 to Largo. There, says Wilson casually, "His parents, who were still living, received him with joy; but his recluse habits induced him to shun the haunts of men, and he constructed a cave in their garden, where he sought repose in solitude. . . ."

The fact is that, far from having been shipwrecked, he had had himself put ashore on a desolate island at his own request—and there he remained alone for four and a half years before being taken off and returned to happy little Largo, his parents' garden, and the cave which he hastened to dig. This voluntary commitment has been amply commented on (although I don't think it has been interpreted quite as I interpret it), but I am unaware that any modern writer has so much as mentioned the cave in the garden, with the exception of Walter de la Mare, in his wonderfully engaging *Desert Islands*. Thomas Wright, in his Bicentennial Edition of *The Life of Daniel Defoe*, does have a fairly thorough account, sans cave, of this peculiar man.

Alexander Selkirk was born Selcraig (just as Robinson Crusoe was born Kreutznaer, and Daniel Defoe, for that matter, was born Foe), like Hans Andersen, as Walter de la Mare points out, and so many folk-tale heroes, the seventh

3

son of a cobbler. "Wild and restless," he ran off to sea for six years after creating a disturbance in church at the age of nineteen. He returned only to beat up his brother for giving him salt water (it was a mistake) and to beat up another brother and his father and finally even his mother for trying to stop him. On Sunday morning, the 30th of November, 1701, he was obliged to stand up in church in front of the pulpit and acknowledge sin, be rebuked in the face of the congregation for it, and promise amendment in the strength of the Lord.

Understandably, this passionate young man went to sea again the following spring, with Dampier, the celebrated buccaneer, who had two ships to plunder French and Spanish vessels. Thomas Stradling, "a man of ferocious and quarrelsome temper," was master of Selkirk's ship, the *Cinque Ports*, and Dampier himself commanded the *St. George*. Arrived at the Juan Fernandez Islands off the coast of Chile early in 1704, the two masters quarreled and separated; but Selkirk, too, became embroiled with Stradling and had himself and his effects rowed ashore to Mas-a-tierra, an island roughly twelve by three miles. "When, however," says Wright,

> . . . he saw the boat returning, the horrors of his situation vividly presented themselves; and, rushing into the surf up to the middle, he stretched out his hands towards his comrades, and implored them to come back and take him on board again. The only answer was a jeer. The boat reached the ship, the ship spread her sails, and Selkirk was alone on his island.
>
> Unable to abandon the hope that Stradling would relent and come back for him, the unhappy Selkirk found himself chained to the beach; and, even when gnawed with hunger, rather than go in search of fruits and other products of the woods, he contented himself with shell-fish and seal's flesh,

4

and whatever else he could obtain without removing inland. He hated even to close his eyes. Often he cursed the folly that had brought him to this terrible solitude, and sometimes, starting up in agony, he would resolve on suicide. Voices spoke to him both in the howlings of the sea in front and in the murmur of the woods behind. The shore was creatured with phantoms. Then—cooling his fevered brain—came sweet visions of his childhood, the home at Largo, his mother, the fields he had rambled in, the words he had heard in the old kirk, thoughts of God.

After eight long months of melancholy and horror, in which he was "scarce able to refrain from doing himself violence," he "vanquished his blues," as De la Mare puts it, and set to work. He burned allspice wood, fed on fish, turnips and goats' meat, and came gradually to cope creatively with life on Mas-a-tierra. He had a couple of narrow escapes, once from a fall of a hundred feet, another time from marauding Spaniards, and when his ammunition ran out he raced barefoot after the island's goats and their kids, capturing and killing no less than five hundred of them.

On the 31st of January, 1709, he was picked up, scarcely articulate but otherwise healthy, by two marauding ships, the *Duke* and the *Duchess,* on one of which was no other than Dampier. Selkirk was made mate of the *Duke,* and subsequently master of one which the marauders captured, and returned home with about £800 of prize money, or plunder. As De la Mare notes, this "prince and prototype of all castaways" was "not so happy, he said, as when he hadn't a farthing." Selkirk enjoyed considerable notoriety after his return to England in October of 1711. He was interviewed by Richard Steele, was made the subject of a paper in *The Englishman,* and had several narratives of his life written, as well as four published accounts of his adventures. Steele, who saw Selkirk quite often, De la Mare says, "believed that even if he had been ignorant of Selkirk's story, he would still have detected the ravages of solitude in his 'aspect and gesture.' He 'showed a certain disregard to the ordinary things about him, as if he had been sunk in thought.' "

De la Mare continues, "After a few months' absence Steele met him again 'in the street, and though he spoke to me I could not recall that I had seen him. Familiar discourse . . . had taken off the loneliness of his aspect, and quite altered the air of his face.' "

It was after this that Selkirk made his way home and constructed the cave which De la Mare oddly glides over (I say "oddly" because it was one of the charms of the late poet that he could seize on an item like this and expatiate on it at great and pleasant length). The cave could not contain Selkirk either, however. This "unsociable" man emerged to fish and to wander around: it was thus that he met a girl named Sophia Bruce, whom he found tending a cow. They eloped to London; but when it was all over, Sophia was left alone and Selkirk continued on his lonely way. He drifted back to Largo, got into another scrape there which sent him packing; and after knocking around Bristol and Liverpool, he went to sea once again. All too fittingly, he died at sea in 1723. "He is said," de la Mare adds, "to have bequeathed his effects to 'sundry loving females'—including two who claimed to be his widows. But of this episode Defoe made no practical use." In 1885 his brooding statue went up on his front lawn. Had I known about the cave when I stared at the statue of Mr. Selkirk, I would certainly have gone around back and tried to discover if any vestiges of it remained, these hundreds of years later.

Now what strikes one immediately is that this man, who had himself put ashore on a desolate island in a moment of anger, who hid in a cave in another moment of anger, who estranged himself from his family and was kicked out of town in another moment of anger, was if not psychotic certainly what we would nowadays term a "seriously disturbed personality." Tempting as it may be to analyze the components of the disturbance, I must resolutely disclaim either the skill or the desire to undertake such an analysis. I am content to point out that the disturbance existed and would rather have you return with me to the period of Selkirk's fame, when journalists chased him for his story much as journalists of the 1950's chased the skipper of the *Flying Enterprise,* Captain Carlsen, who refused to abandon ship after it cracked in a hurricane, but remained aboard alone in a vain effort to save it. One of those journalists was an aging Cockney hack named Daniel Defoe.

Scholars are apparently still arguing as to whether Selkirk and Defoe actually met. Thomas Wright says categorically that Defoe "made a journey from London to Bristol apparently for the express purpose of seeing" Selkirk at the house of a Mrs. Damaris Daniel and that Selkirk "placed in Defoe's hands all his papers." On the other hand, back in 1916 William P. Trent was arguing in his *Daniel Defoe* (an intelligent and enlightening book, but so steeped in the dying genteel tradition that its author could not bring himself to reproduce the full subtitle of *Moll Flanders,* much less to quote from it or to recommend it to general readers) that "the makers of myths have not hesitated to affirm that Defoe made use of the papers of the returned sailor—who has not been shown to have had any—and cheated him into the bargain. A meeting with Selkirk has also been affirmed by some, and the house where the supposed conference took place has been pointed out in Bristol."

Well, whatever the truth as to the possible encounter, we do know that Defoe was thoroughly up on the adventures of the Scottish sailor, that he was a careful researcher, and that in many many of its details *Robinson Crusoe* does parallel Selkirk's story. I would prefer to think that they met, if only because I enjoy imagining the confrontation, in the comfortable home of the lady with the elegant name, of the dour adventurer and the dapper, elderly word-slinger; but I must admit that it really doesn't matter. What counts is that this profile-writer, who was in journalism for money as he had been in half a dozen other enterprises to support his wife and six children, from hosiery to jobbing to spying to editing, worked up yet another in his incredible series of true-life romances, with no other purpose than to pick up some quick cash, and that from his imagined version of the travail of the neurotic castaway came one of the great pure classical tales of all time.

We might pause for just a moment here to glance at Defoe's own life in order to sharpen our perspective on the man who became a great novelist almost in spite of himself and who won immortality by transforming an abnormal episode into a saga of man's conquest of nature. I think the use he made of Selkirk's adventure, or rather his transformation of it, will be somewhat clearer if we locate Defoe and see him as he was when he emerged into the great creative outburst of his sixties.

Defoe's Presbyterian parents trained him for the ministry, and although as a young man he decided that he was not fitted for it, he received a comparatively good education. Apparently he got a good grounding in science, too, and he says of his Colonel Jack at the age of fourteen:

> I loved to talk with seamen and soldiers. . . . I never forgot anything they told me . . . young as I was, I was a kind of an historian; and though I had read no books, and never had any books to read, yet I could give a tolerable

account of what had been done, and of what was then a-doing in the world. . . .

He became a commission merchant, lived in Spain for a time, married (not happily, it is important to note), wrote poor poetry on the side, and by 1692 had failed in business to the extent of about a quarter of a million dollars. Thereafter he was never really out of financial trouble. He got off by making a deal with his creditors; he went into the brick and tile business, became a prolific journalist and pamphleteer, and started to mix in politics. He found—and so did his readers—that he had the ability to write about current issues in a style that was direct, simple, and clear. But with the death of his patron, King William, and the accession of Queen Anne in 1702, Defoe, although an enormously popular Dissenter, became a hunted man. In 1703 he was arrested, thrown in jail, tried, and sentenced to pay a fine, to stand three times in the pillory, to be indefinitely imprisoned, and thereafter to be paroled. The extraordinary thing about this ugly episode, aside from the public humiliation of a man who had already earned certain claims to public distinction, was that Defoe himself managed to turn it to good account: the mob treated him as a hero, instead of being mocked and jeered at he was cheered and feted in the midst of his exposure, and his "Hymn to the Pillory" was very well received indeed.

Thereafter Defoe devoted himself more and more to political journalism. The politest word that can be found for much of his life and work in these middle years is that both were unsavory. He sold his skills to the highest bidder, spied for those in favor and sneered at those out of favor, and year after year churned out economic essays, unsuccessful poetry, humorous tidbits, and political correspondence, feverishly accumulating dowries for his marriageable daughters. The act of writing, apparently of writing *anything* as long as there was money in it, became as ingrained and habitual with him as it has ever been with any hack. Not infrequently he wrote semi-fictional biographical puffs for quacks or odd birds, and he seemed to delight in working up quasi-factual accounts of the lives of unusual characters.

Such was the man who, at the age of sixty, sat down to knock out a lively account of the adventures of a castaway, and who, in the incredible five years that followed, unburdened himself of the three parts of *Robinson Crusoe, Duncan Campbell, Memoirs of a Cavalier, Captain Singleton, Moll Flanders, A Journal of the Plague Year, Colonel Jack, Roxana,* and *A New Voyage Round the World.* No wonder that Trent comments,

> It becomes still more astonishing when we are reminded that during these years Defoe's bibliography must be credited with at least six other volumes . . . that his journalistic labors . . . remained considerable . . . that he wrote at least a score of pamphlets . . . and finally that it seems highly probable that he spent several of his summers taking horseback journeys in order to secure materials for his interesting and valuable *Tour Thro' the Whole Island of Great Britain.* . . .

If we think of Daniel Defoe as a typical Englishman, a typical Londoner, perhaps a typical Cockney (he was even born within hearing of Bow Bells), and of his tale of a man on an island as a typical English novel, with its emphasis on factuality, fortitude, and optimistic common sense, we find that we are cheered on by English critics of all persuasions, from Sam Johnson to Virginia Woolf to V. S. Pritchett (let us except Macaulay, who said coldly of Defoe: "Altogether

I don't like him"). Indeed, it is precisely those writers who one might think would harbor reservations about Defoe's genius who are most fervent in their adulation, who support most fervidly Daudet's estimation of Defoe as England's national author and Robinson Crusoe as "the typical Englishman par excellence, with his adventuresomeness, his taste for travel, his love of the sea, his piety, his commercial and practical instincts," and so on and so on. Thus Virginia Woolf writes of Defoe that "he belongs, indeed, to the school of the great plain writers, whose work is founded upon a knowledge of what is most persistent, though not most seductive, in human nature. . . ."

But it is Walter de la Mare who phrases most precisely this English pride in Defoe's normality, his rationality, his lack of neurotic undertones. Speaking of *Robinson Crusoe,* he says shrewdly,

> It is not so much in spite of its limitations as to a large extent because of them that it remains one of the most famous books in the world. It taxes no ordinary intelligence. There is nothing delicate, abstruse, subtle to master. It can be opened and read with ease and delight at any moment, and anywhere. Its thought is little but an emanation of Crusoe's seven senses and of his five wits. Its sentiments are universal.

I have no intention of calling these verdicts into question. There is no point in forcing a reading of *Robinson Crusoe* which would see it as something other. But I keep harking back to that odd Scotch sailor who hid himself in a cave, and I cannot but suspect that one of the greatest of Defoe's achievements is one which has hardly been touched on by all his admirers in the last few centuries. It is De la Mare, once again, who comes closest to it, and so I must quote him once again:

11

. . . if Defoe had really faced, as he might have tried to face, the problem set in *Crusoe* his solution could not have been in that book's precise terms. All praise and thanks that it is what it is, a triumph in its kind; and yet one may pine for what, given a more creative imagination and a different Crusoe, the book might have been if the attempt had been made to reveal what a prolonged unbroken solitude, an absolute exile from his fellow-creatures, and an incessant commerce with silence and the unknown, would mean at last to the spirit of man. A steadily debasing brutish stupidity? Hallucinations, extravagances, insanities, enravishment, strange guests?

Selkirk after but four years' silence was scarcely articulate. Crusoe after his eight and twenty years, addresses the three strangers whom he finds trussed-up on the beach with the urbanity of a prince, the courtesy of an Oriental, and in faultless Spanish. . . .

Well, this touches more closely on what seems to me to be one of the most intriguing facets of both *Robinson Crusoe* and its author: his ability to *normalize* the *abnormal*, to write of extreme experience in terms of sensible human reaction to it, to describe the lives of extraordinary people in ordinary language and in readily comprehensible but not patronizing terminology. Parenthetically, those who are curious as De la Mare was curious as to how a different Crusoe might have reacted, might consult an eighteenth-century narrative in the form of a journal kept by a sailor who had been put on Ascension Island in May, 1725, by the commodore and captains of the Dutch fleet "for a most enormous crime." The castaway, who lasted apparently until mid-September, left his incomplete journal lying beside his skeleton, where both were found later by Captain Mawson of the *Compton*. He describes in most affecting and horrible detail his inability to catch the island goats which both Selkirk and Crusoe had captured and killed, and his being forced to drink turtle blood mixed with his own urine. It is to be found in Charles Neider's anthology, *Man against Nature*, and is worth examining as one instance of the sufferings of a man on an island who was not blessed with the good fortune, skill and ingenuity of Crusoe.

To return to our theme. What strikes me as extraordinary is Defoe's instinctive ability to take the gruesome self-immolation of a borderline psychotic and convert it into the uplifting tale of a healthy-minded, practical fellow. Isn't this almost the exact opposite of the working method of many modern poets and novelists, who start with the seemingly normal, the deceptively ordinary, and proceed to reveal to our horrified but fascinated gaze (and to the disgust, let it be added, of those trained to appreciate an older, more "positive" kind of writing) that what lies behind the smiling façade is a cesspool, a jungle or a desert strewn with bleached bones? When we give our children *Robinson Crusoe* for their birthdays we are tacitly concurring with Defoe's estimate of himself as a moralizer and purveyor of unexceptionable sentiments, based on splendidly factual narratives—which we now see have been culled from sources as neurotic as the moralities and sentiments of any modern novel.

"The reappearance of Selkirk into the civilized world," De la Mare comments, "was certainly for Defoe a stroke of luck, but then, Selkirk, for full seven years before Defoe made use of him, had been 'a common prey to the birds of literature.' It was sheer ability that not only recognized the literary value of this nugget, but prevented Defoe from being too clever in his tale—though clever in all conscience he could be."

This is so, but it remains to point out that Defoe's seizing upon Selkirk's tale was hardly unique in his literary life, either in the character of the tale itself, or in the use he made of it. Defoe seems to have long been fascinated with those who were cut off from the world either through force of circumstance, by a quirk of nature, or from their own wilfulness. In the midst of one of his most prolific journalistic periods, he was, it is important to bear in mind (the description is Trent's),

> . . . a shunned bankrupt and turncoat, living in chambers in London or with his wife and children in a large house in Newington, seeing little or nothing of the gay society of the epoch, not even acquainted with the fellow men of letters who with himself give the age its chief luster, but, none the less, in no sense a recluse, rather the keenest observer of his day, the most intelligent, alert, and well paid of the prime minister's secret agents and the most accomplished journalist England had produced—perhaps the most remarkable the world has ever seen.

This is the man who in 1719 published a pamphlet entitled *Dumb Philosopher; or, Great-Britain's Wonder*, subtitled "Surprizing Account how Dickory Cronke, a Tinner's Son in the County of Cornwal, was born Dumb, and continued so for 58 years; and how some Days before he died, he came to his Speech."

This is the man who, maintaining his special interest in the plight of those cut off because they were deaf and dumb, became rather dismally embroiled with his beloved daughter Sophia's suitor Henry Baker, a specialist in the training of those so afflicted; and who, in April, 1720, brought out *The History of the Life and Surprising Adventures of Mr. Duncan Campbell*, subtitled, "A Gentleman, who though born Deaf and Dumb, writes down any Stranger's Name at First Sight; and their Future Contingencies of Fortune. . . ."

This is the man who in 1726 brought out *Mere Nature*

Delineated, about a boy who had been found running wild in a German forest and had been brought to London for medical examination. It is interesting to observe how Defoe describes this Peter the Wild Boy:

> . . . they tell us, he was found wild, naked, dumb; known to, and knowing nobody. That he lived a vegetative life, fed on grass, moss, leaves of trees, and the like; that he acted below brutal life, hardly a sensitive, and not at all a rational.
>
> They hardly allow, that he walked or stepped erect, but rather creeping on hands and knees, climbing trees like a cat, sitting on the boughs like a monkey, and the like; tho' in that part we must not carry our fancy beyond the fact, because we see him at present standing upright, as the soul-informed part of mankind do. . . .

This is the man, then, who wrote *Robinson Crusoe.* It is true that my listing of and quotation from his works has been highly selective. But for one thing, others of his works can be interpreted as paralleling, so to speak, those re-marked above; for example, it is hardly stretching the story line of a masterpiece like *Moll Flanders* to see it as Mark Schorer does: "Like *Robinson Crusoe,* this is a desperate story of survival, a story that tries to demonstrate the possibility of success through unremitting native wit." For another, I have wished not to exhaustively analyze Daniel Defoe, but only to indicate that certain personalities and themes fascinated him if not obsessively, at least recurrently, and that this may have been because these people and these notions echoed certain tormenting problems in his own personal life—the problems of the man alone. It is true that Defoe was a busybody, a progressive-minded money-maker, and in many ways a representative man of his time; but it is also true that he was unhappily married, that he was deprived of many of the stimulations he sorely needed, and that he died wretchedly, an old man hiding out from his creditors and abandoned by his ungrateful children.

The theme of *Robinson Crusoe* parallels, in its duality, the life of its author. Crusoe, on the one hand, in the classic posture of human extremity: loneliness; on the other, an unsentimental, hardheaded chap learning to make do with what he salvages from the wreck of the ship and manages to acquire on the island. So Defoe was, as we have seen, at times ostracized and cut off from the best society of his time; and yet, as the judicious biographer James Sutherland observes, he "enjoyed the mere variety of human life, the bustle of active people, the shopkeeper scratching his head with his pen, the fine lady cheapening a piece of silk, the beggar limping by on his crutches, the stir and commotion of market-day in a small town, the forest of shipping on the river at Gravesend." It is no wonder that his readers were "the small shopkeepers and artisans, the publicans, the footmen and servant wenches, the soldiers and sailors, those who could read but who had neither the time nor the inclination to read very much."

The most recent biographer of Defoe, Brian Fitzgerald, writing from what is apparently a Marxist orientation, puts it this way:

> He could compensate himself for all the failures of his life—for his bankruptcy, for the degradation of his imprisonment, and the claustrophobic fear of confinement that haunted him ever afterwards—by becoming the captain of his soul and the master of his fate on an imaginary uninhabited island in the North Atlantic. He could compensate himself for the humiliations he had suffered in public life by doing the actions of government he had never been able to perform in reality, by showing his capacity for ruling and directing and colonising. No longer need he concern himself with the remote and more abstract problems of hu-

man society; he could, through the power of his imagination, become the monarch of all he surveyed. . . .

Whatever our reservations about the manner of Mr. Fitzgerald's expression, we must grant that this does make sense, as does his description of *Robinson Crusoe* as "the great allegory of the capitalist system. Crusoe," he says,

> . . . who was Defoe projected, was the supreme affirmation of the individual. Like the lively, enterprising merchants and tradesmen, the middle class, the bourgeoisie, then in the full flush of revolutionary triumph, Robinson Crusoe renounces the past and prepares to make his own history. . . . Crusoe triumphed—as did the bourgeois capitalist—by his faith in himself, his naive optimism, which enabled him to overcome both his own folly in risking his fortune and the cruelty and the savage hostility of his fellow-men, and to found his ideal colony beyond the seas. He was the empire-builder, the man who challenged nature and won; his reward was calculated down to the last threepence, and it was well earned.

This fits in rather comfortably with Sutherland's assertion that

> . . . if Defoe's public was drawn chiefly from the middle and lower classes, that public had got an epic entirely after its own heart, with a hero it could understand and admire because he was taken from its own ranks. Crusoe may be all Mankind in difficulties, but he is first of all an Englishman of the lower middle classes making the best of things.

His story is told in "the prose of democracy, a prose which in modern England with its inhibitions and its class consciousness has almost been parsed out of existence."

It may be objected that all this accounts for Crusoe's popularity in his own day, but not necessarily thereafter—

the easiest kind of post facto analysis. It may be objected that it borders on the obvious to assert that Daniel Defoe, like so many other creative minds throughout the ages, was piqued (if not tormented) by the problems of loneliness and isolation, but that he turned them to account for the cash customers of his day by presenting them as healthy problems, as susceptible of solution as the problems of trade or empire. The real question, it may be argued, is why *Robinson Crusoe* has persisted in its popularity in the several hundred years since its first printing, down through a time when interest would seem more likely to center not on what this ingenious islander does with his goats and his salvaged tools, but rather on his dreams and nightmares, on what he substitutes for female companionship for more than twenty-eight years, and on the symbolic richness of his punishment and redemption.

I have no answers to this question beyond those which have already been given by time and by scholars and critics. Before the beginning of the twentieth century, we know, there had already appeared at least seven hundred editions, translations, and imitations of the story. In our time their number has multiplied, perhaps beyond counting. In the eighteenth century, Sheridan wrote a popular pantomime, with David Garrick playing Crusoe; in the nineteenth, Offenbach composed the music for an opera based on the adventures of our hero; in the twentieth, Luis Bunuel, the gifted Spanish surrealist movie-maker, was intrigued enough with Robinson Crusoe—despite the fact that he claims not to have liked the book—to make from it a thoroughly absorbing movie, one which has moments of incandescence, with Daniel O'Herlihy as a perfectly right Crusoe. In the eighteenth century Crusoe was used as the basis for lectures in classical political economy; in the twentieth, as we have seen, as ideal fuel for Marxian analysis.

But now, in our own day, something does seem to be happening. The book which Maxim Gorky characterized apothegmatically as "the Bible of the Unconquerable" is being turned over to the kiddies. It is not being shared with them, like *Alice in Wonderland* or even *Huckleberry Finn;* in an age in which hillbillies gape at the Sadlers Wells Ballet on their barroom screens and intellectuals leaf desperately through their expensive paperbacks in search of entertainment which will not be entertaining, *Robinson Crusoe* does not seem to be read often by those past the age of confirmation (even Bunuel's intriguing and sensitive film is recommended for the impressionable young alone).

The reader may now begin to suspect, with reason, that what I have been attempting to do is to push *Robinson Crusoe* for the adult trade. (Children have as yet no need to be so instructed—although even *that* audience is becoming so violently sophisticated that one may tremble for its future capacity to be enthralled by the doings of a single man, neither bubble-headed nor space-gunned, who teaches a parrot to talk and learns by trial and error how to bake bread and fire pottery.) To be sure, there are many ways of awakening, or re-awakening, reader interest in a classic work. We may rhapsodize over the plot, or story development, but only, it seems to me, if we can be reasonably certain—as in a Portuguese or Tibetan classic—that it has remained generally unknown. We may linger admiringly over the author's periods and cherish the subtleties of his rhythmic ebbs and flows, but not, it seems to me, when the author wields the serviceable but uninspiring "prose of democracy." We may fall in with the current fad of playing locksmith, fumbling among the unwieldy bunch of keys that constitute our critical armory for the one that will magically unlock the work and reveal the symbolism presumably hidden within—but Thomas Wright, who maintained stoutly for years (basing himself on an offhand remark of Defoe's) that *Robinson Crusoe* was a deliberate allegory, a direct reflection of Defoe's own life, and that Defoe for nearly twenty-nine years had led a life of silence, was at length forced to admit that he had been the victim of his own theorizing; and I have no desire to lay the foundations for such a future admission.

We may finally—which is what I have attempted—look to see if, how, in what way, the passions and problems of the author have paralleled ours so many years later. If we then find Defoe to be contemporary—not in manner necessarily, nor even in outlook, but in *preoccupation*—then surely he merits pride of place alongside those in our time who have been preoccupied too with loneliness and isolation but who, much more torn than he with the agony of doubt, have hesitated to address themselves to the Unconquerable and so have become the tribunes of the Unsure.

Here, however, we enter other realms. I would not contest the obvious truth that *Robinson Crusoe* has been read over the years not primarily because of what it says, or omits, about loneliness, but because it appeals to the busy child in us all, because it is a practical and entertaining manual in the domestication of nature, and because it is a painless and un-frightening guide to the exotic. To the extent that it continues to be read, it can be seen as still providing the same kind of refreshment to the same kind of people. But I have been addressing myself in these lines, I suppose, to the Unsure, to those who increasingly attempt to distinguish themselves from the masses by ignoring escapist literature, even classical escapist literature, in favor of those books which do grapple with the problem of loneliness.

In the emerging mass society, the *angst* of the solitary intellectual is now being experienced, if confusedly, by ever-lengthening lines of bumper-to-bumper megalopolitans trained to dread nothing more fiercely than loneliness. Will *Robinson Crusoe,* with its cheery accent on the positive, still find acceptance among either the hypersophisticated or the great ordinary anonymous mass who have been its cherishers, as they have been the cherishers—at least until the coming of the mass society—of most great writings throughout the ages? One can only guess. It is entirely possible, for example, that it may be on the verge of yet a new wave of popularity for just these reasons, that now it will be read not as an epic of man's indomitability, but as a nostalgic revery of those old days when it was possible to conceive of the vanquishing of loneliness and the disappearance of doubts, when it was possible to conceive that by conquering nature you had conquered all.

"He who wants to escape the world translates it," said Michaux. If by his translation he conquers, if only for an hour, "the last unknown and insular retreat," has he not earned all over again the honor of our rapt attention, as well as that of our invincible offspring?

FIELDING'S USE OF FICTION:
THE AUTONOMY OF *JOSEPH ANDREWS*

FIELDING, 1742

by Irvin Ehrenpreis

Joseph Andrews, Fielding's first novel, might be
said to progress by shuttling. For, instead of an organic or
cumulative plot of suspense, the structure of this story depends upon small oscillations of emotion which gather, as
the large design, into massive waves of reversal. A good instance of this is the monolog of Lady Booby near the end
of the book (Book IV, Chapter XIII). She decides to sacrifice her reputation and to marry a footman, Joseph Andrews.
On reflection, however, the disgrace soon appears intolerable: she will save her name and remain single. At this junc-
ture, her waiting woman, Slipslop, informs Lady Booby that
Joseph can never marry his own sweetheart, Fanny, because
that beautiful girl has turned out to be his long lost sister.
Her ladyship instantly reverses herself and declares that she
will marry the footman after all.

To a modern reader the changes represent an inward
conflict. Lady Booby would like to enjoy a footman husband, and she would also like to enjoy the prestige of her

23

rank: since the two motives are incompatible, her plight comes close to hysteria. This aspect of her psychology was also present to Fielding and his readers; but a moral aspect, which we might regard as subordinate, would have seemed of primary significance to them. That is the element of un-masking: the baronet's widow would like to believe that she is superior to vulgar passions and that her desires are both respectable and rational. But "in reality" she is dominated by the same "low" impulses which drive all human creatures, and these are made manifest by her incapacity to sustain a rational decision.

Frequently, the unmasking is implicit: Fielding merely juxtaposes two episodes and lets one comment on the other. An elementary case is a prude in a coach, indignant at being asked for a strong drink. A few sentences later, a bandit holds up the coach, grabs a silver flask from the prude, drinks her health out of it, and declares its contents to be brandy (Book I, Chapter XII). In such reversals, Fielding's irony is often too quiet to be noticed without attention. A specimen of his light hand is Lady Booby's mode of addressing Mr. Scout, her lawyer, as she changes from railing at him to feel-ing grateful. "I don't understand your gibberish," she says in her anger, degrading him with a reiterated pronoun; "*you* take too much upon *you*, and are very impertinent . . . . *you* shall be taught better, I assure *you you* shall." In his shrewd reply, Scout queries her ladyship's description of Fanny as a beauty. "Beauties, indeed!" says the lawyer, "your ladyship is pleased to be merry." Suddenly he receives a title: "Pray, what sort of dowdy is it, *Mr. Scout?*" He sums up Fanny as "a poor dirty drab," and the reversal is com-plete: "Well, but *dear Mr. Scout*, let her be what she will, these ugly women will bring children" (Book IV, Chapter III; my italics). Soon after this episode, Fielding noiselessly

24

extends its implications by remarking that Lady Booby "was perfectly polite, nor had any vice inconsistent with good breeding."

Even gross comic effects, like Slipslop's murder of language, glide into subtlety if Fielding wishes, as when the baronet's widow reproaches the waiting woman for not appreciating her ladyship's scruples: "Thou art a low creature . . . a weed that grows in the common garden of the creation." Slipslop's ear is not so dainty that she can distinguish "Covent Garden" from "common garden," and she briskly spurns any link between herself and one of London's centers of debauchery: "I have no more to do with Common Garden than other folks."

Such ironies, unmaskings, conflicts, and reversals stand behind the full pattern of the book. This is a story in which many people set out but few reach their destination, and those get the farthest who have nowhere to go. At the start, Joseph Andrews is a footman in the family of a baronet, Sir Thomas Booby. Joseph loves Fanny Goodwill, an illiterate foundling who has grown up as a servant in the same household. Under the tutelage of the local curate, Abraham Adams, the boy and girl have developed virtuous and chaste characters out of their fundamentally good natures.

But the straight course of their affection is soon reversed. Mrs. Slipslop, waiting woman to her ladyship, has Fanny dismissed on trumped up charges of immorality; for Slipslop covets Joseph herself and feels jealous of Fanny. Shortly after this event, the baronet, his lady, her woman, and her footman all leave their country home and move east to London for the season. Suddenly, Sir Thomas dies, and his widow plays Potiphar's wife with Joseph. When the footman rejects her hinted proposals, she has her steward, Peter Pounce, turn him out of the house.

Here, with Chapter XI of Book I, begins the great geographical countermovement to the original London journey. Instead of remaining in the capital, Joseph starts back to the home parish in the west. After covering a good distance, he is beaten up by thieves and must recuperate at an inn. Meanwhile, two secondary movements have begun. Parson Adams has also set out for London, hoping to sell some volumes of his sermons; and Fanny, who learns of Joseph's accident, goes to find and look after him. Both these journeys are reversed. First, Adams meets Joseph at the inn and, while there, discovers that he has forgotten to bring the nine volumes of sermons with him; therefore, he joins the footman on the road west. Then, having got separated from Joseph, Adams comes across Fanny, whom he rescues from a would-be ravisher. She naturally turns homeward with the parson after he explains what has happened to her lover; and they soon meet up with Joseph himself at another inn.

By this time, Lady Booby has found London unbearable and made plans to establish herself again at her country seat. To prepare the household, she sends ahead first Mrs. Slipslop and then Peter Pounce. The waiting woman overtakes Adams and Joseph before Fanny has joined them; and she remains with Joseph in a coach while Adams gets lost on foot. When the parson, having collected Fanny, is re-united with Joseph, therefore, he is also re-united with Mrs. Slipslop. This foursome quickly dissolves, however, since the waiting woman refuses to travel with the girl. Going on by post chaise, she leaves the three to make the rest of their way on foot.

When Fielding is not advancing by retreats, he is generally continuing by interruptions. One scene commonly breaks in upon its predecessor rather than develops it. Almost every turn of events is due to some unexpected meeting of characters with one another. These encounters are the beginning of a sequential formula which normally stops short of completion. In the proper sequence, a meeting is followed by a second step, conversation. This leads eventually to disagreement, and the fourth stage is an intense verbal argument. If the sequence is permitted to proceed, the final tableau is a ferocious mock-heroic scuffle, uproarious but causing no permanent injury.

Thus, after the waiting woman and Joseph accidentally join forces with Fanny and the parson, Slipslop finds herself engaged in conversation by Adams. Unluckily, he chooses to talk about Fanny. Slipslop condemns his unclerical violence in opposing the girl's ravisher; and as Adams is impenitent, she points out that "want of shame was not the currycuristic of a clergyman." We are thus moving from the third stage of the sequence to the fourth, and should soon be in the last (Slipslop calls Adams a go-between, whereupon he takes "two or three strides across the room"), except for an interruption: the coachman comes to tell Slipslop that he is about to leave.

In the next chapter, Adams makes a surprise visit to a neighborhood clergyman. After a conversation based on a misunderstanding, Adams staggers his involuntary host by requesting a loan of money. The quarrel which follows goes as far as the limits of lawful dialog; and then the second parson assumes the pose of a boxer. But again the sequence is interrupted, by one of Fielding's deadpan ironies: "His wife, seeing him clench his fist, interposed, and begged him not to fight, but show himself a true Christian, and take the law of [Adams]."

After several stormy escapades, Adams and his protégés are once more overtaken—now by Peter Pounce, who delivers them from abundant embarrassments. He seats Adams

27

in his chariot while Fanny and Joseph go along on a single horse. But true to Fielding's pattern, the parson and the steward soon quarrel, and Adams leaps out, to finish his trip with the youngsters.

As the three of them enter their parish, they are passed for the last time, by Lady Booby in her coach and six. Here is the opening of the fourth and final book of the novel. The geographical reversal is over; all the chief characters are at home for the series of episodes which bring about the resolution of their separate dilemmas.

Lady Booby begins with an attempt at bullying Adams into refusing to marry Joseph and Fanny. Since the parson will not oblige her, she has a lawyer arrange for the couple to be jailed by a compliant justice. But this maneuver is also blocked when Squire Booby, her ladyship's newly-wed nephew, arrives, and his wife is revealed to be Joseph's sister Pamela. The squire soon liberates the lovers; their marriage plans are renewed, and Lady Booby finds her jealous agonies redoubled.

To divert the widow's envy of her rival, Fielding employs his meeting-fight formula in a variant peculiar to Fanny. Whenever the girl is approached by strange men, her effect is to provoke first an attempt at seduction through persuasion and then an outright attack. Fanny's main function in the plot is to be nearly raped. Joseph suffers a similar persecution from his employer, from Slipslop, and from the chambermaid at an inn; but he is dextrous enough to end the process short of carnal contact. Fanny, however, has more innocence than agility; and she requires constant rescuing. This is exactly how she joins the great east-west journey; for only after a vigorous nocturnal battle—with her treacherous fellow traveler, who has flung the girl to the ground—does Adams discover that the maiden he has succored is Fanny.

At an inn, much later, Fanny is kidnapped by the agents of a squire who had entertained her party. Peter Pounce in his chariot produces the felicitous interruption of that sequence, and Fanny's virginity is preserved. The very justice who, for Lady Booby's sake, sentences Fanny to jail, does not relinquish the girl without scheming to enjoy her body.

This motif recurs, near the end, at the zenith of Lady Booby's distress. A city fop, who arrives on a visit to her ladyship, sees Fanny alone and tries to win her. Although he fails, his servant is commanded to make fresh efforts. Pimping turns to raping while the servant talks; but Joseph appears in time to stun the villain and save the beauty.

Nevertheless, Lady Booby determines to encourage the fop's designs with the hope of separating the two lovers. Accidents assist her inclinations until she finds herself receiving at dinner not only her nephew, his wife, and the fop—whose name is Beau Didapper—but also Adams, Joseph, and Fanny. Thanks to a stormy night, they are all forced to sleep in the great house. What follows is the antepenultimate chapter of the book, and the one just before the denouement. In it, as Mark Spilka has shown, Fielding symbolically resolves the various roles of the characters. At the same time, he runs through a recapitulation of his narrative motifs. For during the night a whole series of reversals and unmaskings takes place; the chance-meeting-to-fist-fight sequence is played through; and Fanny experiences her last, most paradoxical near-rape.

After bed-time, Beau Didapper tries to sneak between Fanny's sheets; but misjudging the room, he leaps upon Slipslop. This error at three in the morning has a history older than Cervantes and Marivaux, from whom Fielding adapted it; it is spiced with allusions to Richardson's *Pamela*; and it anticipates the comedy of *Tom Jones*, Books IX and X. The scene reverberates across centuries: we have Guzman de Alfarache (Part I, Book II, Chapters VIII–IX) embracing an ass when he expects a maid (or a maid, as in *Guzman*, Part II, Book III, Chapter I, when he expects a lady); Don Quixote grabbing a fellow lodger's doxy and taking her for a princess (Part I, Chapter XVI); Pharsamon at midnight in the boudoir of his mistress's mother, while her "vieille" Marguerite, blunders into the unwilling arms of his valet (Marivaux's *Pharsamon*, Part VI); and "Mr. B——," dressed as a girl and bedded with Pamela (2-vol. Everyman edition, I, 178–87).

Improving on Marivaux, Fielding not only repeats the game immediately with a different couple, but joins the two versions through a causal link and a moral contrast. After a gambol involving Slipslop, Didapper, Adams, and (as a witness) Lady Booby, the light of a lamp corrects the mistaken identities, and all retire again. Adams, however, makes a wrong turn and ends up beside Fanny. When Joseph comes to salute his beloved in the morning, the error is opened and the farce reaches its second denouement.

The language in which the humiliated parson cries out his innocence has reverberations of its own. "As I am a Christian," he says, "I know not whether she is man or woman." In *Shamela*—Fielding's burlesque of *Pamela*—these are the words of the blockhead whom the trollop protagonist has gulled into nearly ravishing her: "By Heaven, I know not whether you are a man or a woman, unless by your swelling breasts." This of course alludes to the speech of Richardson's hero when Pamela has beaten off his attack: "I know not, I declare (beyond this lovely bosom), your sex." But more pertinent than such references is the connection of Adams' speech, at the close of the novel, with Joseph's defense of himself at the beginning.

> "Consider, child," says the new widow (laying her hand carelessly upon his), "you are a handsome fellow, and might do better; you might make your fortune."
>
> "Madam," said Joseph, "I do assure your ladyship, I don't know whether any maid in the house is man or woman."

Joseph's and Adams' honesty meet, across the book, unmasking the frauds of Mr. B——, Shamela, and her ladyship.

To untie the love intrigue, Fielding employs the ancient device of concealed parentage, through what is probably a parody of this convention in the literature of his day. Though there is premeditated comedy in the resulting recognition scene, many readers have found it structurally weak and have wondered why Fielding adopted it. Freud called this motif, when used in fantasies, the "family romance," and he related it to a child's dissatisfaction with his parents (*Collected Papers*, V [1950], 75–76). The motif seems to have had special value for Fielding, not only because he had already embodied it in the ending of his early burlesque, *The Pleasures of the Town* (1729), but also because it was to dominate his longest novel, *Tom Jones*. Similarly, the plot of his comedy *The Temple Beau* (1730) turns on a rightful older brother's regaining his inheritance from a treacherous junior.

In Fielding's childhood we find, as well as grounds for criticizing his parents, strong reasons for molding that criticism into a family romance, since many of his troubles sprang from questions of blood relationship. His mother and father had married the year before Henry was born; it was apparently a runaway match to which the bride's parents had refused their consent. Though the husband, Edmund Fielding, was allied to the aristocracy and was the son of a royal chaplain, his career in the army had not yet proved very profitable. His wife, Sarah Gould, was the daughter of a prosperous, knighted judge with a handsome estate in Somerset—the locale for the village scenes of *Joseph Andrews*—where Henry was actually born. Six children followed Henry in nine years, but only the youngest was again a boy. Colonel Fielding preferred London to the fireside; he would leave his family for long periods and stay in town; he gambled heavily and was fleeced by sharpers.

When Henry was eleven, Sarah (Gould) Fielding died; the colonel handed his brood over to his mother-in-law's sister and went back to London. About a year after the first wife's death, he took a second (but not the last)—a Roman Catholic widow, rumored to be an Italian who had "kept an eating house." According to angry relatives, the children found their stepmother repugnant when she joined them in 1719. Twelve-year-old Henry was said to have been beaten for intransigence. Soon, however, they were dispersed: Henry, to Eton; the girls, to another school; and the littlest to their grandmother, Lady Gould.

When Henry was fourteen, Lady Gould brought suit for custody of the children and for control of the property. Henry sided with her; the colonel threatened to remove him from Eton; and the boy ran away to stay with his grandmother. When he was fifteen, she won the suit, and he thereafter remained in her care. Yet he was a frequent visitor in his father's London house, and the colonel (who died just before the son embarked on *Joseph Andrews*) took a genuine interest in his career.

What Henry thought of Eton is suggested by the discussion of public schools in Book III of *Joseph Andrews* (Chapter V). What judgments he passed on his father are suggested by the endless use of rural society, in his works, to show up defects in the pleasures of the town. Fielding is no simple primitivist; his villagers are neither innocent nor benevolent. Nevertheless, he implicitly asks, What deep rewards has London that make it a more satisfactory residence than Somerset? It seems likely that the confusion of his relationships during puberty would have encouraged reveries of belonging to an imaginary family. The death of the father as Henry was about to begin writing the novel might have revived such reveries. And the parallels, as we shall see, between the life of Joseph's "real" father and that of Edmund Fielding (rather than Henry) would tend to support this theory.

It is even possible that Fielding's childhood may explain his unpleasant use of incest as a device for comic suspense. With five sisters, three mothers, and only a fraction of a father, he must have been exposed to incestuous pressures of an unusual sort; and themes which appear gratuitously offensive to many readers could have been purely comic to him. For this is how he gives a cliff-hanging peripety to *Joseph Andrews*.

In Chapter XII of Book IV occurs the monolog of a pedlar who had befriended the travelers on their way and has just come to call upon Adams. The pedlar reveals that Fanny, known to be a foundling, had been stolen from Joseph's parents. This block to the marriage is removed in the penultimate chapter, XV, when old Andrews and his wife arrive and Joseph is discovered never to have been their child at all. Here his true father also appears, in the character of a prosperous "Mr. Wilson"—who had given the travelers elaborate hospitality and who has also come, in the course of a premeditated western journey, to visit the parson. The last chapter of the novel contains Joseph and Fanny's marriage and the customary string-tying.

Fielding's use of the pedlar and Mr. Wilson touches on some traditional objections to the structure of *Joseph An-*

drews. The first relates to the way Mr. Wilson was originally introduced. Adams, Joseph, and Fanny happen to take
shelter in his house; and here, through by far the longest
chapter of the entire novel (Book III, Chapter III), Mr.
Wilson recounts to them an autobiography which is oppres-
sively detailed: like Colonel Fielding, he had spent much of
his life absorbed in the dissipations of London, but unlike
the colonel he had at last recognized the futility of his existence and withdrawn to a country estate with his wife and
children; unfortunately, his eldest son had been stolen by
gypsies. The common charges brought against this story
are that it has only a weak connection with Fielding's main
plot and that it contains too many particulars. Neither
charge is sound. From a "plot" which marches by reversals,
interruptions, and digressions, the sagacious reader quickly
learns not to expect causal coherence. Similarly, the details
are no more crowded or minute than in the rest of the novel.
The real blemish is that Wilson's tale is dull and repetitious.
The same faults belong to the other tales which are hauled
into the novel: the history of Leonora (Book II, Chapters IV
and VI) and the history of Leonard and Paul (Book IV,
Chapter X).

Yet while these inserted tales do not deserve to be read
in themselves, Fielding was hardly acting without skill in
using them. Not only had he the many picaresque prece-
dents before him. He also constructed the two longer tales
as negative analogues—to use R. S. Crane's expression—of
the main characters' careers. Leonora, the daughter of a
wealthy gentleman, lives in a town and succumbs to the habits which must tempt an urban coquette; her vices finally
ruin her. By implication, the value of Fanny's illiteracy,
poverty, and rusticity appears rather as a shield against such
enticements than as primitivist goods-in-themselves. Wil-

son's story, symmetrically placed at the beginning of Book III, balances Leonora's, which is set at the beginning of Book II; and his life displays a series of perils which Joseph —prudent, devout, and rustic—need not encounter. In the *Brothers Karamazov*, Alyosha's notes on Father Zossima's youth have a similar, though less disjunctive, purpose.

In Fielding's use of the pedlar, one meets another practice condemned by many readers. This character falls into position, toward the end, by a coincidence so flagrant as to trouble even those who have learned to digest the episodic quality of the author's design. Yet the pedlar's figure is in fact employed with several sorts of art. If the solution of the mystery is to be a burlesque of dramas like *Oedipus*, the pedlar acts as a highly ingenious parallel to the messenger in Sophocles' play. Furthermore, the successive allusions to him are an example of Fielding's skill in what George Sherburn calls "neat intercalation." His initial part is significantly providential. The three travelers have run out of money and cannot settle a bill at an alehouse. After other resources have failed, the pedlar, who "chances" to be there and to overhear the conversation, offers to lend Parson Adams' trio the sum needed (Book II, Chapter XV). Before going on, they tell him "where he might call to be repaid." At Wilson's house, Adams' mention of the pedlar's goodness spurs his host to insert a piece of gold among the provisions bestowed upon the travelers when they leave (explained later, in Book III, Chapter V). When he does come to Adams' parish, the pedlar sees a boy struggling in a river. He saves the child, who "chances" to be Adams' son (Book IV, Chapter VIII), and then he meets the father again. Thus Fielding has prepared us for both the pedlar's reappearance and his miraculous role.

It is well known that Fielding's profuse employment of

coincidence is his deliberate way of teaching us to trust in Providence. When the parson assures Fanny that "Providence had sent him to her deliverance," he preaches the basis of Fielding's own creed (Book II, Chapter IX). On that doctrine Fielding builds the principle that active charity—good works, benevolence—and not passive grace or faith, is demanded by the Christian's deity. It is to illustrate this ethical and theological argument that he contrasts Adams, as the ideal Church of England parson, with the other clergymen in the book. For deists, materialistic Anglicans, and Methodists all fall under his condemnation (Book I, Chapter XVII; Book II, Chapter XIV). At the same time, he is willing to allow that good principles may exist outside the Church of England, and exhibits a Roman Catholic as proof (Book III, Chapter VIII). These implications of Fielding's work have been analyzed by Ralph Rader (unpublished dissertation, Indiana University, 1957; see also M. C. Battestin, *The Moral Basis of Fielding's Art*).

Yet it would be dangerous to trust Fielding's exposition of sectarian doctrines. To High Church he assigns a rapacity and luxury which the lives of the High Church leaders themselves repudiated. To the Methodists he attributes an insistence upon the value of grace without good works which neither Wesley nor Whitefield would have preached.

The intricate, arbitrary structure of the novel has another function as well. Reading along and constantly finding that threads like the pedlar's goodness are part of the author's design, we gain a confidence in his control which relieves us from the anxiety otherwise aroused by the dangers recurrently menacing our friends. This confidence is unfortunately damaged by several oversights in Fielding's handling of his plot. But there are so many beautiful examples of apparent irrelevancies becoming pertinent, or apparent mysteries suddenly unraveled, that the comic tone remains securely established.

It is to enhance this comic tone that Fielding uses not only the digressive essays which introduce the first three books but also the many passages where, in his own person, he comments on the course of the history. By reminding us of his presence through these direct interventions, as well as by the complex knottings and unknottings of the plot, he gives us a fatherly reassurance: no matter what miseries seem to approach our friends, we need not worry; the good-natured author can manage.

Fielding's interventions have, in addition, a structural significance which is generally ignored. Of course, there was abundant precedent for them in Cervantes and Marivaux, his models. But in several of his own plays Fielding had employed a "rehearsal" pattern which has the same effect. *Pasquin* and *The Historical Register* are two examples. Here the scene is supposed to be behind stage at a theater where a new play is being rehearsed. While some of the characters act out the play-within-a-play, the rest of the cast discuss its value as drama and its connection with politics or morality. The "frame" characters can thus deliver precisely the mixture of literary criticism and general reflection which the narrator provides in the digressive passages of *Joseph Andrews*. By moving from the theater to the novel, Fielding was giving scope to a multiple viewpoint for which dramatic technique seems repressive.

A glance at these early plays may also loosen the chains which conventionally bind Fielding's genius to Richardson's chariot. To treat *Joseph Andrews* (or even *Shamela*) as dependent upon *Pamela* is a treacherous starting point for criticism. The idea of a man being menaced with rape by a woman had been realized long before, in Fielding's *The*

Coffee-House Politician (1730). Here also are several quasi-rapes, such as one scene in which a magistrate tries to seduce a woman who has been brought before him and another in which a man about town (like Didapper) accosts an honest woman as if she were a whore. To build the love intrigue around servants had been the resource of Fielding's *Grub-Street Opera* (1731), where the conquest of the profligate young squire by the virtue of an humble tenant's daughter anticipates both Squire Booby's marriage to Pamela and the passion of Booby's aunt for Joseph. In *An Old Man Taught Wisdom* (1734) a rich squire's daughter marries her footman. A whole set of Fielding's plays have parsons like those (apart from Adams) in *Joseph Andrews;* and one play presents Don Quixote (the avowed model for Adams) in an English setting.

Of course, to analyze all the foreshadowings of the novel in the writer's earlier works could be as misleading as the ordinary obsession with *Pamela*. Anticipations are not meanings, and to study them is no substitute for examining the book itself. Yet this method may possibly account for another defect in the narrative pattern, and explain what perhaps is a miscalculation, by the author, of certain effects. It is not merely Fielding's oversights that break into the comic tone. It is also the few incidents where violence or cruelty is extended too far for good humor. With the episode of the squire who lures Adams into his home for the purpose of sadistically hoaxing him, the farce miscarries: the squire means to be unkind; the slapstick is not due to unforeseeable accident or anger; the painful suspense lasts too long. For such excesses we might excuse Fielding by remembering his models. Rabelais repeatedly exposes innocents to the most extravagant torments, and Cervantes is often pitiless to Don Quixote. However, their victims are portrayed so one-sidedly or so inconsistently that they do not attract the kind of self-identification evoked by a man like Adams; Don Quixote is a more profound conception than the parson, but he has the indestructibility of comic strip caricatures.

Fielding may have failed to appreciate the degree of distress that he was eliciting because in theatrical farces many sorts of stage business are available to qualify the surface cruelty of slapstick gestures: the victim is manifestly unharmed, and shows more indignation than misery; the attacker is grotesque and primitive, a symbol rather than a "real" person. In Fielding's story, furthermore, there are other turns which would be striking as spectacle but have little point as narrative. One is the calculation by which Adams, Joseph, and Fanny are united in time to be passed by Lady Booby (with her coach and six) just as they enter their parish. The symbolism here is scenic rather than narrative; since Fielding mentions it in a phrase, and does not follow it up, the effect is negligible. On the stage, of course, the unity of such an impression would be immediately felt as significant. Similarly, many of the slapstick gestures would have a far sharper impact in a theater than they have when summarized as fiction. At times, in the great fisticuff sessions, one seems almost to be reading stage directions.

But Fielding's most beautiful achievement in this novel, the refined quixotism of Abraham Adams, is a work of prose fiction. Like his forebears in the tradition, Adams is uncompromising. Outsiders must enter his fantasy; he rarely steps out of it or accepts their world. For sympathetic, "humorous" comedy of this kind (as opposed to the "rejective" satire of a Juvenal), the author must accomplish at least two feats. He must yoke together, harmoniously and in the same person, major virtues and minor faults which are conventionally treated as incompatible; for it is thus that he creates a possible focus of such humor. He must also show other characters—with whom the reader may readily identify himself—constantly, willingly, crossing over and accepting the fantasy of the humorist, who is not self-conscious. This principle of course is what Fielding learned from Cervantes. In Adams' display of erudition without dignity, benevolence without prudence, major courage and trivial vanity, the parson makes an irresistible mixture of moral incongruities. His complete acceptance by simpler characters (Joseph, Fanny, the pedlar, Wilson) and his humiliation or rejection by unsympathetic characters, lure the reader into measuring him by Adams' own standards and not by common sense.

It would be unjust to make the value of the novel depend on the moral stature of Abraham Adams. Rather it lies in Fielding's power to move other characters into and out of the parson's world so as to produce a deeply symbolic comedy which does not alienate us from the comic protagonist. Perhaps Fielding does this without regarding principles of consistency, verisimilitude, or point of view which some judges assume as fundamental to the novel form. If he does so, however, he thereby marks the limits of those principles rather than the defects of his work.

Critics as magisterial as Henry James have preached the doctrine, for example, that a novelist commits a fault when he speaks directly, in his own character as author; i.e., when he either ignores the pretense that the story is telling itself or confesses "that the events he narrates have not really happened, and that he can give the narrative any turn the reader may like best." James (with, one supposes, deliberate humor) indulges this scruple so far as to say, "Such a betrayal of a sacred office seems to me, I confess, a terrible crime." Yet Proust—in a masterpiece popularly associated with the same tradition as James and opposed to that of Fielding—has passages like the following:

> In this book of mine, in which there is not one fact that is not imaginary, nor any real person concealed under a false name, where everything has been invented by me to meet the needs of my story, I ought to say in praise of my country that, at any rate, these millionaire relatives of Françoise . . . really are alive and, convinced that their modesty will never take offence because they will never read this book, it gives me a childish pleasure and deep emotion to record here their real name, Larivière (*Remembrance of Things Past*, Random House 2-vol. ed., II, 976).

It would be presumptuous of us to defend Proust or to accuse James. Their kinds of comedy have assuredly more in common than either has with Fielding's; and James himself remarks, "The house of fiction has in short not one window, but a million" (Preface to *The Portrait of a Lady*). It is only necessary for us to recognize that the work of all three is better understood as an elaborate parable than as a pseudo-document. To our patterned memory of chaotic life, they appeal with the great, symbolic abstractions of their intricate drama. To make consistency—whether of tone, moral insight, or point of view—a yardstick of their literary value seems to me as naive as to suppose that Giotto was more limited than Ingres. Draughtsmanship, linear perspective, *trompe-l'oeil*, are techniques of painting but not the purpose of painting. Morality is a necessary means of aligning human forces in tragedy, but it is not the value of tragedy. If we reduce the art of fiction to some few techniques of certain novelists, we destroy the very insight which art alone can provide.

TRISTRAM SHANDY'S ANTI-BOOK

STERNE, 1760–67

by Gerald Weales

"Of all the cants which are canted in this cant-ing world—though the cant of hypocrites may be the worst —the cant of criticism is the most tormenting!" So says Tris-tram Shandy. With Shandy standing behind one's chair, what can one ("*i.e.*, an author," says Tristram, making fun of writers who say *one* when they mean *I*)—with Tristram at my elbow, probably, like Uncle Toby, whistling "Lilli Bullero," what can I say about *The Life and Opinions of Tristram Shandy, Gent.*, by the Reverend Mr. Laurence Sterne? There are certain stock things that can be said, that have been said. The pattern of criticism was set with the publication of the first two volumes in 1760. At about that time, Samuel Richardson, the fame of having protected Pamela's virtue for so many pages heavy about his shoulders, wrote, in the guise of a young lady in London, that the book was built of "unaccountable wildness; whimsical incoher-encies; uncommon indecencies. . . ." *Tristram Shandy* was to be much loved and much laughed at, but the author was

Gerald Weales

to be harried for structural perversities, apparently as arbitrary as e. e. cummings' predilection for the lower case. Although we have come to accept the notion that there is method in Sterne's chaos, the criticism—somewhat watered —still persists. George Sherburn wrote in *The Restoration and Eighteenth Century* (1948), his volume of *A Literary History of England:* "One tolerates his use of blank pages, black pages, and marbled pages, his placing his preface in the middle of the book, his dots, dashes, and index hands, and other tricks that Joseph Addison would have classed as 'false wit.'"

Judging from his letters and the later volumes of the book itself, Sterne was as sensitive to the criticism aimed at *Tristram Shandy* as any author is likely to be. The entire work is sprinkled with asides to critics, advice to critics, quarrels with critics, defenses against critics. At one point in the last volume, for example, Tristram refuses to praise the widow Wadman, even though he is convinced that an apostrophe would be the making of his chapter: "let the chapter go to the devil; provided any damned critic in keeping will be but at the trouble to take it with him." The criticism of *Tristram Shandy* and the author's annoyance at it thus becomes one of the jokes in the book. Today, however, Tristram appears to be facing quite another indignity, one that would have been less easy for the author to absorb, even though, not quite seriously, he had predicted its coming:

As my life and opinions are likely to make some noise in the world, and, if I conjecture right, will take in all ranks, professions, and denominations of men whatever,—be no less read than the *Pilgrim's Progress* itself—and in the end, prove the very thing which Montaigne dreaded his Essays should turn out, that is, a book for a parlour-window. . . .

The prophecy has proven itself. In the eighteenth century Sterne was often attacked, but more often read; today his novel is an accepted classic, but in the acceptance (turn away, Mr. Shandy) lies good-humored indifference. A casual, non-statistical enquiry indicates that of all the books that call forth easy protestations of love—excepting probably Robert Burton's *The Anatomy of Melancholy*—Sterne's novel must be the least read. The modern reader, like the lady whom Tristram reprimands for "reading straight forwards, more in quest of adventures, than of the deep erudition and knowledge," is likely to become impatient, not just with the tricks that offend Professor Sherburn (as Joseph Addison), but with the digressive structure—the starts and stops, the interruptions, the false promises, the asides. Yet, digressions are "the life, the soul of reading," as Tristram says; "take them out of this book, for instance,—you might as well take the book along with them. . . ." In this sentence, Sterne is doing more than laughing at Tristram's apparently pointless garrulity. He is pointing out that the digressions, like the mechanical surprises, are basic to the form and intention of *Tristram Shandy*, that those devices which annoy and repel some readers are precisely the instruments that make the book most attractive.

More than a century ago Walter Bagehot tried to rule out the possibility of a pattern in Sterne's novel: "No analysis or account of 'Tristram Shandy' could be given which would suit the present generation; being, indeed, a book without a plan or order, it is in every generation unfit for analysis." The present present generation (Bagehot could not have known) can find plan or order in any work, given the inclination and a little careful distortion. With *Tristram Shandy* definition, not distortion, is needed—for *plan* or *order*, read *attitude*. The nine volumes with all their twists and turns are held together by the fact that they are so obviously products of a single imagination and a single method, which is, I suppose, what Sterne meant when he wrote to David Garrick (sending him the first two volumes): " 'tis however a picture of myself, & so far may bid the fairer for being an Original." *Tristram Shandy* is Sterne's comic view of the world and of his own place in it. The recurring references to Cervantes and Rabelais, the writers from whom he seems to have gained the greatest inspiration and the most enjoyment, imply what Sterne is trying to do in the novel. He is specific about it in a letter to Robert Dodsley, his first publisher: "The Plan, as you will percieve [*sic*], is a most extensive one,—taking in, not only, the Weak part of the Sciences, in wch the true point of Ridicule lies—but every Thing else, which I find Laugh-at-able in my way. . . ." It is impossible to read very far in *Tristram Shandy* without realizing that Sterne finds laugh-at-able all human pretension —social, intellectual, artistic, personal—and, by extension, all human activity. He is not an angry satirist; his laughter is good humored. He knows, as he says in his sermon, "The Levite and His Concubine," that "certainly there is a difference between *Bitterness* and *Saltness*,—that is,—between the malignity and the festivity of wit."

Sterne's use of digression cannot be explained simply by recognizing that his book reflects the humorist's laughing fondness (with only occasional dips into venom) for men and the preposterous ways in which they think, talk and act. He can raise laughter at the foibles of human behavior by describing a brief scene; he can mock a man's special knowledge (his hobby-horse) by parody or quotation. The endless interruption serves these two comic methods by giving them greater employment, by dragging more and more subjects in by the heels. Sterne's digression, however, does more than open doors. It is a comic method itself and its butt is Sterne and his novel. He can best make fun of himself and the incredible idea that he, like all the other hobby-horse riders, is writing a book, by defying every convention of the eighteenth-century novel and memoir (of which *Tristram Shandy* is a distant relative), by going beyond the defiance even—by breaking his work into fragments that shoot off in all directions. *Tristram Shandy* is essentially an anti-book. When that fact is recognized, every irrelevance becomes relevant, not to the book's plot, but to its narrator-hero, Sterne's instrument for achieving order by making disorder, for displaying a mind by pretending that minds are so beset by vagaries that their likenesses can never be caught.

Before looking at the ways in which Sterne avoids telling his story, I should point out that there is a story to be told, that *Tristram Shandy* has a plot. Supposedly the novel was to describe the life (and the opinions) of a country gentleman whose character had been formed by a number of accidents that befell him before, at or shortly after his birth. The nine volumes (published two at a time between 1760 and 1767) never get the narrator-hero beyond his childhood. The first four volumes form the most obvious unit; primarily concerned with getting Tristram born and named, the real or non-digressive action of these volumes takes place within a year. There are four main incidents—the begetting of Tristram, the decision that his mother shall have her lying-in in the country, the mashing of his nose by Dr. Slop's forceps and the mix-up at the christening which gives him his name —which serve as anchors to hold in place the rest of the material—the story of Yorick, the presentation of Uncle Toby and Corporal Trim and their passion for playing soldier, the ideas of Tristram's father, Yorick's sermon and the asides of the narrator. The fifth and sixth volumes jump to Tristram's childhood, using the death of his brother Bobby, the preparation of Mr. Shandy's educational system (the *Tristra-paedia*) and the unfortunate affair of the falling window which gives Tristram an accidental circumcision as the weak wall of plot on which to hang the comic decoration. The three years that passed between the publication of Books V and VI (1762) and Books VII and VIII (1765) took Sterne to France in search of health, which he never found. The seventh volume is a complete digression, an account of the narrator's sudden trip to France to escape death, the result probably of an inability to get on with the book as he had planned it. The eighth volume takes up the story of Uncle Toby's courting of the widow Wadman, hinted at in Book I, promised in Book III and begun at the end of Book VI, and the ninth volume, published singly, finishes the courtship. The novel ended at this point not because it had come to a conclusion in any conventional sense, but because Sterne had turned to his *A Sentimental Journey through France and Italy* and because he died before he could turn back to Tristram—as he suggested he would in a letter written in 1766.

These few high points in Tristram's embryonic and infant life and the courtship of Uncle Toby (a flashback to the year before Tristram was born) are held together by continual glances ahead and to the rear. They are the beads through which the string of the narrative is to run, but it is Sterne's business to knot the string as often as possible between beads, to loop it, tangle it, break it completely and retie it as neatly as possible. To drag his feet between incidents, Sterne uses four kinds of interruption: (1) conversation with imagined readers; (2) false starts, promises that are never kept; (3) the structural play that Professor Sherburn lists; and (4) digressions which often, like Chinese boxes, become digressions within digressions within digressions. The conversations with the reader are simply over-extensions of the eighteenth-century fondness for speaking directly to the audience. Where Fielding might introduce a chapter by taking his readers into his confidence, Sterne is more likely to command them ("Lay down the book, and I will allow you half a day to give a probable guess at the grounds of this procedure"), to ask their advice ("What would your worships have me do in this case?") and to get it ("Tell it, Mr. Shandy, by all means.—You are a fool, Tristram, if you do"), to discuss their competence as readers, to give them age, sex, position, personality. At one point, he sends the inattentive lady back to reread a chapter because he is convinced that she has missed an important point: "I told you in it, That my mother was not a papist.—Papist! You told me no such thing, Sir."

A variation on this familiarity with the reader is Sterne's continued assurances that a matter will be made clear farther on, that a story will be told in a later volume, that a character will finally be explained. It is possible that some of the hints would have materialized, like Toby's affair with Mrs. Wadman, had the book really run on to more volumes, but it is apparent throughout that Sterne is starting hares that he has no intention of running to ground. He promises chapters on chambermaids and button holes, although later he begs off, asking if he might substitute a chapter on chapters instead. Tristram often looks forward to his account of his travels with Mr. Noddy, but since Tristram never gets out of childhood, Mr. Noddy never becomes more than a name. The most pervasive of Sterne's false starts is Jenny, a character to whom he often speaks or whose actions he describes, but who is never identified. She appears casually in the first volume, where Tristram stops to reprimand the reader for jumping to conclusions in assuming that he must be married because he addresses a "dear, dear Jenny." Jenny may be his kept mistress, his child, a friend of the opposite sex, he suggests, but although Jenny is still turning up in the ninth volume, she is still carefully unidentified.

The structural and typographical trickery is more than the adolescent high spirits that some of Sterne's critics have implied that it is. His mechanical jokes are not always funny and they are sometimes used too repetitiously, but even more than the unresolved promises and the arguments with imaginary readers, they are aimed at the pretensions and the fastidiousness of both readers and writers. The book is sprinkled with asterisks to replace material which ostensibly Sterne considers too delicate for the ears of his readers. Since he often uses the word *spade*, and not *****, when he means *spade*, the scattering of asterisks is, in fact, a laugh at the gentility which insisted that its mild scatology and pornography are more becoming dressed in typographical veils. Sterne's mock nicety is most evident in the wonderfully funny scene in which the hot chestnut rolls into the open fly of Phutatorius, at the gathering of the divines; "Zounds!" cries Phutatorius, and then, "Z—ds!" Similarly, Sterne's placing of the dedication in the eighth chapter of the first volume and the preface in the middle of Book III is not sheer perversity; in playing with their position in his novel, he satirizes the whole process of dedications and prefaces, just as the matter of the first thrusts at the venality of dedications and of the second at the pomposity of prefaces.

Sterne is structurally most cavalier in his treatment of chapters. Their length has nothing to do with the material they contain; occasionally a single sentence or a very short paragraph becomes a complete chapter. Even when he restrains the digressions, he often, for no apparent reason, breaks a single incident into several chapters. "A sudden impulse comes across me," he explains, "drop the curtain, Shandy—I drop it—Strike a line here across the paper, Tristram—I strike it—and hey for a new chapter." He leaves one chapter blank so that the reader can fill in his own description of Mrs. Wadman, just as, at another spot, he leaves a space for the reader to swear in. He passes over two chapters because his Uncle Toby is whistling and he cannot concentrate (although he does give the music for "Lilli Bullero" in one of them) and then, pages later, inserts the missing chapters under their original numbers, going back to pick up the material that he left out. He leaves out a chapter in the fourth volume because its description of the journey of Mr. Shandy and Toby is so beautifully done that it will make the rest of the book weak by comparison. "A dwarf who brings a standard along with him to measure his own size—take my word, is a dwarf in more articles than one.—And so much for tearing out of chapters." Sterne's toying with the length, position, even the necessity of chapters is more than harmless personal pleasure, although he obviously enjoys the joke involved. It is a slap at the order implied in the division of material into suitable working units. It is a demonstration of his claim, made early in the book when he introduces and dismisses Horace: "for in writing what I have set about, I shall confine myself neither to his rules, nor to any man's rules that ever lived."

The first three of Sterne's interruptive methods contribute to the planned disorder of his book, but, by comparison with the fourth, they are merely surface mannerisms. Digression ("the life, the soul") is obviously basic to the structure of a novel that is going to take until the middle of

its third volume to get its hero born. Sterne's disgressions are
not the conventional, neat insertions of picaresque novels,
like the goat-herd's story in *Don Quixote* or Mr. Wilson's
account of his misspent youth in *Joseph Andrews*. *Tristram
Shandy* does have such set pieces—Slawkenbergius's tale
about the man with the long nose—but these are as subject
to interruption as anything else in the book. Trim's story of
the King of Bohemia and his seven castles, for example, is
halted first in an attempt to date the action, then to allow
Toby to discuss the origin of gunpowder, next to let Trim
describe his wound and his love for the young Beguine.
"What became of that story, Trim?" asks Toby pages later.
"We lost it, an' please your honour, somehow betwixt
us. . . ." Sterne's digressive technique can be seen at its most
flamboyant when he interrupts a remark of Uncle Toby's
("I think, says he") near the beginning of Book I, Chapter
XXI. The narrator leaves Toby's words hanging in the air
while he proceeds to describe the speaker, a description that
is stopped immediately by some general remarks on climate
and writing. Having returned to Uncle Toby's history and
character, Sterne (or Tristram) gets involved in the story of
Aunt Dinah and the coachman, with some side remarks on
formal argumentation. What with a chapter on digressions,
a chapter on ways of drawing character ("I have a strong
propensity in me to begin this chapter very nonsensically")
and a minute and round-about account of Uncle Toby's
wound in the groin, his convalescence, his preoccupation
with fortification and his servant Trim, it is not until Book
II, Chapter VI that the poor man finished his sentence: "I
think, replied he,—it would not be amiss, brother, if we rung
the bell." In his chapter on digressions, Sterne offers his own
explanation, at once comic and accurate, of his digressive
method. He finds "truly pitiable" the ordinary author. "For,

if he begins a digression,—from that moment, I observe, his whole work stands stock still;—and if he goes on with his main work,—then there is an end of his digression." As for himself, "I have constructed the main work and the adventitious parts of it with such intersections, and have so complicated and involved the digressive and progressive movements, one wheel within another, that the whole machine, in general, has been kept a-going. . . ." The splendor of Sterne's digressions, aside from their intrinsic wit and humor, is that they do keep the machine a-going even while they appear to be poking sticks in the spokes of its wheels; they get Tristram's story told even while they seem to be insisting that storytelling is as laughable an activity for a man as any other.

If *Tristram Shandy* as a whole, its structure and its style, becomes Sterne's humorous view of himself and his world, there are within it specific satirical thrusts at the conventional butts of satire, at "the Weak part of the Sciences, in wch the true point of Ridicule lies." Toward the end of the fourth volume, Tristram comments on the wild ride he has taken through the first four volumes of his life and admits cheerfully that some by-standers have been brushed as he passed by:

> Now ride at this rate with what good intention and resolution you may—'tis a million to one you'll do some one a mischief, if not yourself—He's flung—he's off—he's lost his hat—he's down—he'll break his neck—see!—if he has not galloped full among the scaffolding of the undertaking critics!—he'll knock his brains out against some of their posts—he's bounced out!—look—he's now riding like a madcap full tilt through a whole crowd of painters, fiddlers, poets, biographers, physicians, lawyers, logicians, players,

schoolmen, churchmen, statesmen, soldiers, casuists, connoisseurs, prelates, popes, and engineers—Don't fear, said I—I'll not hurt the poorest jack-ass upon the king's highway—But your horse throws dirt; see you've splashed a bishop—I hope in God, 'twas only Ernulphus, said I.—But you have squirted full in the faces of Mess. Le Moyne, De Romigny, and De Marcilly, doctors of the Sorbonne.—That was last year, replied I.—But you have trod this moment upon a king.—Kings have bad times on't, said I, to be trod upon by such people as me.

Tristram's horse is not quite so out of control as he makes it sound in this paragraph; Sterne holds the reins and if Tristram rides close enough to splash a bishop, it is because Sterne sees something in the bishop that is obviously splashable. Yet, it is certainly true that he has no intention of hurting the "poorest jack-ass" on the road. Sterne's satire is not the reforming anger of Ben Jonson or Jonathan Swift; it is the good-natured satire of a man who is amused at jackasses, expects them to go on being jackasses and is cheerfully willing to admit that he is something of a jackass himself. Oliver Goldsmith accused Sterne of having "contempt for all but himself, smiling without a jest, and without wit professing vivacity." "Contempt" is too harsh a word for Sterne's amusement at men, and Goldsmith is quite inaccurate when he suggests that Sterne exempts himself from the general laughter. Not only is he a butt implicitly; he is one specifically. Sterne uses one of his own sermons, "The Abuses of Conscience Considered," when he reaches the scene in *Tristram Shandy* in which the sermon is to become the target of satire.

The specific objects of Sterne's satire are no longer of interest to anyone except scholars and antiquarians. He was obviously attracted to arcane volumes of all kinds, treatises written in the excluding jargon of the professions, the special language of what Gerard Manley Hopkins called, in another context, "áll trádes, their gear and tackle and trim." Sometimes Sterne quotes directly from his sources, as when he gives, in Latin and English, the anathema of Ernulphus, the twelfth-century Bishop of Rochester. Sometimes he parodies; sometimes he invents. The book is awash with references, both genuine and fictitious; the classical authors are called on to uphold positions they may or may not have supported. This ambiguous richness has been a blessing to academic detectives who have hunted out sources with diligence; Wilbur L. Cross's standard biography of Sterne discusses a number of the works that found their way into Sterne's mind and book, particularly those that gave Uncle Toby his military knowledge, and since the Cross biography was published in 1929, other scholars have continued to work over the body of Tristram Shandy in an attempt to identify the marks on it. This process, which would probably have amused Sterne, is the business of scholarship, but it can have very little importance to the general reader of *Tristram Shandy*. Uncle Toby and his sieges are not more or less funny when the reader knows that there was a Comte de Pagan and that Sterne had read (had heard of, at least) his *Traité des Fortifications* (1645). Actually the list of readings that Sterne gives for Uncle Toby in *Tristram Shandy* becomes a little wearing, even when we know that they are real; it is the situation that is funny: that a man with a wound in his groin has to read treatises dating back two centuries to explain what has happened to him. Toby is funny because, like Don Quixote, he is a man possessed by his reading, and his descriptions are funny (the *double entendre* aside) because they ridicule the kind of military writing which displays a garrulous concern for detail and terminology and an indifference to the human activity of the battlefield. One of the few times that Sterne becomes acid in *Tristram Shandy* and the only time the acidity splashes on Uncle Toby is when he casually comments on a battle that Toby is about to re-enact in his own backyard:

> As this was the most memorable attack in the whole war,— the most gallant and obstinate on both sides,—and I must add the most bloody too, for it cost the allies themselves that morning above eleven hundred men,—my uncle Toby prepared himself for it with a more than ordinary solemnity.

Sterne uses a variety of methods of mocking the pretensions that he wants to explode. One of the most consistent and most effective is to turn the specialist's knowledge over to Walter Shandy and let him run it quickly into absurdity. Mr. Shandy is fascinated by matters medical, theological, philosophical; he is addicted to argument and explanation. As a result, he presents his theories about the importance of an uninterrupted begetting, of a feet-first birth, of a long nose, of a name with implicit power to greatness and of the auxiliary verb as the key to education with the proper consideration of the authorities and the rejection or acceptance of them. In the course of Mr. Shandy's thinking, the medical theorist, the theologian and the philosopher become so removed from practical matters that their disciplines become ridiculous. In some of its details, the scholastic argumentation that Walter Shandy plays havoc with is no longer pertinent, but it is a relatively simple matter to recognize that the satire is easily transferable to our own time, to the sometimes picayune concerns of the literary critic, the analytic philosopher, the educationist and the social scientist. In turning Walter Shandy loose on those disciplines that are supposedly most concerned with men but which have invented a special language that excludes the bulk of men, Sterne has created a situation that is valid far beyond Mr. Shandy's immediate cogitations. There are always small bands of men who take shelter in the bastions of jargon and run up flags of complacency; there is always the need of a Walter Shandy to blow up these redoubts, not by attacking them but simply by entering them.

Although Walter Shandy is Sterne's chief satirical weapon, he has others. One is the simple statement, sometimes in the mouth of a character, sometimes from the narrator himself, which in summarizing a pompous passage destroys the material it is concerned with. The best example follows the article in his mother's marriage-settlement that Tristram quotes in Book I. The article, full of the repetitions, the re-identifications, the *to wits* and *whereases* that are standard for a satire on the legal style runs for three tiresome pages (Modern Library ed.); at the end Tristram adds, "In three words—'My mother was to lay in, (if she chose it) in London.' " A third device of Sterne's, the one that he uses with his own sermon, is to present the material that is to be laughed at in a dramatic situation in which the behavior of the characters points up the absurdity of what is being said. Sterne's sermon is not absurd in itself; it lacks the ornateness of classical and theological reference that would have made of it the kind of joke that we get in the philosophical ruminations of Mr. Shandy. "The Abuses of Conscience Considered," like most of Sterne's sermons, is a straightforward pleading for morality, touched here and there with evidences that it was written by the author of *Tristram Shandy*, but for the most part it is simply competently dull. Sterne thought enough of it to have it printed later in a volume of his sermons. He is, then, not specifically satirizing the material or the style of his sermon; he is satirizing the whole idea that one man—especially himself—should get up and preach morality at another. This becomes clear as we realize that Sterne is more interested in the delivery of the sermon and its reception than he is in the sermon itself. He takes great pains to get Corporal Trim in the correct oratorical position to read the sermon; he allows frequent interruptions from Mr. Shandy, Uncle Toby and Dr. Slop; he lets the sermon anger the Roman Catholic doctor and then put him to sleep; he makes Trim break down before the end of the sermon, convinced that the general description of the Inquisition is a factual account of what has befallen his unfortunate brother Tom, and give way to Mr. Shandy, who finishes the reading. Although some of the eighteenth-century reviewers expressed an admiration for the sermon itself, the actual effect of the scene is to lose the sermon in its reading. So much for the preaching of morality, Sterne seems to say.

Although *Tristram Shandy* is spotted with laughter at particular professions and disciplines, it is filled also with thrusts at a more general erudition, the kind of intellectual ornamentation that eighteenth-century authors delighted in and that modern authors use almost as frequently but more self-consciously, the learned additions that are dragged in by the heels, like my introduction of Gerard Manley Hopkins three paragraphs back. Sterne makes fun of this kind of pretension by allowing his narrator to call up classical analogies which he only vaguely remembers. The most extended example comes after the death of his brother Bobby when Tristram runs through a whole list of authors, pagan and Christian, ancient and modern, in an attempt to put his finger on the depiction of grief that best describes Walter Shandy's reaction to his son's death. At another point, Tristram says of one of his learned references, "I have not the time to look into Saxo-Grammaticus's Danish history to know the certainty of this;—but if you have leisure, and can easily get at the book, you may do it full as well yourself." Tristram's pose, the knower who is not really certain that he knows, is the standard comic way of satirizing the writer who is happier with a quotation than with a straightforward observation.

There are two aspects of Sterne—Sterne the sentimental and Sterne the prurient—that deserve special consideration. To some of Sterne's critics, in his own and later centuries, his sentiment has seemed the most admirable thing in his book and his bawdy the most deplorable. This kind of criticism implies that neither the sentiment nor the bawdy quite belongs in *Tristram Shandy*, and such an implication is false. Sterne uses both kinds of writing in a special way in his novel, so that the sentiment does not become sentimental and the bawdy does not become dirty.

Sterne's sentiment is neither the utilitarian nicety of Sir Richard Steele nor the genteel glorying in a polite emotion for the emotion's sake that characterized the sentimentalists who sighed over his counting the pulse of the lovely glove seller in *A Sentimental Journey*. His biography is full of attachments to ladies, sentimental affairs that never apparently went beyond the letter-writing stage; yet although he affected passions, and perhaps believed in the affectation, he never ceased to see himself, even in his letters to the ladies, as something of a comic figure. *Tristram Shandy* has its sentimental, its pathetic passages, but even the most celebrated of them—the death of Le Fever—is not pure pathos. Much was made when Book VI first appeared of the exquisiteness of the line that follows on Uncle Toby's oath ("He shall not die, by G——") on hearing that Le Fever must die: "The Accusing Spirit, which flew up to heaven's chancery with the oath, blushed as he gave it in;—and the Recording Angel, as he wrote it down, dropped a tear upon the word, and blotted it out for ever." It was possible for the eighteenth century to take this kind of excess seriously, even though it is hard to do so today, but there is evidence that Sterne, although he was eighteenth-century enough to write it, was realistic enough to know that it was humorous. The scene in which Toby speaks his oath is one in which he is struggling, half-in, half-out of bed, marching forward, one shoe off, one on, at each repetition of "He shall march," and shouting hopeful defiance above each of Trim's matter-of-fact statements that the lieutenant must die. The scene is essentially comic, and all the pathos of the dying lieutenant and Uncle Toby's concern for him cannot erase the comedy. There is no laughter in the story of Le Fever, but there are smiles at least because Toby and Trim insist on being Toby and Trim even at the dying man's bedside. Sterne never sees any action simply through the eyes of the actor and, as a result, even his sentiment is tinged with a mild and loving mockery.

In the same way, the other pathetic or potentially pathetic scenes are touched with comedy. Yorick's death is lightened by the high rhetoric of Eugenius at his bedside, by the byplay with the night cap as the parson says farewell and by the presentation of the inscription on his grave: "Alas, poor Yorick!" The death of Bobby is completely lost in the classic definitions of Mr. Shandy and the scene in the kitchen in which Trim moralizes (a below-stairs Mr. Shandy) and Susannah can think of nothing except the green satin nightgown which will come to her when Mrs. Shandy goes into mourning. As the pathetic scenes are touched into comedy by the behavior of the characters who play them, so Sterne's flights of sentimental rhetoric are consciously undercut when he gives lavishly of his eloquence, only to withdraw the gift with a single capping sentence. He ends an apostrophe on the simple worth of Trim with "O Trim! would to heaven thou had'st a better historian!—would thy historian had a better pair of breeches!" In the last volume, he follows a paragraph, addressed to Jenny, on the sadness and shortness of life with a one-sentence chapter: "Now, for what the world thinks of that ejaculation—I would not give a groat." Sterne is too much of a realist to take his sentiment and his pathos without comedy; the impulse that produced *Tristram Shandy*, the inclination to laugh in delight at the strange humors of the world, operates on Sterne the sentimentalist, just as it operates on Sterne the writer and Sterne the preacher.

Sterne's "uncommon indecencies," as Richardson called them, are absorbed into the texture of *Tristram Shandy* as surely as his sentiment is. Thackeray, in his famous hatcheting essay on Sterne in *The English Humourists of the Eighteenth Century*, speaks of "that dreary *double entendre*" and complains that the "foul Satyr's eyes leer out of the leaves constantly." Some of Sterne's readers who are not so fastidious as Richardson and Thackeray were, and I am one of them, are likely to find the *double entendre* almost as funny as Sterne himself obviously did. In the description of the terrible accident in which Trim and Bridget break down the bridge in Toby's garden the slapstick of the scene is heightened by the fact that the author appears to be talking about a completely different kind of maneuver than the surface meaning of his words denotes. If this scene is in the novel for its own sake, there are others in which the *double entendre* heightens the satire. That the monumental nose in Slawkenbergius's tale may be no nose at all gives more than a prurient fillip to the story; the double meaning makes that much more ridiculous the curiosity of the townspeople of Frankfort and the abstruse university arguments on the reality or the false-ness of the nose. In the same way, the Italian wind-instrument ("I dare not mention the name of the instrument in this place") that Sterne introduces into his scholarly analysis of the ways of drawing character emphasizes the foolishness of the whole discussion. If the more accepting reader has a complaint against Sterne, it is not that he uses *double en-tendre,* but that he sometimes, almost coyly, insists on hint-ing that the reader may miss something. These suggestions, however, like the passages they accompany, are aimed at the kind of nicety that likes references to the bedroom and the bathroom if they are cloaked in polite enough language. "Why the most natural actions of a man's life should be called his Non-naturals,—is another question," says Tris-tram. At the end of his story about the court of Navarre, in which the word *whiskers* gains a double meaning and then reverts to a single meaning, although not the denotative one, Sterne comments on the kind of thinking that is the real butt of all his *double entendre:* "And when the extremes of deli-cacy, and the beginnings of concupiscence, hold their next provincial chapter together, they may decree that bawdy also."

If Sterne worked only in hints, suggestions, double meanings, he might in one sense deserve the prurient label that is sometimes fastened on him. In *Tristram Shandy,* how-ever, the dainty suggestions are balanced with downright frankness. In a letter to William Warburton, who had of-fered Sterne unwanted advice on how to make his novel more acceptable to the tender-minded, Sterne says, "I may find it very hard, in writing such a book as 'Tristram Shandy' to mutilate everything in it down to the prudish humour of every particular." He finds mutilation not hard, but impos-sible, for he is working not in genteel comedy, but in an older tradition that takes in the Elizabethans, his beloved Rabelais and the first important comedian, Aristophanes. He is the kind of comic writer who does not put on blinkers, does not choose to work a small plot delicately. For this reason, he takes the reader to the Shandy bedside at the moment of Tristram's begetting to hear Mrs. Shandy say, "Pray, my Dear, have you not forgot to wind up the clock?" He lets the window fall on the exposed Tristram and lets the hot chestnut roll into the front of Phutatorius' trousers. He makes the widow Wadman worry greatly about the extent of the wound in Uncle Toby's groin. He understands and uses low comedy and, by allowing his characters to moralize, philosophize and categorize all around these actions, he makes clear and comic the dichotomy between the functions and passions of the body and the idealizing vagaries of the mind.

Sterne also uses the frankly sexual and scatalogical, as he sometimes uses his *double entendre*, as a satirical device. A bald line at the end of a pompous passage can bring the pretentious down from its self-supplied pedestal. After printing in French the discussion by the doctors of the Sorbonne on the methods by which a child may be baptized while still in its mother's womb, Tristram suggests that baptizing all the homunculi at once might be a safer and more effective course: "And provided, in the second place, That the thing can be done, which Mr. Shandy apprehends it may, *par le moyen d'une petite canulle,* and *sans faire aucun tort au pere.*" Similarly Uncle Toby puts an end to a discussion between Walter Shandy and Yorick on prodigies and the ages at which they first make their genius known. The two disputants, displaying their learning, attempt to cap each other's examples, moving with each exemplary prodigy to an earlier age. Yorick finally tops Mr. Shandy. "But you forget the great Lipsius, quoth Yorick, who composed a work the day he was born." But the victory is Uncle Toby's. "They should have wiped it up, said my uncle Toby, and said no more about it." These lines are the verbal equivalent of the dung beetle on which Trygaeus flies to heaven in Aristophanes' *Peace*. Sterne does not use his "uncommon indecencies" exactly as Aristophanes and Rabelais did before him, but, like the earlier comic writers, he uses them for more than their own sake. He is not a teller of dirty stories; he is a humorist who is aware that men do not spend the whole of their lives in drawing-rooms.

For the bulk of this essay I have been concerned with *Tristram Shandy* as one man's laughing attempt to look closely at the world he lived in. From time to time, I have referred to the book as a "novel"—the label it customarily wears. Since little of the material and method discussed above has close relevance to that genre, I should perhaps say something about *Tristram Shandy* as a novel. Although it looks back to *Don Quixote* and forward to *Ulysses,* it is plainly unlike most of its generic brothers. It can best be described in Huey Long's famous words: "Just say I'm *sui generis,* and let it go at that."

Without attempting a detailed explanation of what I think constitutes a novel, I should like to suggest that in two important ways *Tristram Shandy* fits that genre. Sterne creates genuine characters and places them in a concrete setting, and when he chooses to put aside digression, he involves his characters in dramatic situations that forward whatever plot the book has. Although the reader is likely to come away from *Tristram Shandy* with a generalized sense of the bemused and amused view of the world that is the book's primary quality, the specific things that stick in his mind are probably the characters, Tristram's relatives and neighbors, rather than the satiric points that Sterne makes. When Ignatius Sancho, the ex-slave, wrote to Sterne, "I declare I would walk ten miles in the dog days, to shake hands with the honest Corporal," he was expressing the kind of fondness for Trim, and for Uncle Toby, that Sterne's readers have always come away with. The reason is that Trim and Toby are so carefully delineated in the course of the book—their habits, their foibles, their tics, their little vanities, their strong loyalties—that they become more than the caricatures they would have been had Sterne allowed them simply to represent their primary passion for mock warfare and left them at that. The other figures—Mr. and Mrs. Shandy, Yorick, Dr. Slop, the widow Wadman—are as completely presented; starting with a particular characteristic—Mr. Shandy's fondness for argumentation, Mrs. Shandy's happy inability to grasp any idea, Yorick's cheerful irreverence—Sterne builds on and around it until a palpable character emerges. Even the minor characters—the disputing divines, the gossiping servants—take on flesh. Sterne, like Dickens, uses comic overstatement in painting his characters, but he never allows them to become stereotypes. They are human enough to need a place to live. Sterne provides a real countryside, real houses and gardens and, what is more important, real relationships for them to thrive in. His use of detail provides the furnishings (material and emotional) that make the settings believable. The reader not only hears the squeaking hinge on the Shandy parlor door and sees the converted bowling green where Toby and Trim hold their maneuvers; he knows clearly the relationship of Mr. Shandy to his wife and his brother, of Dr. Slop to the neighborhood, of Yorick to his parishioners, of the servants to the Shandy family, of Trim to Uncle Toby.

One of the reasons that the characters are such solid creations is that Sterne places them, and often arrests them, in scenes that define them dramatically. When Hogarth chose to draw Trim reading Yorick's sermon for a second edition of volume one, he picked a scene that had already caught Trim as clearly as a painter could. The novel is full of such scenes: Yorick riding into the village on his skinny horse, Mrs. Shandy stooping at the keyhole, Mr. Shandy reaching for his handkerchief, Obadiah riding wildly with Dr. Slop's bag flying at his neck, Uncle Toby looking for a mote in Mrs. Wadman's eye, Trim dropping his hat to illustrate the transience of human life. These are short scenes in which the gestures of the actors are indications of personality. In the more sustained narrative passages—Uncle Toby's courtship, for instance—the characters are revealed more fully, but they never act in a way that contradicts anything that the reader knows of their history or their mannerisms. Sterne gets all the humorous and satiric effects that he wants from his characters, not at their expense.

Those short scenes in which the characters are allowed to act can do more than put the actors on display. When Sterne chooses to let the digression rest, he can advance the narrative action of the novel with a few sentences—a gesture, an alarm, a confrontation, a line of dialog. He knows, as good novelists always do, that action is at the heart of every novel, although in *Tristram Shandy*, unlike most novels, the action is not going anywhere in particular. There are temporary stops—the birth of Tristram, the death of Bobby, Uncle Toby's breaking off with Mrs. Wadman—but there is no final destination. The end of *Tristram Shandy* is that there shall be no end. In this sense—for all that is novelistic about it—it is an anti-novel as much as it is an anti-book.

With Tristram still at my shoulder, his whisper of cant

still in my ear, I had better drop all this talk of anti-novel and anti-book, and go back to the work itself. At the end of the last volume, after Toby has escaped Mrs. Wadman, Obadiah comes into the Shandy parlor to complain that Mr. Shandy's bull has failed to provide his cow with a calf. Obadiah's accusation sets Mr. Shandy off on one of his rhetorical flights, which is interrupted, as they so often are, by Mrs. Shandy's failure to understand what is going on:

> L—d! said my mother, what is all this story about?—
> A Cock and a Bull, said Yorick—And one of the best of its kind, I ever heard.

And so it is.

THE WORLD OF *PRIDE AND PREJUDICE*

AUSTEN, 1813

by Leo Kirschbaum

It is often maintained that Jane Austen in *Pride and Prejudice* was neither a romantic nor a visionary, that she felt no revolutionary compulsion to change the social scene, country gentry society, which she described so wittily. I find this not a completely satisfactory statement. For if she accepts that society, she also implicitly damns it. On a deeper level still, her caustic account of family life probably deserves the designation of cynical. Similarly, she is credited with a cool rational perception that never deviates into passion. This is not completely true either. There are two kinds of portraiture in the novel: one, that customary to the comedy of manners, a rather easy classification of a character into unchanging, general characteristics; two, a mode in which the author at the moment seems to know as little about her characters as they know about themselves.

The style of *Pride and Prejudice*—so reasonable, so just—invites the reader, as it were, not to react outside the arbitrary but convenient boundaries set by the author. It seems impolite to Miss Austen to wince at what is being said. Yet one does. That indomitable hypnotic style does not always prevent the reader from feeling something very close to disgust.

Everything ends so beautifully. Jane gets Bingley, Elizabeth marries Darcy. What more can one ask? The answer is—less contrivance. It is not probability but accidental meetings, the author's machination, that carries these two affairs to a happy close. Jane Austen, the *régisseur*, pushes these two Bennet daughters into happiness. But they have enough of life and emotion, especially Elizabeth, to awaken pity in their confusions and defeats. They become somewhat too real to fit completely the auctorial design for them. What life usually is is bracketed by one of the minor characters, Elizabeth's friend, Charlotte Lucas. She is a "sensible, intelligent young woman, about twenty-seven." She is fully as sensitive and rational as Elizabeth Bennet, but accident does not control *her* career. Listen to her at the beginning of the book. "There is so much of gratitude and vanity in almost every attachment that it is not safe to leave any to itself. We can all *begin* freely—a slight preference is natural enough; but there are very few of us who have heart enough to be in love without encouragement. In nine cases out of ten, a woman had better show *more* affection than she feels." That the individual ego is almost incapable of distinterested choice could hardly be stated more trenchantly or brutally. When Elizabeth, with private scorn, and of course the reader's approval of our heroine, declines the hand of the Reverend William Collins, a stupid, pompous, toadying ass, Charlotte grabs at the opportunity—to Elizabeth's amazement. "Miss Lucas, who accepted him solely from the pure and disinterested desire of an establishment, cared not how soon that establishment were gained."

Her reflections were in general satisfactory. Mr. Collins to be sure was neither sensible nor agreeable; his society was irksome, and his attachment to her must be imaginary. But still he would be her husband. Without thinking highly of men or of matrimony, marriage had always been her object; it was the only honorable provision for well-educated young women of small fortune, and however uncertain of giving happiness, must be their pleasantest preservation from want. This preservative she had now obtained. And at the age of twenty-seven, without having ever been handsome, she felt all the good luck of it.

In contrast with this, Jane's final euphoria seems bovine, and Elizabeth's mature love, rarefied. "I am not romantic, you know," Charlotte says to Elizabeth. "I never was. I ask only a comfortable home; and considering Mr. Collins' character, connections, and situation in life, I am convinced that my chance of happiness with him is as fair as most people can boast on entering the marriage state." When Elizabeth leaves after a visit to the Derbyshire parsonage, where Mrs. Collins has arranged to avoid her husband's proximity as much as possible, Elizabeth thinks:

> Poor Charlotte! it was melancholy to leave her to such society! But she had chosen it with her eyes open; and though evidently regretting that her visitors were to go, she did not seem to ask for compassion. Her home and her housekeeping, her parish and her poultry and all their dependent concerns had not yet lost their charms.

Towards the end of the novel, we hear that she is pregnant. The story of Charlotte Collins is important in *Pride and Prejudice*. It is severe, uncompromising realism—life, not romance.

Not even David Ricardo could have been more conscious of the role which money plays in life than Jane Austen in this novel. It is financial security that holds together the social edifice, country gentry society, which she is describing, and she knows this in every drop of her ink. The book may be said to labor the point. The very first sentence of the novel is: "It is a truth universally acknowledged, that a single man in possession of a good fortune must be in want of a wife." It is not avarice, as in *Volpone,* that propels the characters. Rather, it is the financial, social, and psychological security (remember Charlotte) which the possession of money accomplishes. Mothers do not seek psychologically or morally eligible husbands for their daughters: there are a limited number of opportunities of financial security, and these must be grasped quickly. Who the man is, what he is are almost totally irrelevant. Of course, it is best if the man have enough fortune to be idle, for idleness is the accompaniment of position and respect. (How much was Jane Austen herself in her treatment of character bedazzled by Bingley and Darcy's coin, I wonder!) These idle people, always on the verge of being completely bored, must be able to afford establishments, big or small, run by servants, who are almost always nameless. Great emphasis is laid on the past; it is the most respectable of the foundations of wealth and breeding, but there is no attempt to investigate it or understand it. Ultimately there is a social hierarchy which is seemingly based on family and tradition but which is really based on income. Those who have the most are at the top, with the largest houses and parks, the best furniture and paintings, and the best streams for fishing. Money that comes from trade is looked on somewhat askance, but its origins are hastily forgotten in the passage of generations. To escape present vulgarity, however, it is generally advisable to give up business or profession and settle in the country.

On the first page the first thing we hear of Bingley is

that he is "a young man of large fortune." Mrs. Bennet immediately wants to get him for one of her five daughters. She as quickly distrusts Mrs. Long because the latter "has two nieces of her own." At the assembly, where we first meet him, "Mr. Darcy soon drew the attention of the room by his fine, tall person, handsome features, noble mien; and the report which was in general circulation within five minutes after his entrance, of his having ten thousand a year." Here is Jane Austen's vignette of the Bingleys, brother and two sisters:

> They were in fact very fine ladies, not deficient in good humor when they were pleased nor in the power of being agreeable when they chose it, but proud and conceited. They were rather handsome, had been educated in one of the first private seminaries in town, had a fortune of twenty thousand pounds, were in the habit of spending more than they ought and of associating with people of rank, and were therefore in every respect entitled to think well of themselves and meanly of others. They were of a respectable family in the north of England, a circumstance more deeply impressed on their memories than that their brother's fortune and their own had been acquired by trade.
>
> Mr. Bingley inherited property to the amount of nearly a hundred thousand pounds from his father, who had intended to purchase an estate but did not live to do it. Mr. Bingley intended it likewise, and sometimes made choice of his county; but as he was now provided with a good house and the liberty of a manor [the right to hunt], it was doubtful to many of those who best knew the easiness of his temper whether he might not spend the remainder of his days at Netherfield, and leave the next generation to purchase.
>
> His sisters were very anxious for his having an estate of his own; but though he was now established only as a tenant, Miss Bingley was by no means unwilling to preside at his table, nor was Mrs. Hurst, who had married a man of more

fashion than fortune, less disposed to consider his house as her home when it suited her. Mr. Bingley had not been of age two years when he was tempted by an accidental recommendation to look at Netherfield House. He did look at it and into it for half an hour, was pleased with the situation and the principal rooms, satisfied with what the owner said in its praise, and took it immediately.

On such gentry do the innumerable housekeepers, cooks, maids, servants, stable-boys, tenants in their cottages, the farms and sheepcotes, the mills and forges, the weak and poor, and old, the children, of the novelist's unpeopled rural England depend. To go an inch beyond the view Miss Austen allows is to become depressed.

The beginning of the social process is illustrated by a Bennet neighbor.

> Sir William Lucas had been formerly in trade in Meryton, where he had made a tolerable fortune and risen to the honor of knighthood by an address to the King, during his mayoralty. The distinction had perhaps been felt too strongly. It had given him a disgust to his business and to his residence in a small market town; and quitting them both, he had removed with his family to a house about a mile from Meryton, denominated from that period Lucas Lodge, where he could think with pleasure of his own importance and, unshackled by business, occupy himself in being civil to all the world.

The attitude of such to the lower classes around them is given in these remarks on Lady Catherine de Burgh:

> Elizabeth soon perceived that though this great lady was not in the commission of the peace for the county, she was a most active magistrate in her own parish, the minutest concerns of which were carried to her by Mr. Collins; and whenever any of the cottagers were disposed to be quarrelsome, discontented, or too poor, she sallied forth into the

village to settle their differences, silence their complaints, and scold them into harmony and plenty.

The paramount importance of money in the mores of this society is perhaps best exampled by the Wickham-Lydia Bennet scandal. Unmarried, they run away together from Brighton. He is charming and utterly immoral, financially irresponsible, with gambling debts and no ability to pay them. She is an empty-headed flirt, whose sexual proclivities would appear even more reprehensible were Miss Austen at all inclined to spell things out. They are eventually discovered in London. Wickham, a fortune hunter, has no intentions of marrying the baggage. But Darcy secretly intervenes:

> [Wickham] confessed himself obliged to leave the regiment on account of some debts of honor which were very pressing, and scrupled not to lay all the ill-consequences of Lydia's flight on her own folly alone. He meant to resign his commission immediately; and as to his future situation, he could conjecture very little about it. He must go somewhere, but he did not know where, and he knew he should have nothing to live on. Mr. Darcy asked him why he had not married your sister at once. Though Mr. Bennett was not imagined to be very rich, he would have been able to do something for him, and his situation must have been benefited by marriage. But he found, in reply to his question, that Wickham still cherished the hope of more effectually making his fortune by marriage in some other country. Under such circumstances, however, he was not likely to be proof against the temptation of immediate relief. They met several times, for there was much to be discussed. Wickham of course wanted more than he could get, but at length was reduced to be reasonable.

And so Wickham marries Lydia, society is sufficiently appeased, and Mrs. Bennet is violently happy. Lest the reader believe what occurs here unique, consider the dialog between the honorable Colonel Fitzwilliam and Elizabeth. Money by marriage must be the overriding concern not only of females but of younger sons:

> "I do not know anybody who seems more to enjoy the power of doing what he likes than Mr. Darcy."
>
> "He likes to have his own way very well," replied Colonel Fitzwilliam. "But so we all do. It is only that he has better means of having it than many others, because he is rich, and many others are poor. I speak feelingly. A younger son, you know, must be inured to self-denial and dependence."
>
> "In my opinion, the younger son of an earl can know very little of either. Now, seriously, what have you ever known of self-denial and dependence? When have you been prevented by want of money from going wherever you chose or procuring anything you had a fancy for?"
>
> "These are home questions—and perhaps I cannot say that I have experienced many hardships of that nature. But in matters of greater weight I may suffer from the want of money. Younger sons cannot marry where they like."
>
> "Unless where they like women of fortune, which I think they often do."
>
> "Our habits of expense make us too dependent, and there are not many in my rank of life who can afford to marry without some attention to money."

The problem of what is meant by Jane Austen's "acceptance" is aggravated by her treatment of family. If we are to take the Bennets as typical—and why should we not?—then *Pride and Prejudice* presents this basic human institution as quite repugnant. Consanguinity seems to be the sole adhesive among the seven Bennets we meet. The mother is "a woman of mean understanding, little information, and uncertain temper." Mr. Bennet despises his wife but gets some amusement out of her, as he does out of the rest of the activities of his family and neighborhood; nevertheless, his ability to be witty does not in the author's eyes excuse him for a complete lack of responsibility and discipline. His three youngest daughters are presented as deplorably silly. Lydia and Kitty are incapable of thought or true morality and are interested only in dances, admiration, and millinery shops. Mary, the book reader, is portrayed as even more foolish than the other two.

> When supper was over, singing was talked of, and [Elizabeth] had the mortification of seeing Mary, after very little entreaty, preparing to oblige the company. By many significant looks and silent entreaties did she endeavor to prevent such a proof of complaisance, but in vain; Mary would not understand them; such an opportunity of exhibiting was delightful to her, and she began her song. Elizabeth's eyes were fixed on her with most painful sensations. . . . Mary's powers were by no means fitted for such a display; her voice was weak and her manner affected. Elizabeth was in agonies.

This leaves us with Jane and Elizabeth. Jane is beautiful, good-natured, and sentimental. She is mature enough to value her sister, Elizabeth, but, for this reader at least, she never comes wholly to life. She is almost an exemplification of the Pelagian heresy. Her incessant goodness and placidity become boring. Of Elizabeth, I shall speak next, but what must be said now is that with the exception of the words on Jane, the opinions above are those she herself possesses, and which she shares with Darcy. Bluntly, she is for the most part strongly ashamed of her immediate family.

> They were hopeless of remedy. Her father, contented with laughing at them, would never exert himself to restrain the wild giddiness of his youngest daughters; and her mother, with manners so far from right herself, was entirely insensible of the evil. Elizabeth had frequently united with Jane

in an endeavor to check the imprudence of Catherine and Lydia; but while they were supported by their mother's indulgence, what chance could there be of improvement? Catherine, weak-spirited, irritable, and completely under Lydia's guidance, had always been affronted by their advice; and Lydia, self-willed and careless, would scarcely give them a hearing. They were ignorant, idle and vain. While there was an officer in Meryton, they would flirt with him; and while Meryton was within a walk of Longbourn, they would be going there forever.

Elizabeth, at a remark of her mother, "was in such misery of shame that she could hardly keep her seat!" She "had never been blind to the impropriety of her father's behavior as a husband. She had always seen it with pain. . . ." When Elizabeth sees Darcy in conversation with her uncle, Mr. Gardiner, she thinks, "It was consoling that he should know she had some relations for whom there was no need to blush." But Darcy's relationship with her aunt, Mrs. Philips, is not so consoling:

> Mrs. Philips's vulgarity was another and perhaps a greater tax on his forbearance, and though Mrs. Philips, as well as her sister, stood in too much awe of him [Darcy] to speak with the familiarity which Bingley's good humor encouraged, yet whenever she *did* speak, she must be vulgar. Nor was her respect for him, though it made her more quiet, at all likely to make her more elegant. Elizabeth did all she could to shield him from the frequent notice of either, and was ever anxious to keep him to herself and to those of her family with whom he might converse without mortification; and though the uncomfortable feelings arising from all this took from the season of courtship much of its pleasure, it added to the hope of the future; and she looked forward with delight to the time when they should be removed from society so little pleasing to either, to all the comfort and elegance of their family party at Pemberley.

This is a family party of three, including Darcy's sister—not his aunt Lady Catherine, whom he dislikes as much as Elizabeth dislikes her mother. Jane and Bingley move from Netherfield to get away from *her* family.

As I have remarked, there are two modes of characterization in *Pride and Prejudice*. The first is applied to *all* the characters, pleasant or unpleasant, who inhabit the book—with the exception of Elizabeth and Darcy. Once established, character by this first mode is fixed. There is nothing more to be learned essentially about such a person; whatever he says or does only exemplifies what we originally have been given. This, of course, gives a stability and inevitability not merely to Miss Austen's perception but also to *what* is being perceived. But at the heart of the novel is another mode of characterization, that applied to Elizabeth and Darcy. It says that human nature is both unknowable and fluid, that in a relationship of two, for example, neither may understand himself or the other. How much employment of this mode destroys the air of unchangeableness in *Pride and Prejudice* cannot be measured mathematically. But it seems to me that such characterization does tend to invalidate the notion of a Jane Austen always looking at life knowingly, imperturbably, and patiently. Elizabeth says, "There are few people whom I really love and still fewer of whom I think well. The more I see of the world, the more am I dissatisfied with it; and every day confirms my belief of the inconsistency of all human characters, and of the little dependence that can be placed on the appearance of either merit or sense." This could almost be the motto of the story of Elizabeth, herself, and Darcy.

From the start he is irrationally, emotionally entangled:

Occupied in observing Mr. Bingley's attentions to her sister, Elizabeth was far from suspecting that she was herself becoming an object of some interest in the eyes of his friend. Mr. Darcy had at first scarcely allowed her to be pretty; he had looked at her without admiration at the ball; and when they next met, he looked at her only to criticize. But no sooner had he made it clear to himself and his friends that she had hardly a good feature in her face, than he began to find it was rendered uncommonly intelligent by the expression of her dark eyes. To this discovery succeeded some others equally mortifying. Though he had detected with a critical eye more than one failure of perfect symmetry in her form, he was forced to acknowledge her figure to be light and pleasing; and in spite of his asserting that her manners were not those of the fashionable world, he was caught by their easy playfulness. Of this she was perfectly unaware; to her he was only the man who made himself agreeable nowhere and who had not thought her handsome enough to dance with.

Darcy continues to be attracted, without being able either to plumb or measure his own feelings. He "had never been so bewitched by any woman as he was by her. He really believed that were it not for the inferiority of her connections, he should be in some danger." He begins "to feel the danger of paying Elizabeth too much attention." "She attracted him more than he liked. . . ." Elizabeth, however, is much more self-blind than her lover. Wickham asks her, "Are you much acquainted with Mr. Darcy?" "As much as I ever wish to be," cried Elizabeth warmly. "I have spent four days in the same house with him, and I think him very disagreeable." (How much one is reminded of Shakespeare's Beatrice!)

But in Elizabeth, too, a stronger force than prejudice is operating. At a ball he asks her to dance. She is so surprised that "without knowing what she did, she accepted him."

After dancing, they part in silence, "on each side dissatisfied, though not to an equal degree, for in Darcy's breast there was a tolerable powerful feeling towards her, which soon procured her pardon. . . ." While Elizabeth is the guest of Charlotte and Mr. Collins, Darcy *accidentally* comes to the manor house, Rosings—and so their acquaintance is renewed. Here he reveals his love to her, to her astonishment! "In vain have I struggled. It will not do. My feelings will not be repressed. You must allow me to tell you how ardently I admire and love you." Unfortunately he dwells, too, on her social inferiority and on the disadvantages of her family. She refuses him.

> "And this is all the reply which I am to have the honor of expecting! I might, perhaps, wish to be informed why, with so little *endeavor* at civility, I am thus rejected. But it is of small importance."
> "I might as well inquire," replied she, "why with so evident a design of offending and insulting me, you chose to tell me that you liked me against your will, against your reason, and even against your character?"

With Darcy's letter to Elizabeth explaining his part in advising Bingley to leave Netherfield and his past relations with Wickham, Miss Austen turns her attention more to Elizabeth's confused involvement with Darcy. In this letter, he admits to "the utmost force of passion" that led him, unwillingly, to his proposal. He was not "master enough of myself." But Elizabeth has always believed herself to be "a rational creature speaking the truth from her heart." Darcy's letter forever destroys this illusion:

> She grew absolutely ashamed of herself. Of neither Darcy nor Wickham could she think without feeling that she had been blind, partial, prejudiced, absurd.

"How despicably have I acted," she cried. "I, who have prided myself on my discernment! I, who have valued myself on my abilities! who have often disclaimed the generous candor of my sister and gratified my vanity in useless or blamable distrust. How humiliating is this discovery! Yet how just a humiliation! Had I been in love, I could not have been more wretchedly blind. But vanity, not love, has been my folly. Pleased with the preference of the one and offended by the neglect of the other, on the very beginning of our acquaintance, I have courted prepossession and ignorance and driven reason away where either were concerned. Till this moment I never knew myself.

Nevertheless, her feelings toward Darcy "were at times widely different." She begins to lose some of her self-esteem. At one of Lydia's remarks, "Elizabeth was shocked to think that, however incapable of such coarseness of *expression* herself, the coarseness of the *sentiment* was little other than her own breast had formerly harbored and fancied liberal!" Darcy begins to rise in her esteem.

Again, *accidentally* they meet at his estate, Pemberley. "The few minutes in which they continued together were some of the most uncomfortable of her life. Nor did he seem much more at ease. . . ." But Elizabeth remarks that he has changed, that he no longer has his usual hauteur. She watches him being gracious to her relatives, the Gardiners. "Never . . . had she seen him so desirous to please, so free from self-consequence or unbending reserve, as now." Elizabeth now endeavors to understand her present feelings toward him, and the result is a paragraph that might have been written by Stendhal:

As for Elizabeth, her thoughts were at Pemberley this evening more than the last; and the evening, though as it passed it seemed long, was not long enough to determine her feelings toward *one* in that mansion; and she lay awake two whole hours, endeavoring to make them out. She certainly did not hate him. No, hatred had vanished long ago, and she had almost as long been ashamed of ever feeling a dislike against him that could be so called. The respect created by the conviction of his valuable qualities, though at first unwillingly admitted, had for some time ceased to be repugnant to her feelings; and it was now heightened into somewhat of a friendlier nature by the testimony so highly in his favor, and bringing forward his disposition in so amiable a light, which yesterday had produced. But above all, above respect and esteem, there was a motive within her of good will which could not be overlooked. It was gratitude. Gratitude, not merely for having once loved her, but for loving her still well enough to forgive all the petulance and acrimony of her manner in rejecting him, and all the unjust accusations accompanying her rejection. He who, she had been persuaded, would avoid her as his greatest enemy, seemed on this accidental meeting most eager to preserve the acquaintance, and without any indelicate display of regard or any peculiarity of manner where their two selves only were concerned, was soliciting the good opinion of her friends and bent on making her known to his sister. Such a change in a man of so much pride excited not only astonishment but gratitude—for to love, ardent love, it must be attributed; and as such its impression on her was of a sort to be encouraged as by no means unpleasing, though it could not exactly be defined.

But though she knows he loves her, Elizabeth does not as yet admit she loves him. It is when she thinks that she has lost him because of the Lydia-Wickham scandal, that, in a queer psychological turnabout, she partially discovers *her* feelings:

Her power was sinking; everything *must* sink under such a proof of family weakness, such an assurance of the deepest disgrace. She could neither wonder nor condemn, but the belief of his self-conquest brought nothing consolatory to her bosom, afforded no palliation of her distress. It was, on the contrary, exactly calculated to make her understand her own wishes; and never had she so honestly felt that she could have loved him as now, when all love must be vain.

At this moment I must admit that the Jane Austen who tries to understand character is less fluent, less able than the customary Jane Austen who defines a character once and for all. For Miss Austen even when dealing with the irrational must perforce be rational. She senses the passion and the hidden complexity of the Elizabeth-Darcy relationship but she does not feel it enough. For to *feel* it this polite, general, impersonal style would not do. A kind of poetry was required, and Miss Austen in her control chose not to be a poet. Here is the final declaration of the love of Elizabeth and Darcy. I find it pedestrian, pedantic, an evasion, a missing of her opportunity.

> "If you *will* thank me," he replied, "let it be for yourself alone. That the wish of giving happiness to you might add force to the other inducements which led me on I shall not attempt to deny. But your *family* owe me nothing. Much as I respect them, I thought only of *you*."
> Elizabeth was too much embarrassed to say a word. After a short pause, her companion added, "You are too generous to trifle with me. If your feelings are still what they were last April, tell me so at once. *My* affections and wishes are unchanged, but one word from you will silence me on this subject forever."
> Elizabeth, feeling all the more-than-common awkwardness and anxiety of his situation, now forced herself to speak, and immediately, though not very fluently, gave him to understand that her sentiments had undergone so material a change since the period to which he alluded, as to make her receive with gratitude and pleasure his present assurances. The happiness which this reply produced was such as he had probably never felt before; and he expressed himself on the

occasion as sensibly and warmly as a man violently in love can be supposed to do.

Pride and Prejudice represents Jane Austen's attempt to see the real currents beneath a world she chose to regard as frozen into immobility. She sees, and yet she does not see.

JANE EYRE: A ROMANTIC EXEMPLUM WITH A DIFFERENCE

BRONTË, 1847

by Joseph Prescott

I

"For fiction—read Scott alone; all novels after his are worthless," wrote Charlotte Brontë at eighteen. Twelve years later, she had defied the romantic establishment sufficiently to match plain Jane Eyre with unhandsome Rochester, at the same time avoiding in other points, as critics have shown, the large gestures of romance. Having recognized this much, one is struck by the considerable residue of romantic convention which, finally, dominates the novel. Most striking is the recurrence of what may be called the superlative mode in characterization, style, and incident.

The character who comes to mind at once is Blanche Ingram, the work clearly of a romantic amateur. So blatantly odious a creature becomes a physically and socially attractive rival not of Jane Eyre but of Mrs. Rochester, whose private attack upon her husband appropriately precedes Miss Ingram's social "attack." The difference between monsters is that the mad and matted one can be shut away whereas the sane and curled one cannot. The extremity of the latter's objectionableness is measured by the fact that Jane, aware of her master's "perfect, clear consciousness of his fair one's [Blanche's] defects," abdicates her usual unblinking good sense to resort to casuistry in extenuation of Rochester's apparent intention:

> It seemed to me that, were I a gentleman like him, I would take to my bosom only such a wife as I could love; but the very obviousness of the advantages to the husband's own happiness, offered by this plan, convinced me that there must be arguments against its general adoption of which I was quite ignorant: otherwise I felt sure all the world would act as I wished to act.

When Rochester later recounts that he found Miss Mason " 'a fine woman, in the style of Blanche Ingram; tall, dark, majestic,' " the comparison, dropped with seeming casualness, sets up ripples of further association in the reader's mind: Miss Mason was a beauty, Miss Ingram is; Miss Mason made a hell of Rochester's life, Miss Ingram. . . .

The large gestures of romance affect the style continually. Straight out of romance is the prancing arrival at Thornfield of Rochester and his guests:

> . . . at last wheels were heard; four equestrians galloped up the drive, and after them came two open carriages. Fluttering veils and waving plumes filled the vehicles; two of the cavaliers were young, dashing-looking gentlemen; the third was Mr. Rochester, on his black horse, Mesrour; Pilot bounding before him: at his side rode a lady, and he and she were the first of the party. Her purple riding-habit almost swept the ground, her veil streamed long on the breeze; mingling with its transparent folds, and gleaming through them shone rich raven ringlets.

It hardly needs Mrs. Fairfax's identifying exclamation for us to know that the final impression marks the entrance of "Miss Ingram!"

But it is not only the narrator's prose that runs the color of Miss Ingram's riding-habit; Jane Eyre's and Rochester's speeches to one another also do. Consider whether a really plain real Jane would speak to her bridegroom in this style:

". . . Sophie called me upstairs to look at my wedding-dress, which they had just brought; and under it in the box I found your present—the veil which, in your princely extravagance, you sent for from London: resolved, I suppose, since I would not have jewels, to cheat me into accepting something as costly. I smiled as I unfolded it, and devised how I would tease you about your aristocratic tastes, and your efforts to masque your plebeian bride in the attributes of a peeress. I thought how I would carry down to you the square of unembroidered blond I had myself prepared as a covering for my low-born head, and ask if that was not good enough for a woman who could bring her husband neither fortune, beauty, nor connections. I saw plainly how you would look; and heard your impetuous republican answers, and your haughty disavowal of any necessity on your part to augment your wealth, or elevate your standing, by marrying either a purse or a coronet."

Or consider the relation which Rochester's operatic style in the following passage bears to living speech:

"Never," said he, as he ground his teeth, "never was anything at once so frail and so indomitable. A mere reed she feels in my hand!" (And he shook me with the force of his hold.) "I could bend her with my finger and thumb: and what good would it do if I bent, if I uptore, if I crushed her? Consider that eye: consider the resolute, wild, free thing looking out of it, defying me, with more than courage—with a stern triumph. Whatever I do with its cage, I cannot get at it—the savage, beautiful creature! If I tear, if I rend the slight prison, my outrage will only let the captive loose. Conqueror I might be of the house; but the inmate would escape to heaven before I could call myself possessor of its clay dwelling-place. And it is you, spirit—with will and energy, and virtue and purity—that I want: not alone your brittle frame. Of yourself, you could come with soft flight and nestle against my heart, if you would: seized against your will you will elude the grasp like an essence—you will vanish ere I inhale your fragrance. Oh! come, Jane, come!"

Again, in the choice and disposition of incident, the superlative mode is amply illustrated. Jane, in flight from Thornfield, having left the coach at Whitcross "without another shilling in the world," discovers that she forgot to take her parcel out of the pocket of the coach. ". . . and now," she announces, "I am absolutely destitute. . . . Not a tie holds me to human society at this moment. . . ." The romantic author pushes the situation to a theatrical extreme. It is of course credible that, in her disturbed state, as Jane herself explains, she should forget the parcel; but, for her situation to be dramatically effective without excess, it is not necessary that she should be absolutely money-less, parcel-less, tie-less.

At the other extreme of fortune, as the novel draws to a close, Jane, holding herself "supremely blest," paints, in the account of her ten years of married life, a cloudless picture of ideal felicity.

En route to this conclusion, the plot breaks through the framework of a "reasonably" romantic novel with a thumping piece of Gothic claptrap. An exchange of cries between Rochester and Jane might have been acceptable enough had they experienced, waking or dreaming, a general sense of communion. But to postulate communication complete, in the verbatim reports of both characters, with Western Union accuracy, is to stagger even a romantic reader. The author's admitted superstitiousness apart, her claim that the scene in which Jane hears Rochester's voice "really happened," is, as Aristotle would have pointed out, irrelevant.

II

This rousing dream of passion—the invention of a thirty-year-old virgin—is shot through with a didacticism which finally suggests that her father misplaced parts of his weekly sermons among the manuscript sheets of the unsuspected novel.

A strain of the platitudinous runs through the narration. Waiting at an inn before she is taken to Thornfield for the first time, Jane Eyre remarks:

> It is a very strange sensation to inexperienced youth to feel itself quite alone in the world, cut adrift from every connection, uncertain whether the port to which it is bound can be reached, and prevented by many impediments from returning to that it has quitted.

When Jane returns to Gateshead, she is inspired by the Reed sisters to observe:

> True, generous feeling is made small account of by some; but here were two natures rendered, the one intolerably acrid, the other despicably savourless for the want of it. Feeling without judgment is a washy draught indeed; but judgment untempered by feeling is too bitter and husky a morsel for human deglutition.

Having fled the temptation of Thornfield after Rochester's secret is out, Jane, wishing for death, reflects:

Joseph Prescott

Life, however, was yet in my possession: with all its require-
ments, and pains, and responsibilities. The burden must be
carried; the want provided for; the suffering endured; the
responsibility fulfilled. . . . I must struggle on: strive to live
and bend to toil like the rest.

Shortly afterward, in a discouraged moment, she solilo-
quizes: " 'Why do I struggle to retain a valueless life? Because I know, or believe, Mr. Rochester is still living:' " and,
as if this might not be sufficient reason after what we have
seen of her passion for her master, she adds for good measure: " 'and then, to die of want and cold, is a fate to which
nature cannot submit passively. . . .' "
     Among the many Biblical allusions which point up the
narrative, one is especially premonitory: Rochester's identification of Thornfield, after Jane has learned its secret, with
the tent of Achan. Soon afterward, Rochester asks: " '. . .
What shall I do, Jane? Where turn for a companion, and
for some hope?' " Her exhortatory reply is as smug as it is
staccato: " 'Do as I do: trust in God and yourself. Believe
in heaven. Hope to meet again there.' "
     There is, in fact, in this novel a deal of amateurish ser-
monizing, and the homilist grows tedious. When St. John
Rivers brings Jane *Marmion*, she takes time to deliver, as
from a pulpit, an irrelevant discourse on modern literature:

Alas! the readers of our era are less favoured. But, courage!
I will not pause either to accuse or repine. I know poetry
is not dead, nor genius lost; nor has Mammon gained power
over either, to bind or slay: they will both assert their existence, their presence, their liberty and strength again one day.
Powerful angels, safe in heaven! they smile when sordid
souls triumph, and feeble ones weep over their destruction.
Poetry destroyed? Genius banished? No! Mediocrity, no:
do not let envy prompt you to the thought. No; they not

only live, but reign, and redeem: and without their divine
influence spread everywhere, you would be in hell—the hell
of your own meanness.

The didacticism gains in volume, and the narrative, as
it approaches its conclusion, takes on the character of an
exemplum in which Jane's autobiography becomes an illustration of divinity's ends. Had he remained identical with
Achan, Rochester must have died a violent death. But quite
early the author has laid the groundwork for a commutation
of sentence to another Biblical retribution. For all her use of
the superlative mode, Charlotte Brontë carefully qualifies
Rochester's defections. Where Rochester is concerned,
Jane's judgment is early swayed by her feeling. "I was growing very lenient to my master:" she considers, "I was forgetting all his faults, for which I had once kept a sharp look-
out." Even at her most vigilant, however, she is discouraged
by the author from finding Rochester thoroughly objection-
able. Thus, in the account of their first meeting, Jane says, "I
think he was swearing, but am not certain. . . ." The question of Adèle's paternity is so managed that Rochester may
be innocent of the charge: " '. . . the Varens, six months
before, had given me this fillette Adèle; who she affirmed
was my daughter; and perhaps she may be, though I see no
proofs of such grim paternity written in her countenance:
Pilot is more like me than she. . . .' " A moment later, he reverses himself with the categorical denial, " 'I am not her father. . . .' " Jane then seeks in Adèle's "countenance and
features a likeness to Mr. Rochester, but found none: no
trait, no turn of expression announced relationship."
Later Rochester asserts that Adèle is " 'not my own child' "
but rather " 'a French dancer's bastard.' " (Presumably an
English dancer's bastard would have been more acceptable.)

Consequently, Rochester, having taken in a *foreign waif*, appears in a positively charitable light. In the account of his ten years' search for his ideal of a woman, Rochester reports: " '. . . Disappointment made me reckless. I tried dissipation —never debauchery: that I hated, and hate. That was my Indian Messalina's attribute: rooted disgust at it and her restrained me much, even in pleasure. . . .' " Again, by contrast with his *Indian* Messalina, his French, Italian, and German mistresses suggest that there is virtue in him. Such a sinner may be spared even as he is punished.

The innkeeper who describes the Thornfield disaster to Jane comments: " 'Poor Mr. Edward! . . . Some say it was a just judgment on him for keeping his first marriage secret, and wanting to take another wife while he had one living: but I pity him, for my part.' " Almost immediately afterward, it appears that God has joined the innkeeper in pity, though not before He has fulfilled for Rochester the appropriate Biblical injunction:

> But I say unto you, That whosoever looketh on a woman to lust after her hath committed adultery with her already in his heart.
> And if thy right eye offend thee, pluck it out, and cast it from thee: for it is profitable for thee that one of thy members should perish, and not that thy whole body should be cast into hell.
> And if thy right hand offend thee, cut it off, and cast it from thee: for it is profitable for thee that one of thy members should perish, and not that thy whole body should be cast into hell.

How well the punishment fits the offense may be seen at a glance: " '. . . one eye was knocked out,' " the innkeeper reports, " 'and one hand so crushed that Mr. Carter, the surgeon, had to amputate it directly. The other eye inflamed:

he lost the sight of that also . . .' "—but not for long. The author sees to it that Rochester recovers the sight of his one eye, and all's well that ends well.

The qualified rake has become the very model of a Christian gentleman. It is therefore religiously as well as romantically acceptable that, when Jane first saw him at Ferndean,

> His form was the same strong and stalwart contour as ever: his port was still erect, his hair was still raven-black; nor were his features altered or sunk: not in one year's space, by any sorrow, could his athletic strength be quelled, or his vigorous prime blighted.

Romance and *exemplum* blend. Physically, Rochester makes an impression rather like that of the Hollywood heroine who comes through flood and mud with hair unruffled. Spiritually, he has achieved a homiletically articulate grace:

> "Jane! you think me, I daresay, an irreligious dog: but my heart swells with gratitude to the beneficent God of this earth just now. He sees not as man sees, but far clearer: judges not as man judges, but far more wisely. . . . Of late, Jane—only—only of late—I began to see and acknowledge the hand of God in my doom. I began to experience remorse, repentance; the wish for reconcilement to my Maker. I began sometimes to pray: very brief prayers they were, but very sincere.

Then follows the story of his prayer that he be joined in death with the presumably dead Jane, and of her reply to his distant cry. Romance and *exemplum* unblend long enough for the following sequence:

> He put me off his knee, rose, and reverently lifting his hat from his brow, and bending his sightless eyes to the

earth, he stood in mute devotion. Only the last words of the worship were audible.

"I thank my Maker, that in the midst of judgment he has remembered mercy. I humbly entreat my Redeemer to give me strength to lead henceforth a purer life than I have done hitherto!"

After which, it remains only to draw the curtain. This the author does in a chapter which moves from joy to joy: Jane's marriage, the disposition of Adèle (among other things, "a sound English education corrected in a great measure her French defects"), the "perfect concord" of the Rochesters' ten years together, the birth of their first child, the happy marriages of the Rivers sisters, and, crowning all with an aureole of holiness, the missionary career of St. John Rivers. The description of his work reads disconcertingly like a citation for an honorary degree: "Firm, faithful, and devoted; full of energy, and zeal, and truth, he labours for his race: he clears their painful way to improvement: he hews down like a giant the prejudices of creed and caste that encumber it." Then, with rather unseemly alacrity, the author, in the concluding lines of the novel, martyrizes the missionary:

And why weep for this? No fear of death will darken St. John's last hour: his mind will be unclouded; his heart will be undaunted; his hope will be sure; his faith steadfast. His own words are a pledge of this:—

"My Master," he says, "has forewarned me. Daily he announces more distinctly,—'Surely I come quickly!' and hourly I more eagerly respond,—'Amen; even so come, Lord Jesus!' "

The *exemplum* is complete, and the romance no less. Each to his own: Rivers to his Lord, Rochester to his lady.

III

Reader, she married him—but not before her story had achieved a peculiar difference from other romances, not to mention *exempla*. I refer to an erotic strain [1] which grows more and more pronounced as the narrative unfolds.

That there should be a series of generally and mildly sexual allusions in this novel should of course come as no surprise. Thus, after Rochester has spoken to Jane as his " 'cherished preserver' " with "strange energy . . . in his voice; strange fire in his look," she describes a restless night:

> I regained my couch, but never thought of sleep. Till morning dawned I was tossed on a buoyant but unquiet sea, where billows of trouble rolled under surges of joy. I thought sometimes I saw beyond its wild waters a shore, sweet as the hills of Beulah; and now and then a freshening gale, wakened by hope, bore my spirit triumphantly towards the bourne: but I could not reach it, even in fancy,—a counteracting breeze blew off land, and continually drove me back. Sense would resist delirium: judgment would warn passion. Too feverish to rest, I rose as soon as day dawned.

I would suggest that Jane is too feverish to rest not only because of what preceded her retirement, but also because, like her creator, she knows the Bible well enough to feel, at her deepest level, the full force of her allusion:

> Thou shalt no more be termed Forsaken; neither shall thy land any more be termed Desolate: but thou shalt be called Hephzibah and thy land Beulah: for the Lord delighteth in thee, and thy land shall be married.

[1] The following observations were made independently of Wayne Burns's kindred discussion of a passage in *Jane Eyre* in "Critical Relevance of Freud," *Western Review,* XX (1956), 301–14.

For as a young man marrieth a virgin, so shall thy sons marry thee: and as the bridegroom rejoiceth over the bride, so shall thy God rejoice over thee.

Images of sexual fulfilment abound. After Jane, still unaware of Rochester's secret, has consented to marry him, she speaks of being "called to the paradise of union" and thinks of "the bliss given me to drink in so abundant a flow." Again, she says, ". . . my eyes seemed as if they had beheld the fount of fruition. . . ."

Feminine images occur so frequently that it becomes difficult to understand why readers should ever have had any doubt about the sex of the author. On Rochester's return to Thornfield Hall following Jane's arrival, Jane says, ". . . a rill from the outer world was flowing through [the hall]; it had a master: for my part, I liked it better." As the master becomes cordial, Jane reports, "So happy, so gratified did I become with this new interest added to life, that I ceased to pine after kindred: my thin crescent-destiny seemed to enlarge; the blanks of existence were filled up; my bodily health improved; I gathered flesh and strength."

Is it likely that the gentlemanly Rivers would describe to a girl his vision of married life in these terms: " '. . . I rested my temples on the breast of temptation. . . . The pillow was burning . . .' "? Is not this rather a wishful feminine image given Rivers by an author who, if unconsciously, wrote more truthfully than she had known? Finally, Jane resists Rivers' proposal in peculiarly feminine terms: " '. . . Nothing speaks or stirs in me while you talk. I am sensible of no light kindling—no life quickening. . . .' " The images grow out of the womanly mind and heart of the narrator like leaves from a tree—naturally. Only a man of extraordinary insight into and sympathy with the feminine point of view might hope to achieve the authenticity of this feature of the narrator's diction.

Beyond such imagery, there are a number of passages in which ambiguity, compact or extended, subserves the full expression of the mind of a female author writing under known constraints. The question which Jane asks herself, "With whom will Blanche Ingram pair?" in a social gathering is resonant with personal meaning. When Blanche has paired with Rochester, and just after Rochester, following the charade of "Bridewell," has said to her in Jane's hearing, " '. . . remember you are my wife . . . ,' " Jane describes them in an extended *double entendre* applicable at once, in what may be called "Victorian," to social intercourse and sexual:

> . . . I still see the consultation which followed each scene: I see Mr. Rochester turn to Miss Ingram, and Miss Ingram to him; I see her incline her head towards him, till the jetty curls almost touch his shoulder and wave against his cheek; I hear their mutual whisperings; I recall their interchanged glances. . . .

Rochester himself, disguised as the gypsy fortune-teller, speaks to Jane obliquely of their relationship: " '. . . If you knew it, you are peculiarly situated: very near happiness; yes; within reach of it. The materials are all prepared; there only wants a movement to combine them. Chance laid them somewhat apart; let them be once approached and bliss results.' " Later, as Rochester hurries her to church, she thinks, "I wonder what other bridegroom ever looked as he did—so bent up to a purpose, so grimly resolute. . . ." He describes his love for her: " '. . . a fervent, a solemn passion is conceived in my heart; it leans to you, draws you to my centre and spring of life, wraps my existence about you—and, kindling in pure, powerful flame, fuses you and me in one. . . .' " Soon afterward, Rochester's voice becomes "the pant of a lion rising," as, toward the conclusion, "He looked and spoke with eagerness: his old impetuosity was rising" immediately after he has said, " '. . . we must be married instantly,' " and before he repeats, " 'We must become one flesh without any delay, Jane. . . .' "

Whether or not Charlotte Brontë guided her pen consciously in these passages, I cannot believe that she did not when Jane, in an intimate scene in which she wished " 'to tease [Rochester] a little,' " said of Rivers' proposal of marriage, " '. . . he asked me more than once, and was as stiff about urging his point as ever you could be.' " The author here, I submit, is not only having Jane tease Rochester but is herself, under cover of her epicene pseudonym, thumbing her nose at conventional constraints upon feminine expression. We are now as far from innocent romance as from otherworldly sermon.

This aspect of the author's mind seems to me best understood in the light of two private revelations which she made in letters written in early maturity. At twenty, she confided: "If you knew my thoughts; the dreams that absorb me; and the fiery imagination that at times eats me up and makes me feel Society as it is, wretchedly insipid, you would pity and I dare say despise me." At twenty-two, she discussed her reasons for declining her first proposal of marriage:

> Moreover, I was aware that Henry knew so little of me he could hardly be conscious to whom he was writing. Why, it would startle him to see me in my natural home character; he would think I was a wild, romantic enthusiast indeed. I could not sit all day long making a grave face before my

husband. I would laugh, and satirise, and say whatever came
into my head first.

As a woman, Charlotte Brontë realizes the femininity of
Jane Eyre with perfect naturalness. As "Currer Bell," I suggest, she writes with a freedom which she could not otherwise permit herself. And, perhaps now unconsciously, now
consciously, she is laughing and satirizing, flouting the
larger husband-dominated literary world with its restric-
tions upon her passionately guarded independence of mind
and expression. Did she not write to G. H. Lewes: "Come
what will, I cannot, when I write, think always of myself
and of what is elegant and charming in femininity; it is not
on those terms, or with such ideas, I ever took pen in hand:
and if it is only on such terms my writing will be tolerated,
I shall pass away from the public and trouble it no more"?

Within the novel itself, Jane pauses long enough to
editorialize:

> It is in vain to say human beings ought to be satisfied
> with tranquillity: they must have action; and they will make
> it if they cannot find it. Millions are condemned to a stiller
> doom than mine, and millions are in silent revolt against their
> lot. Nobody knows how many rebellions besides political
> rebellions ferment in the masses of life which people earth.
> Women are supposed to be very calm generally: but women
> feel just as men feel; they need exercise for their faculties,
> and a field for their efforts as much as their brothers do; they
> suffer from too rigid a constraint, too absolute a stagnation,
> precisely as men would suffer; and it is narrow-minded in
> their more privileged fellow-creatures to say that they ought
> to confine themselves to making puddings and knitting stock-
> ings, to playing on the piano and embroidering bags. It is
> thoughtless to condemn them, or laugh at them, if they seek
> to do more or learn more than custom has pronounced neces-
> sary for their sex.

Lest this attitude be considered incompatible with romance and *exemplum*, let us hear from one who knew the
author, her biographer, Mrs. Gaskell:

> One day, during that visit at the Briery when I first met her,
> the conversation turned upon the subject of women's writ-
> ing fiction; and some one remarked on the fact that, in
> certain instances, authoresses had much outstepped the line
> which men felt to be proper in works of this kind. Miss
> Brontë said she wondered how far this was a natural con-
> sequence of allowing the imagination to work too constantly
> . . . I remember her grave, earnest way of saying, "I trust
> God will take from me whatever power of invention or
> expression I may have, before He lets me become blind to
> the sense of what is fitting and unfitting to be said!"

DICKENS' *GREAT EXPECTATIONS:* A KAFKAN READING

DICKENS, 1860–61

by Mark Spilka

In discussing the connection between Dickens and modern times, Lionel Trilling links the English author with the Czech genius, Franz Kafka, through their common preoccupation with childhood problems. For both writers, that is, the violation of childhood peace defines existence; their heroes never escape from that experience, but continually repeat it in later life, under the dominance of harsh parental figures. This was what Kafka had in mind, apparently, when he called his first novel, *Amerika,* a "sheer imitation" of *David Copperfield* on five specific counts, but "above all" in method. He had little use for Dickens' rambling, sentimental style, his repetitious effects, and his plethora of rude characterizations; but he did like the series of familial traps through which the hero passes, in his quest for maturity and belonging. This method seems far more explicit, however, in *Great Expectations,* where the faults of *Copperfield* have been largely stripped away and where the hero moves in a direct line of march through similar predicaments. Indeed, the grotesque, dreamlike quality of this sequence, with its heightened sense of ambiguity and guilt, comes especially close to Kafka's fiction.[1] It should prove rewarding, then, to examine the book through Kafkan eyes, so as to reveal a depth and subtlety in Dickens which are usually denied him, and to demonstrate his kinship with the modern world.

Great Expectations is one of the dark novels of Dickens' later period. Its dreamlike quality is not accidental, since it is based on the author's growing conviction that life itself is like a nightmare. As with *David Copperfield*, the novel is written in the first person, from the point of view of a young boy called Pip. He is an orphan, like David, but he is raised by a harsh elder sister and her childlike husband, the blacksmith Joe Gargery. Pip's youth is filled with a variety of "mortal terrors"; but the things which terrify him then are no different, essentially, from the ordeals of early manhood. This is what Dickens seems to discover here: that the oppressed and lonely child remains oppressed and lonely, even as an adult, and that he inflicts upon others the very wrongs from which he suffers.

Pip's guilty feelings help to explain his terrors. Imposed on him, in part, by parental figures like his sister, they are also the result of his own material expectations, or of his participation in the general social guilt of the nineteenth century. They serve to focalize the dreamlike atmosphere, so that we stand behind him in his passage through a world made evil by multiple crimes against humanity, while the most guilty figure of all is Pip himself, at the center of the nightmare. As the novel opens, for instance, he is seized by a

---

[1] A great many readers have seen this parallel, but for the record, it was first noted publicly by E. W. Tedlock, Jr., in "Kafka's Imitation of *David Copperfield*," *Comparative Literature*, VII (Winter, 1955), 61.

convict in the graveyard where his parents are buried. This is his first "vivid and broad impression of the identity of things," his first awareness of the end of childhood innocence. In this respect, it resembles those wonderful opening scenes in Kafka, where a groom and horses rise up out of a pigsty, or where a man wakes up to find himself a cockroach, or to face arrest for an unnamed crime.

> "Hold your noise!" cried a terrible voice, as a man started up from among the graves at the side of the church porch. "Keep still, you little devil, or I'll cut your throat!"
>
> A fearful man, all in coarse grey, with a great iron on his leg. A man with no hat, and with broken shoes, and with an old rag tied round his head. A man who had been soaked in water, and smothered in mud, and lamed by stones, and cut by flints, and stung by nettles, and torn by briars; who limped, and shivered, and glared and growled; and whose teeth chattered in his head as he seized me by the chin.

The man is Abel Magwitch. His cuts and fetters have been inflicted by society, which has reduced him to a rigid, lumpish object, who shakes and rattles like a machine, and whose very feelings are expressed by clicking noises in his throat. Pip reacts to the man with mingled sympathy and terror, as the convict sends him home to steal "vittles" from the pantry and a file from the blacksmith shop. This is his first experience with actual guilt, and as most Dickensians would agree, it springs from the traumatic period in the author's youth, when his father was placed in a debtor's prison, and the boy was sent to work in a blacking warehouse, to help support the family. His shock and resentment then would recur, in later years, through projections like the convict, for his father; the blacksmith shop, for the blacking warehouse; and the file and vittles, for his father's "irons" and his family's support. Along with these came feelings of complicity in the father's "crime." When Pip is seated at the dinner-table, for instance, he slips some bread-and-butter for the convict down his trousers' leg. First he compares his secret burden with the burden on his conscience; then it makes him "think afresh of the man with the load on *his* leg." When he returns to the convict with his loot, the wooden finger on a direction post seems to point at him. As he moves through the marsh, the landscape bursts at him through the mist, and a black ox stares at him with accusing eyes. "I couldn't help it, sir!" he blubbers back. "It wasn't for myself I took it!"

This is Dickens saying, "It wasn't for myself I labored!" He wants to express the bewildered innocence of a child, appalled by his first exposure to social degradation. But in the child's desire to exonerate himself, and to insist on perfect innocence, he sees the embryonic desire to establish moral isolation, in later years, at the expense of common humanity. Thus, as the novel develops, Pip enters a world where money and respectability seem to insure protection from degrading contacts. Now he does take money for himself, takes it unearned, and comes to believe in it to the exclusion of human love. Yet even at this later stage, he insists on perfect innocence: he merely wants to "get ahead" in life, without realizing that getting ahead, in a materialistic world, means leaving others behind—means leaving them stranded on the marsh, without food or file or solace.

So the opening scene contains the seeds of later conflict. A young boy, faced with another person's need, wants to avoid the stigma of irons and prison-ships. At first his better nature wins out, since he does signal to the convict, at a crucial moment, that he hasn't betrayed him. But engulfed by new perplexities, he soon forgets his compassion, and only his sense of guilt remains. He feels troubled about keeping a secret from Joe Gargery; he is alarmed by the appearance of a second convict, who brings a gift from the first; when his sister is beaten with the discarded leg-iron, he feels implicated in the attack; and when he defeats a young boy in a fistfight at Miss Havisham's, he is obsessed with the bloodstains on his trousers. At the same time he wants Joe's confidence at any cost; he is ashamed now of his kindness to the convict; he decidedly hates his sister; and more than anything else, he wants the kiss from the girl Estella, which is awarded him for his success at fisticuffs. These subtle touches at the beginning of his life forecast his later recognition of his own unworthiness—and come remarkably close to Kafka's view of moral ambiguity as an inherent part of human relations.

But if Pip, like all of us, is exposed to Kafkan ambiguities, he is also the victim of plain injustice. In his own home his sister treats him like a criminal.

> As to me, I think my sister must have had some general idea that I was a young offender whom an Accoucheur Policeman had taken up (on my birthday) and delivered over to her, to be dealt with according to the outraged majesty of the law. I was always treated as if I had insisted on being born in opposition to the dictates of reason, religion, and morality, and against the dissuading arguments of my best friends. Even when I was taken to have a new suit of clothes, the tailor had orders to make them like a kind of Reformatory, and on no account to let me have the free use of my limbs.
>
> Joe and I going to church, therefore, must have been a moving spectacle for compassionate minds.

Anyone familiar with Kafka's early life, with his suppression by an insensitive and demanding father, will recognize the similarity in situation. The charge is original sin, and in each case the culprit makes it stick in later life. There is even a striking parallel in the matter of clothes:

> I endured always having to go around dressed in the wretched clothes which my parents had made for me by one customer after another, longest by a tailor in Nusle. I naturally noticed—it was obvious—that I was unusually badly dressed, [but] I was convinced that it was only on me that clothes assumed this appearance, first looking as stiff as a board, then hanging in wrinkles. . . . As a result I let the awful clothes affect even my posture, walked around with my back bowed, my shoulders drooping, my hands and arms at awkward angles, was afraid of mirrors because they showed in me an ugliness which in my opinion was inevitable. . . .

To the sensitive child, the clothes become the visible sign of his indictment. But Pip responds to such measures through another Kafkan trait: he develops a fine sense of injustice, which is further refined by the charges of his sister's friends, "that the young are never grateful," that they are "naterally wicious," and readily comparable to swine. Thus, when an uncle takes him to court, to be bound over as a blacksmith's apprentice, he views the scene at once for what it is:

> I say, we went over, but I was pushed over by Pumblechook, exactly as if I had that moment picked a pocket or fired a rick; indeed, it was the general impression in Court that I had been taken red-handed; for, as Pumblechook shoved me before him through the crowd, I heard some people say, "What's he done?" and others, "He's a young 'un, too, but looks bad, don't he?" One person of mild and benevolent aspect even gave me a tract ornamented with a a woodcut of a malevolent young man fitted up with a perfect sausage-shop of fetters, and entitled, TO BE READ IN MY CELL.

Such crudeness on the part of his elders tends to maim Pip emotionally. If he is sensitive to injustice, he becomes ugly and insensitive when he tries to escape from it. With the convict-father he has already learned to assert his innocence and will later reject the man as basely criminal. Now he looks on the rich, elderly spinster, Miss Havisham, as a weird fairy godmother who will whisk him away from servitude and give him the better life he thinks he deserves. About a year after the marsh episode, he is invited to play at Miss Havisham's, along with her adopted charge, Estella. This lovely, scornful girl arouses an exorbitant passion in Pip, but it is the spinster herself who seems to capture his imagination. Deserted on her wedding day, she has lived for years in a timeless past, shutting out daylight from her rooms, never leaving her home, dressed still in her bridal gown, and with her banquet table still set for the guests who never came. Since her own heart was broken by a faithless lover, she has raised Estella to break all men's hearts, including Pip's. Accordingly, she takes pleasure in watching him play with the girl, who wounds him emotionally at every turn. But the banquet scene itself defines her perverseness. In a darkened chamber, a long table is covered with dust, mold and cobwebs; across its yellow expanse, spiders with blotchy bodies run back and forth, while mice rattle behind the panels and beetles grope about the hearth. As Miss Havisham explains to Pip, these objects represent her soul:

> On this day of the year, long before you were born, this heap of decay . . . was brought here. It and I have worn away together. The mice have gnawed at it, and sharper teeth than teeth of mice have gnawed at me. . . . When the ruin is complete . . . and when they lay me dead, in my bride's dress on the bride's table . . . so much the better if it is done on this day.

Here the table serves as an image of self-decay, the projection of a subjective state onto surrounding objects. As Pip gazes at it, moreover, he is possessed by "an alarming fancy that Estella and [he] might presently begin to decay." His fancy seems a bit belated, since the two have already been touched by the witch's poking stick. Pip has been roused to new aspirations, while Estella has become a lovely manikin, a jewelled object of desire who fits in perfectly with Pip's new dreams: hence his later confession, that "it was impossible to dissociate her presence from all those wretched hankerings after money and gentility that had disturbed my boyhood—from all those ill-regulated aspirations that had first made me ashamed of home and Joe." So Estella is only a part of his material expectations, and his passion for the girl is chiefly boyish lust: for in qualitative terms, love is reserved for living entities; and lust, for mere objects of desire—even romantic objects, like the heartless Estella.

It is Miss Havisham, then, and not Estella, who generates Pip's suffering. The banquet table, the mysterious corridors, the covetous relatives, and the provocative servant-girl, are all part of a web which catches Pip's desires and converts them to her own corruption. But such interpenetrations of scene, action and feeling are more than local devices in this novel; they apply to every stage of Pip's development: to his graveyard awakening, where his latent guilt seems written into the landscape; to his home-life with his sister, where his insecurity is expressed through comic chaos; to his time at Miss Havisham's, where his lust and folly are tainted with surrounding decay; and to the later scenes in London, where his priggery and repentance are part of the urban shabbiness and gloom. Thus, if Pip seems to lack a complicated inner life, his feelings are actually concretized through macabre scenes and images; as in a

Kafka novel, we can see what happens within him, as it happens *around* him. One need only add a few qualifications here: in Kafka, inner states are projected through fantastic metaphors, which are treated in realistic detail; while in Dickens, outer realities are made to seem fantastic through projected feelings, but there is nothing unreal about the total scene. "Without benefit of Freud or Jung," writes Dorothy Van Ghent, "Dickens saw the human soul reduced *literally* to the images occupying its 'inner life' " (my italics).

As I have already shown, Pip's year at Miss Havisham's distorts his values and exalts his sense of personal worth. He no longer feels content with his homely surroundings, which now seem "common and coarse." His glimpse of refinement makes him think with shame of the blacksmith shop and of his friend Joe Gargery. And so his apprenticeship seems catastrophic, as if a thick curtain had fallen on his life, shutting him out from Estella and "from anything save dull endurance any more." Again there are similar lines in Kafka: "I . . . remained wearily behind, barred forever—everything happened to me forever—from girls, an elegant appearance, and dances." Pip too is barred forever from such things, until another aspect of the childhood world begins to operate. At the behest of a fairy godparent, he is to receive a handsome property: "Further . . . it is the desire of the present possessor of that property, that he be immediately removed from his present sphere of life and from this place, and be brought up as a gentleman—in a word, as a young fellow of great expectations."

Here Dickens' childhood dream, to be removed from the blacking warehouse and granted special schooling, is given its trial-by-fiction and utterly exploded. For Pip now enters his fourth and broadest form of imprisonment. He has already been seized by the convict on the marsh; he has suf-

fered punishment at the hands of his unjust sister; and he has
served as a plaything for Miss Havisham. Now he comes to
London, at the heart of English culture, to train for the life
of an English gentleman. His ill-fitting clothes, his dull endurance at the forge, are exchanged for an elaborate ward-
robe and a racy social existence, but without any real in-
crease in freedom. At the center of his world, moreover,
stands another ominous "father," his legal guardian, Mr.
Jaggers. This popular lawyer is noted for his ability to save
criminals from justice, and accordingly his office is always
surrounded by fawning clients. Pip notes one of them, "a
red-eyed little Jew," who performs an anxious jig beneath
the lamppost, and accompanies himself with the words: "Oh
Jaggerth, Jaggerth, Jaggerth! all otherth ith Cag-Maggerth,
give me Jaggerth!" In his servile homage he resembles Block,
the commercial traveller in *The Trial*, who debases himself
with equal zest before the popular Advocate Huld. Even the
setting suggests the atmosphere of *The Trial:*

> Mr. Jaggers's room was lighted by a skylight only, and
> was a most dismal place; the skylight, eccentrically patched
> like a broken head, and the distorted adjoining houses look-
> ing as if they had twisted themselves to peep down at me
> through it. . . . Mr. Jaggers's own high-backed chair was
> of deadly black horse-hair, with rows of brass nails round
> it, like a coffin; and I fancied I could see how he leaned back
> in it, and bit his forefinger at the clients. The room was but
> small and the clients seemed to have had a habit of backing
> up against the wall: the wall, especially opposite to Mr.
> Jaggers's chair, being greasy with shoulders.

On the shelves stand two dreadful casts of convicts,
their faces swollen from hanging. Similar casts appear in
Jaggers' room, in the dark, shabby house where he lives, and
clerks from the court inhabit surrounding chambers. The

trials are on when Pip first comes to London, and for half a crown he is offered the chance of "a full view of the lord chief justice in his wig and robes." Later on in the book, he ruminates on his strange connection with Jaggers:

> I consumed the whole time in thinking how strange it was that I should be encompassed by all this taint of prison and crime; that, in my childhood, out on our lonely marshes on a winter evening I should have first encountered it; that it should have reappeared on two occasions, starting out like a stain that was faded but not gone; that it should in this way pervade my fortune and advancement.

At this point Pip is unaware of the connection between Jaggers and Magwitch. He knows, however, that Jaggers stands at the heart of a vast scheme of social injustice, as an advocate for its more reprehensible victims. His offices are located in Little Britain, and his clerks have an air about them "of knowing something to everybody else's disadvantage." They seem like national brokers in guilt, and Jaggers himself gives the sign of this, as he washes his hands obsessively after dealing with each client. Hence Pip's remark, on coming of age: "It was an uncomfortable consideration on a twenty-first birthday, that coming of age at all seemed hardly worth while in such a guarded and suspicious world as [Jaggers] made of it."

This is Kafka's verdict on the world of his elders, and the point is worth making since Dickens is using the legal muddle, as in Bleak House,[1] to reveal a much deeper muddle in human relations. Of course, his premise is social rather than religious; yet the problem he poses is not simply one of injustice, but of the dehumanization of man. We get an

---

[1] *Bleak House* is, incidentally, a more obvious source for *The Trial* in its use of the snarls and enigmas of the law to symbolize a universal condition.

image of this in Wemmick's metamorphosis, as he walks from the serenity of his home towards Jaggers' office: "By degrees, Wemmick got dryer and harder as we went along, and his mouth tightened into a post-office again." But Wemmick is merely Jaggers' assistant in mechanistic law. It is the connection between Pip and Jaggers which finally yields the key to the puzzle. Pip's crimes are personal, that is, not legal; they suggest that society itself is the trap which dehumanizes man and that the legal mechanism is only its concrete metaphor. When Joe Gargery visits Pip in London, for instance, the wall between them is the wall of class distinction. Joe stumbles in speech between "Sir" and "Pip," between form and affection. He wears his holiday clothes like a trap, and his table manners are execrable. Pip feels ashamed of him, and he especially fears being seen with him by his social rivals. Joe leaves with a dignified defense of his position as blacksmith, but as Pip later realizes, the damage to their friendship is irreparable:

> I would not have gone back to Joe now . . . for any consideration; simply, I suppose, because my sense of my own worthless conduct . . . was greater than every consideration. No wisdom on earth could have given me the comfort that I should have derived from [his] simplicity and fidelity; but I could never, never, never, undo what I had done.

There is an echo of this in Kafka: "A false alarm . . . once answered—it cannot be made good, not ever." Pip's false alarm seems almost as final; it can never be undone, though it is partly atoned for, later on, through suffering and forgiveness. In the meantime, when Magwitch makes his second abrupt appearance, he serves to confirm Pip's actual crimes against humanity. For the legal and personal elements are now joined, and the rejection of Joe Gargery is now connected, through Jaggers and the legal metaphor, with Pip's excessive desire to rid himself of his secret benefactor. His early fear on the marsh, that the convict might consider him guilty of betrayal, is given an ironic twist: he is now on the side of his elders; he has inherited their world, and has himself become, not merely a snob, but an agent of dehumanization.

Even more ironically, Magwitch is the source of all his wealth and status. As the toiling worker, he stands behind the gentleman, and his strength and endurance make possible the life of frivolity and empty form. At one level, then, he represents the socially repressed classes and serves to illustrate their ironic role in the social structure. But at another and deeper level, he represents the kind of psychological repression we find in Kafka: he is the rejected father, the monstrous, shackled, mudstained figure who veritably rises from the parents' grave, first to demand Pip's help, and finally to command his love. This greedy animal, who bolts his food like a dog and who bears the stigma of early crimes, is less the victim of Pip's social snobbery than of his hatred for all fathers and for the world they have left him. For Pip, his appearance signifies the falseness of this world, and his revulsion from the convict, like his revulsion from Jaggers and from the blacksmith shop in the country, is grounded in his disillusionment with adult experience. He is appalled by the ramifications of crime in London; his gentleman's life repeats those crimes on a different level, and spoils him for the humble life behind him; worst of all, his chance of love with Estella seems blasted by this new discovery—that Magwitch, not Miss Havisham, is his benefactor, that the weird fairy godmother has been replaced by an uncouth convict. What a grim, sordid world, indeed, for the childish Pip to grow up in!

But Magwitch has grown up in the same world and in essentially the same manner. Abandoned as a child, he has been in jail and out all his life. "This is the way it was," he explains to Pip, "when I was a ragged little creetur as much to be pitied as ever I see . . . I got the name of being hardened. 'This is a terrible hardened one,' they says to prison wisitors, picking out me. 'May be said to live in jails, this boy.' " Pip too has been in jails all his life, though of a different order; but his experience with his elders has been the same, and his contact with Jaggers has given him the same insight into social repression. Thus his final reconciliation with his "father" is based on shared experience. Just as their paths crossed on the marsh, so they now cross in the city: their point of contact is Jaggers, who is the neutral agent for every level of the social prison; their common bond is the desire to be a gentleman, whether in fact or by proxy; and this bond originates with their common need to be accepted, in love and trust, as human beings. Both father and son are the victims, then, of the same gigantic swindle; they are equally guilty of all manner of crimes, and almost equally innocent in their baffled attempts to find happiness. In their reconciliation Dickens reveals far more maturity than Kafka was ever able to achieve in a lifetime devoted to the same problem.

Dickens makes a sharp distinction, in this novel, between the world made by the fathers and a world where reconciliation with the father is at least possible. This last domain is Wemmick's house in Walworth, where he lives in harmony with his Aged Parent. The house itself is a small cottage, decorated like a miniature Gothic castle, complete with moat, drawbridge and cannon. Wemmick even calls it his "castle," and he guards it jealously from the world below: "No; the office is one thing, and private life is another. When I go into the office, I leave the castle behind me, and when I come into the castle, I leave the office behind." This castle functions in the novel as an ideal which Pip never attains. But he is able to learn a lesson there, as he watches Wemmick's relations with his Aged Parent.

"You wouldn't mind being at once introduced to the Aged, would you? It wouldn't put you out?"

I expressed the readiness I felt, and we went into the castle. There, we found, sitting by a fire, a very old man in a flannel coat: clean, cheerful, comfortable, and well cared for, but intensely deaf.

"Well, aged parent," said Wemmick, shaking hands with him in a cordial and jocose way, "how am you?"

"All right, John; all right!" replied the old man.

"Here's Mr. Pip, aged parent," said Wemmick, "and I wish you could hear his name. Nod away at him, Mr. Pip; that's what he likes. Nod away at him, if you please, like winking!"

"This is a fine place of my son's, sir," cried the old man, while I nodded as hard as I possibly could. "This is a pretty pleasure-ground, sir. This spot and these beautiful works upon it ought to be kept together by the Nation, after my son's time, for the people's enjoyment."

"You're as proud of it as Punch; ain't you, Aged?" said Wemmick, contemplating the old man, with his hard face really softened; "*there's* a nod for you;" giving him a tremendous one; "*there's* another for you," giving him a still more tremendous one; "you like that, don't you? If you're not tired, Mr. Pip—though I know it's tiring to strangers— will you tip him one more? You can't think how it pleases him."

I tipped him several more, and he was in great spirits. We left him bestirring himself to feed the fowls, and we sat down to our punch in the arbour; where Wemmick told me, as he smoked a pipe, that it had taken him a good many years to bring the property up to its present pitch of perfection.

Clearly Wemmick's father is reduced to his second childhood. He is trapped by age, deafness, and a rather comical senility; but his pride beams forth as a revelation of inner life, and Wemmick matches it through his own concern for his parent's feelings. There is a bond between them which includes the old man's follies, for the humor here is much more akin to love than ridicule. There is nothing this warm or gentle in Kafka, except perhaps in the famous "Letter to His Father":

> Fortunately there were . . . exceptions to all these things, mostly when you suffered in silence, and affection and kindliness by their own strength overcame all obstacles, and moved me immediately. . . . For instance, when in earlier times, in hot summers, when you were tired after lunch, I saw you having a nap at the office, your elbow on the desk; or when you joined us in the country, in the summer holidays, on Sundays, worn out from work at the office; or the time when Mother was gravely ill and you stood holding on to the bookcase, shaking with sobs; or when, during my last illness, you came tiptoeing to Ottla's room to see me, stopping in the doorway, craning your neck to see me, and out of consideration for me only waved your hand to me. At such times one would lie back and weep for happiness, and one weeps again now, writing it down.

This is gentle and loving enough, but it was the kind of experience which he could never reflect in his writing, perhaps because of its rarity or because of the immense superiority of his father's strength. Still, it helps to explain the nature of Dickens' comic triumph: the nap at the office, for instance, or the wave from the doorway, which indicate that a bridge of feeling has been thrown across the most formidable barriers. This is what Dickens achieves in *Great Expectations*, and by doing so, he is able to break through the terrible sense of isolation which seems to characterize his world, as well as Kafka's. That Wemmick is fatherly toward his childish father is the point to grasp. For the love between them is made possible only by an exchange of roles, or by the revelation of the father's vulnerability and of his need for love and care. Such an exchange never took place in Kafka's life, but Dickens was apparently able to achieve it, spiritually, in his later years. He was mature, as Kafka never was, in his final relations with his parents, and he found an "objective correlative" for that maturity in *Great Expectations*.

Of course, the castle episode has no connection with Kafka's novel, *The Castle*. Dickens' fathers are not divine, and there is no obsessive quest to obtain their favor. But the rough parallels are at least interesting: the split between castle and city, for example, or the fact that Pip, like K., is never able to reach his own particular castle or to secure a vital place in the world below. That Dickens asked to be buried at the foot of a castle near his home, and that Forster recorded this fact in his biography (which Kafka seems to have read), is also interesting. The important thing, however, is the common sense of defeat and world-weariness which marks the end of both novels, and the brief moment of acceptance for the dying K., which corresponds with the more solid union between Pip and Magwitch. Yet, according to Max Brod, K. "was not to relax in his struggle, but was to die worn out by it"; while Dickens' hero learns to accept his defeat with humility, and retires to a quiet bachelor life —at least in the original ending.

This change in Pip is accomplished gradually, in the

form of an ordeal. He decides to hide his benefactor from the legal authorities, until he can safely smuggle him out of England. In this way he is thrown into close contact with the man, first in his rooms, then on their trip together down the Thames, and finally during his last days in the prison hospital. During this same period Pip is almost murdered by the brutal Orlick; his hands are burned as he attempts to rescue Miss Havisham from fire; and his strength is later consumed by raging fever. It is an atonement process, one which melts away both the repulsion within him and the rigid, heavy bonds, imposed by society, which weigh so heavily upon his father:

> For now my repugnance to him had all melted away, and in the hunted, wounded, shackled creature who held my hand in his, I only saw a man who had meant to be my benefactor, and who had felt affectionately, gratefully, and generously toward me with great constancy through a series of years. I only saw in him a much better man than I had been to Joe.

With the father's vulnerability established, Pip is able to acknowledge his actual worth. Abandoning his gentleman's role, he stands beside him through the final ordeal. There is even a scene in court, when Magwitch is sentenced along with other prisoners, which gives a religious cast to the play of darkness against light, or of guilt against redemption, which informs their whole relationship:

> The sun was striking in at the great windows of the court, . . . and it made a broad shaft of light between the two-and-thirty [prisoners] and the judge, linking both together. . . . Rising for a moment, a distinct speck of face in this way of light, the prisoner said, "My lord, I have received my sentence of death from the Almighty, but I bow to yours," and sat down again.

In his last hours of life, Magwitch gives Pip his paternal blessing and thanks him for his belated faith. Then, as if to complete his punishment, Pip succumbs to a fever which seems
to burn away his guilt. When he comes out of it, he finds
himself in the care of Joe Gargery. He fancies himself a child
again, and essentially he remains a chastened child in later
life. His great expectations have dissolved "like . . . marsh
mists before the sun"; but he has made his peace with his
father, atoned for his sins, and arrived at real humility. To
Joe and his new wife, Biddy, he even asks to be received
"like a forgiven child." With his old friend Herbert, whom
he had once beaten at fisticuffs and whom he always considered as impractical, he enters into a modest business venture;
and though he marvels at his friend's mysterious loss of inaptitude, he now reflects "that perhaps the inaptitude had
never been in him at all, but had been in me."

With Miss Havisham the redemption process works
both ways. Before her death (which precedes that of Magwitch), Pip is able to show her "that, in shutting out the
light of day . . . she had secluded herself from a thousand
natural and healing influences; that her mind, brooding solitary, had grown diseased, as all minds do . . . that reverse
the appointed order of their Maker." Again the play of light
against dark is given a religious cast, as Miss Havisham admits her crimes against herself and Pip, and forgives Estella
(a part of whose "right nature" she has also denied) for her
heartless conduct. A short time later, when her clothes catch
fire, Pip wraps the burning woman in the rotten cloth of the
banquet table and is himself caught up in the conflagration,
as the sign of his complicity in her guilt and of his need for
purification. They are both "tried" by the fire, though again
the parent faces death, after a brief moment of grace when
Pip touches her lips in forgiveness.

The same form of grace has been granted, in the early chapters, to Pip's paralyzed sister, Mrs. Gargery; while in later scenes the stolid Jaggers receives more comic redemption, when forced to confess (obliquely) that he once committed an act of kindness. In these several ways, Dickens reclaims the foster parents and completes his penance for youthful sins. But the novel ends on a more wishful note, as the two foster children meet again at Miss Havisham's, in a romantic garden setting. Since Estella's husband is dead, and since she has learned, through suffering, to understand "what [Pip's] heart used to be," their eventual marriage is assured. Most critics agree, however, that the book should close with the explosion of this last and perhaps most foolish expectation. Dickens had actually planned it this way, and had then changed the ending under the pressure of his friend, Bulwer Lytton. But his original ending had avoided storybook romance, and had fixed the nature of Pip's youthful heart in exactly the right context.

It was two years more before I saw herself. I had heard of her as leading a most unhappy life, and as being separated from her husband, who had used her with great cruelty, and who had become quite renowned as a compound of pride, brutality, and meanness. I had heard of the death of her husband from an accident consequent on ill-treating a horse, and of her being married again to a Shropshire doctor who, against his interest, had once very manfully interposed on an occasion when he was in professional attendance upon Mr. Drummle, and had witnessed some outrageous treatment of her. I had heard that the Shropshire doctor was not rich, and that they lived on her own personal fortune. I was in England again—in London, and walking along Piccadilly with little Pip [Joe Gargery's son]—when a servant came running after me to ask would I step back to a lady in a carriage who wished to speak to me. It was a little pony carriage which the lady was driving, and the lady and I looked sadly enough on one another.

"I am greatly changed, I know; but I thought you would like to shake hands with Estella too, Pip. Lift up that pretty child and let me kiss it!" (She supposed the child, I think, to be my child.) I was very glad afterwards to have had the interview; for, in her face and in her voice, and in her touch, she gave me the assurance that suffering had been stronger than Miss Havisham's teaching, and had given her a heart to understand what my heart used to be.

Here Estella sits, as appealing as ever, though still enclosed within formidable barriers. Yet in the course of their talk, Pip is able to sense the change within her; there is a wave of feeling between them, a suggestion of sympathy and good will, which is all that Pip can expect for the mistaken agonies of adolescent love. Indeed, the warm, appreciative kiss for the pretty child, the very emblem of his youthful heart, is Pip's reward for his early suffering; even at his best, this is all he ever deserved (or wanted) from Estella. Nor can Dickens take him beyond this childlike need and still speak with authority to his readers: for the complexities of adult love are beyond his depth, as they are for Kafka. But he can at least convey that bond of feeling which obtains between two fellow creatures, in the face of shared distress; for it is the same bond which accounts for the special warmth of his comic figures, and for the special poignance of his comic world, where forgiveness and redemption are revealed as human possibilities.

As for the value of that world, Max Brod comes close to defining it in his analysis of the "infantile complex" in literature. He shows that the child's conflict with his parents is the model for his later conflicts with the world: he looks for love and trust from the family and often fails to get it;

he looks for mutual trust in the world at large and meets with similar opposition. Thus, Brod argues, the work of an infantile writer

> . . . is only a more honest, a more serious comprehension of the fatal fundamental constellation of existence, in which we all stand opposed to one another, all mistrusting one another, each one with the secret plea in his heart that one should after all have faith in him, even though he can give no proof of himself.

In a world informed by pain and isolation, such faith is the first step, at the least, toward fuller, deeper communion. We feel the lack of it most sharply through Kafka's fiction; but in Dickens we can also feel its absence, and we can even measure the latter by its hardwon presence—by the nods to Wemmick's father, by the convict's deathbed blessing, and by Estella's final kiss. These actions give his world an added dimension, and make it seem considerably richer, warmer, and more true to our own experience.

RESOLUTION AND INDEPENDENCE:
A READING OF *MIDDLEMARCH*

ELIOT, 1871–72

by Newton P. Stallknecht

George Eliot characterized her favorite novel by appending the subtitle, *A Study of Provincial Life*. It was her avowed purpose, following in the spirit of modern geology, "to show the gradual action of ordinary causes rather than exceptional, and to show this in some directions which have not been from time immemorial the beaten path." In this she has been signally successful; and yet we may, I think, do well to shift our perspective and, if only temporarily and for dialectical purposes, notice that George Eliot's statement may be challenged as too general.

After all, *Middlemarch*, despite its title and its bulk, centers upon a history—or, one might say, a genetic study —of a single human decision. Furthermore, the novel as a whole constitutes an argument devoted frankly to the defense of this decision, which is presented in what seems to George Eliot the most favorable light possible. Rarely has a novelist striven harder to protect the good name of a heroine than George Eliot has done throughout the last chapters of this ample history telling her readers of Dorothea's second marriage. The embarrassed concern felt by Mr. Brooke, Dorothea's "leaky-minded" and carelessly tolerant uncle, while imparting the news of her decision, reflects a problem that has occurred to George Eliot, who feels that she must spring to Dorothea's defense. It is almost as if she dreaded to hear the comment that her own creature, the sprightly and sharp-tongued match-maker, Mrs. Cadwallader, was bound to contribute. In any case, never has a mature and accomplished author gone further in defense of a character than George Eliot in the brief Prelude to the first volume. This little essay has seemed to many readers downright inept, a piece of special pleading sadly ill-conceived in strategy. Certainly the Prelude should never have appeared as such, but its content is interesting nonetheless. Here George Eliot describes Dorothea as a *grande religieuse,* a Saint Theresa, who has lost her way in an uncongenial epoch, blundering into an ambiguous situation as tangled circumstance thwarts her effort "to shape thought and deed in noble agreement."

This apology is, it might seem, an effort to make the best of a bad job. George Eliot's persistent attempt to interpret Dorothea as a genuine heroine reminds us that for many Victorian readers the young matron must have appeared as an object of commiseration, no true heroine but rather an impetuous sentimentalist whom friends and relatives had failed to restrain from headstrong, even questionable, conduct; her uncle, as in the case of her first marriage, being "all the more blamed in neighboring families for not [having secured] some middle-aged lady as guide and companion to his nieces."

There is, indeed, still some danger that today's reader will agree with Leslie Stephen, whose misgivings, recorded in a famous essay, are now published as an introductory note to the Everyman edition of *Middlemarch*, thus becoming, I think most unfortunately, the standard evaluation of the book available to the general reader. Having briefly sketched the circumstances of Dorothea's two marriages, Leslie Stephen writes:

> Had *Middlemarch* been intended for a cutting satire upon the aspirations of young ladies who wish to learn Latin and Greek when they ought to be nursing babies and supporting hospitals, these developments of affairs would have been in perfect congruity with the design. As it is, we are left with the feeling that aspirations of this kind scarcely deserve a better fate than they meet, and that Dorothea was all the better for getting the romantic aspirations out of her head. Have not the commonplace people the best of the argument?

Certainly we cannot ignore the question here implied: Has George Eliot created a tragic princess, a pedantic and sentimental Antigone, whose fate is only to appear ridiculous? As we finish reading the novel, it would hardly seem so. At this stage of the story, the family chorus is unsympathetic. But it is baffled and indignant, hardly amused. The reader may share this attitude but he will not find the situation ridiculous. Dorothea's stand is modest and dignified; and after all, to renounce a fine home, a secure social position, and a fortune is not usually a laughing matter; nor is George Eliot so inept as it makes it appear in this light. She does, however, make quite clear how the people of Middlemarch feel about Dorothea.

> Sir James never ceased to regard Dorothea's second marriage as a mistake; and indeed this remained the tradition concerning it in Middlemarch, where she was spoken of to a younger generation as a fine girl who married a sickly

clergyman, old enough to be her father, and in little more than a year after his death gave up her estate to marry his cousin—young enough to have been his son, with no property, and not well-born. Those who had not seen anything of Dorothea usually observed that she could not have been "a nice woman," else she would not have married either the one or the other.

Here we have the case of the opposition in its extreme form. Its existence, however, qualifies or characterizes Middlemarch itself and not Dorothea, who by the "resolution and independence" of her mature decision has put Middlemarch behind her. To be sure, for Celia, Sir James, and Mr. Brooke, Dorothea never ceases to be a "nice woman." For them her mistake lies primarily in that she is willing to appear otherwise, although of course her attitude toward a handsome inheritance is puzzling; and in any case there is nothing heroic about her obstinate refusal to profit by their common sense.

But after all, these good people can hardly be expected to have shared the wisdom of their author who looks back upon their provincial situation from the point of view of a metropolitan *intelligentsia* of a later generation. This generation has had time to profit by the wisdom of the great romantics and has tempered their philosophies of individualism and self-realization with a growing understanding of the workings of a modern society. Thus George Eliot, although an uncompromising idealist, is no mere Bohemian rebel. She possesses a mature sense of history and is well aware that her heroine must appear in modern dress.

Certainly those determining acts of [Dorothea's] life were not ideally beautiful. They were the mixed result of young and noble impulse struggling amidst the conditions of an imperfect social state, in which great feelings will often take the aspect of error, and great faith the aspect of illusion. For there is no creature whose inward being is so strong that it is not greatly determined by what lies outside it. A new Theresa will hardly have the opportunity of reforming a conventual life, any more than a new Antigone will spend her heroic piety in daring all for the sake of a brother's burial: the medium in which their ardent deeds took shape is for ever gone. But we insignificant people with our daily words and acts are preparing the lives of many Dorotheas, some of which may present a far sadder sacrifice than that of the Dorothea whose story we know.

The plot, or shall we say the argument, of *Middle-march* is intended to carry us to this sober conclusion. In such a case, clearly to understand is to sympathize. We are meant to see Dorothea's decision in the making; or better, since George Eliot is hardly an out and out determinist, we are to see Dorothea make the decision. Thus we must come to discern the shape of the ideals and the alternatives that confronted her as she made up her mind. In explication of this decision, George Eliot offers us a panorama of Middlemarch and the lives of its people. "For," as we have just heard, "there is no creature whose being is so strong that it is not greatly determined by what lies outside it." This thought, appropriate surely from the pen of one who, like George Eliot, had long pondered Spinoza's study of human bondage and human freedom, is well supported by the following observation, that is, nonetheless, perhaps more characteristic of the novelist than of the philosopher.

. . . any one watching keenly the stealthy convergence of human lots, sees a slow preparation of effects from one life on another, which tells like a calculated irony on the indifference or the frozen stare with which we look at our un-introduced neighbour.

It is from such observations as also from an awareness of the "shifting boundaries of social intercourse," of the arbitrariness, artificiality, and the unsteadiness of class distinctions, that we acquire a "new consciousness of interdependence." George Eliot has contributed toward the emergence of this consciousness with consummate skill. As F. R. Leavis has pointed out, her

> . . . sheer informedness about society, its mechanism, the ways in which people of different classes live and (if they have to) earn their livelihoods, impresses us with its range, and it is real knowledge; that is, it is knowledge alive with understanding. George Eliot had said in *Felix Holt*, by way of apology for the space she devoted to "social changes" and "public matters": "there is no private life which has not been determined by a wider public life." The aim implicit in this remark is magnificently achieved in *Middlemarch*, and it is achieved by a novelist whose genius manifests itself in a profound analysis of the individual.

The result is an exhaustive study of human motivation, of the interdependence of people, and their mutual influence upon one another. Such influence is most clearly apparent in family relations, but George Eliot follows its currents and cross-currents far beyond the limits of family life. It is, if we may shift our metaphor, from such a sub-soil that the independence, the autonomy, and responsibility of the mature individual must emerge if it is to exist at all.

The author's intention is accordingly often analytic, and the tone of the work is firmly intellectual. This has, over the years, disappointed a good many readers who, unless these books were forced upon them too early in their school days, remember with pleasure the lyricism, the warmth and depth of feeling of *Silas Marner* and the joyously detailed picture of the childhood of Tom and Maggie

Tulliver in *The Mill on the Floss*. These people find *Middlemarch* far too objective, even too clinical, a study. Here again Leslie Stephen's comment comes to mind.

> *Middlemarch* is undoubtedly a powerful book, but to many readers it is a rather painful book, and it can hardly be called a charming book to any one. The light of common day has most unmistakably superseded the indescribable glow which illuminated the earlier writings.

Well, this is as may be and, after all, pretty much a matter of taste. For my part, I find that I enjoy re-reading *Middlemarch* rather more than *Silas Marner* and that, although the later novel may lack the poetry of its predecessors, its quiet thoughtfulness is far from prosaic. As Virginia Woolf has insisted, *Middlemarch* was written for grown-up people. Its clarity and firmness reward continued study, and the lack, throughout many chapters, of any very dramatic incident, is compensated by the three-dimensional —or should we say *four*-dimensional?—detail, the unity of whose development grows increasingly self-explanatory as we study George Eliot's narrative and commentary.

Again, although lyric intensity may be for the most part lacking, there is an abundance of wit and an irony often at its best when projected into conversation obviously intended otherwise by the speaker. Thus Mr. Brooke's rambling monologs are always amusing and sometimes spectacular in their left-handed significance. Brooke remains throughout, despite his grave shortcomings as a guardian, a landlord, and a politician, a delightful character—at least on the printed page and in small doses. George Eliot does not make the mistake that Jane Austen falls into when she allows the garrulous Miss Bates at last to bore us with her total recall of commonplace incidents.

"Sir Humphry Davy?" said Mr. Brooke, over the soup, in his easy smiling way, taking up Sir James Chettam's remark that he was studying Davy's Agricultural Chemistry. "Well, now, Sir Humphry Davy: I dined with him years ago at Cartwright's, and Wordsworth was there too—the poet Wordsworth, you know. Now there was something singular. I was at Cambridge when Wordsworth was there, and I never met him—and I dined with him twenty years afterwards at Cartwright's. There's an oddity in things, now. But Davy was there: he was a poet too. Or, as I may say, Wordsworth was poet one, and Davy was poet two. That was true in every sense, you know."

Dorothea felt a little more uneasy than usual. In the beginning of dinner, the party being small and the room still, these motes from the mass of a magistrate's mind fell too noticeably.

And again from the same chapter:

"Young ladies don't understand political economy, you know," said Mr. Brooke, smiling towards Mr. Casaubon. "I remember when we were all reading Adam Smith. *There* is a book, now. I took in all the new ideas at one time—human perfectibility, now. But some say, history moves in circles; and that may be very well argued; I have argued it myself. The fact is, human reason may carry you a little too far—over the hedge, in fact. It carried me a good way at one time; but I saw it would not do. I pulled up; I pulled up in time. But not too hard. I have always been in favour of a little theory: we must have Thought; else we shall be landed back in the dark ages. But talking of books, there is Southey's 'Peninsular War.' I am reading that of a morning. You know Southey?"

Dorothea is certainly a victim of her uncle's wool-headed confusion. A very young lady, sensitive and thoughtful, who has listened with growing embarrassment to months of such chatter may be pardoned if she pays a naive respect to the scholarly platitudes of an austere, middle-aged clergyman whose haggard dignity resembles a famous portrait of John Locke. Like Milton's "affable archangel," the Reverend Mr. Casaubon is glad to enlighten so earnest and attractive a listener; and in contrast to Mr. Brooke's "scrappy slovenliness" of mind he appears as a man of high purpose and monumental learning. Poor Dorothea is quite unable to take his measure.

Her imagination rushes toward the theological heroes of her youthful studies. She thinks herself in the presence of a Bossuet or a "living Augustine who unite[s] the glories of doctor and saint."

> It had now entered Dorothea's mind that Mr. Casaubon might wish to make her his wife, and the idea that he would do so touched her with a sort of reverential gratitude. How good of him—nay, it would be almost as if a winged messenger had suddenly stood beside her path and held out his hand towards her! For a long while she had been oppressed by the indefiniteness which hung in her mind, like a thick summer haze, over all her desire to make her life greatly effective. . . . The intensity of her religious disposition, the coercion it exercised over her life, was but one aspect of a nature altogether ardent, theoretic, and intellectually consequent: and with such a nature, struggling in the bands of a narrow teaching, hemmed in by a social life which seemed nothing but a labyrinth of petty courses, a walled-in maze of small paths that led no whither, the outcome was sure to strike others as at once exaggeration and inconsistency. The thing which seemed to her best, she wanted to justify by the completest knowledge; and not to live in a pretended admission of rules which were never acted on. Into this soul-hunger as yet all her youthful passion was poured; the union which attracted her was one that would deliver her from her girlish subjection to her own ignorance, and give her the freedom of voluntary submission to a guide who would take her along the grandest path.

George Eliot makes very clear that Dorothea has been cruelly misled. Hardly for a moment are we allowed to suppose that Casaubon is genuine. The contrast between his semblance and the sorry substance beneath it is a constant source of irony, and George Eliot's expressions of pity for either member of this ill-matched pair are at first almost perfunctory. Both Casaubon's learning and his matrimonial intentions—the latter amounting to little more than a desire for an admiring satellite that will not disturb the dreary orbit of his own existence—are targets for her but thinly veiled contempt. And yet Dorothea in her bookish idealism is entranced. For her, Casaubon is the very embodiment of piety and wisdom. To marry him "would be like marrying Pascal." She is too starry-eyed, too stubborn, and too ill-informed to listen to the obvious and unanswerable objections of her friends and relatives. She ignores their protests with a well-bred composure. Her mind is courteously but firmly closed and she accepts Casaubon's luke-warm proposal, at the same time snubbing the more gallant advances of that most eligible young baronet, Sir James Chettam, who has wooed her by sharing her concern for the proper housing of his tenants. So Dorothea marries Casaubon; and Celia, her amiable and practical sister, gladly accepts Sir James and lives, it would seem, quite happily ever after.

Our attention now becomes focused upon Casaubon and the grim tragedy of his disintegration. A wealthy man and a person of some distinction in provincial life, Casaubon enjoys the respect of his neighbors and of his profession. He may indeed someday become a bishop. His research, although incomplete, is known to the learned world. But this reputation has preceded performance and as a result he is "nervously conscious that he [is] expected to manifest a powerful mind." This is all the more embarrassing since in reality he is little more than a learned crank misled by that dream of the older mythologists, the gratuitous assumption that all myths of whatever date or place of origin are "erratic fragments" or corruptions of a great religious tradition originally revealed to all men. In support of this sweeping hypothesis—an hypothesis, incidentally, especially questionable in the eyes of a humanist like George Eliot—Casaubon has gathered his voluminous notebooks and then —has lost his nerve. His *magnum opus*, unfinished and rendered obsolete by continental scholarship, has become a burden and a rebuke. Like many scholars before and after him, Casaubon is disconcerted by the mirage of a reputation that he cannot achieve. At this point, Dorothea innocently urges him to complete his work, eagerly offering her services as *amanuensis*. Her interest only forces Casaubon the more clearly to recognize his predicament so that her concern heightens his sense of defeat and isolation. "Dorothea was not only his wife: she was a personification of that shallow world which surrounds the ill-appreciated or desponding author."

In these last days, Casaubon suffers acutely. His defenses shattered, lonely, and in miserable health, he is imprisoned within his own suspicion and despair. He allows his dislike for his charming and lively *protégé*, his cousin Will Ladislaw, to degenerate into jealousy and he bullies the young man stupidly. The result, a clear indication of his moral bankruptcy, is the disgraceful clause in his will, added shortly before his death, restraining Dorothea, on pain of forfeiting her ample inheritance, from marrying Ladislaw. Casaubon's agony explains but cannot excuse this vindictive action; but his suffering is so manifest that at last he appears to the unprejudiced reader almost as a sympathetic character. George Eliot finds herself capable of genuine pity where for so long she has been tersely ironical. The image of the broken Casaubon possesses her imagination and she sees him as a victim of circumstance. Her sympathy takes the form of rebuking the physician Lydgate, whose pity for Casaubon in his last days approaches contempt. Lydgate, she notes, was "at present too ill acquainted with disaster to enter into the pathos of a lot where everything is below the level of tragedy except the passionate egoism of the sufferer."

These words, quoted by Mr. Leavis, writing on *Middlemarch* in *The Great Tradition*, command our attention. In large measure, they summarize the magnanimous wisdom of their author and declare her purpose. Mr. Leavis comments that "the essential predicament" here described "involves the insulation of the egoism from all large or heroic ends." Casaubon, despite his learned busy work, has been thus insulated for years, and Lydgate himself is in a similar predicament since he has been unwilling to make the sacrifices necessary to follow his scientific interests. Here, I think, we are close to the heart of the matter—to a theme of psychological and moral significance that is developed in various ways throughout the intricate structure of *Middlemarch*. It may be stated as follows: Every human being is prone to see his world and the possibilities that mark its horizons through the lens of an egoism that blurs, distorts, and foreshortens, sometimes in quite unexpected ways. Such egoism stands in the way of any genuine self-realization; and it is the fate of many "to be present at this great spectacle of life and never to be liberated from a small hungry shivering self." Hence the truth that lies in the paradox of self-transcendence as in Seneca's

Unless above himself he can
Erect himself, how poor a thing is man,

or in that supreme maxim of Christian morality, "Whosoever will save his life shall lose it, and whosoever will lose
his life shall find it." As A. E. Housman once put it, this
is "the most important truth which has ever been uttered,
and the greatest discovery ever made in the moral world."
It is in illustration of this theorem of human nature that
George Eliot develops the frankly didactic portions of her
marginal commentary. Her admonitions are Christian in
spirit. A true non-conformist, she has carried the spirit
of non-conformism to its logical conclusion, and she offers
us a non-institutional Christianity purged of mythology.
Today, when almost everyone is once again fascinated by
mythology and when whole novels are built upon symbolic
themes, her didactic realism is out of fashion; but it remains nonetheless the best of its kind: impartial, humane
without being sentimental, psychologically accurate and
intellectually consistent, and often, because of some turn of
phrase or thrust of emphasis, memorable for its cogency.

Suppose we turn from outside estimates of a man, to wonder, with keener interest, what is the report of his own consciousness about his doings or capacity: with what hindrances
he is carrying on his daily labours; what fading of hopes, or
what deeper fixity of self-delusion the years are marking
off within him; and with what spirit he wrestles against universal pressure, which will one day be too heavy for him,
and bring his heart to its final pause. Doubtless his lot is important in his own eyes; and the chief reason that we think
he asks too large a place in our consideration must be our
want of room for him, since we refer him to the Divine regard with perfect confidence; nay, it is even held sublime

for our neighbour to expect the utmost there, however little he may have got from us. Mr. Casaubon, too, was the centre of his own world; if he was liable to think that others were providentially made for him, and especially to consider them in the light of their fitness for the author of a "Key to all Mythologies," this trait is not quite alien to us, and, like the other mendicant hopes of mortals, claims some of our pity.

Against this egocentric fallacy George Eliot marshals her full powers of argument and illustration. This is especially the case in *Middlemarch*. As a result, this novel stands, if we may borrow a phrase from Henry James, as "the last word of a philosophy endeavoring to teach by example." In one way or another, George Eliot drives home the truth that we will pay dearly if we distort our view of things by thinking of ourselves as the center of our world.

Once again we may be reminded of Spinoza who, in formulating the first principles of his philosophy, undertook to rebuke our egocentric appeals to a providence that but reflects our own narrow concerns. The world was not built to order to suit the taste of any finite being. With such principles in mind, George Eliot consciously brings the wisdom of the philosophers to bear upon the lives of her compatriots. "Pledged to the school teachers' virtues," she openly and frankly evaluates the conduct and the achievements of her *dramatis personae*. Since her characters are clearly conceived and fully realized and her judgment penetrating, the result is capital and her modern readers are reminded that human morality is a fascinating subject.

But let us return to the egocentric fallacy. Even the young Fred Vincy, in his misguided innocence, displays this all too human presumption. In him it is not malignant as in Casaubon or in Bulstrode. It is for Fred merely the penalty of Adam, taking such form as is most natural in the character of a thoughtless young man, for the time being, "addicted to pleasure." Thus, as Fred Vincy slides optimistically into debt, George Eliot offers a characteristic comment.

> On both occasions Fred had felt confident that he should meet the bill himself, having ample funds at disposal in his own hopefulness. You will hardly demand that his confidence should have a basis in external facts; such confidence, we know, is something less coarse and materialistic: it is a comfortable disposition leading us to expect that the wisdom of providence or the folly of our friends, the mysteries of luck or the still greater mystery of our high individual value in the universe, will bring about agreeable issues, such as are consistent with our good taste in costume, and our general preference for the best style of thing. Fred felt sure that he should have a present from his uncle, that he should have a run of luck, that by dint of "swapping" he should gradually metamorphose a horse worth forty pounds into a horse that would fetch a hundred at any moment—"judgment" being always equivalent to an unspecified sum in hard cash.

Although rich in comedy, the story of Fred Vincy's redemption through the patience and example of Caleb Garth, supported by the affection and the clear common sense of his daughter, contains a stinging rebuke of the *snobisme* of Middlemarch, so well represented by the Vincys, and of the traditional notions prescribing the pattern of a young gentleman's education. This story happily centers our attention upon the only people in the novel who are from the start so mature that their virtues need not be distinguished from their common sense: Caleb Garth, his wife and his daughter, Mary.

As a steward of other men's land, Caleb is used to being trusted and his egoism has been purified by his self-respect.

It is significant that "by 'business' Caleb never meant money transactions, but the skillful application of labor." His admirable advice to Fred, the most didactic passage in a didactic novel, contains his own *Apologia*.

> "You must be sure of two things: you must love your work, and not always looking over the edge of it, wanting your play to begin. And the other is, you must not be ashamed of your work, and think it would be more honourable to you to be doing something else. You must have a pride in your own work and in learning to do it well, and not be always saying, There's this and there's that—if I had this or that to do, I might make something of it. No matter what a man is—I wouldn't give twopence for him"—here Caleb's mouth looked bitter, and he snapped his fingers—"whether he was the prime minister or the rick-thatcher, if he didn't do well what he undertook to do."
>
> "I can never feel that I should do that in being a clergyman," said Fred, meaning to take a step in argument.
>
> "Then let it alone, my boy," said Caleb abruptly, "else you'll never be easy. Or, if you *are* easy, you'll be a poor stick."

George Eliot's admiration, springing perhaps from a reminiscence of her own father, is unqualified even when Caleb's amiable shortcomings are to be noticed.

> He was one of those rare men who are rigid to themselves and indulgent to others. He had a certain shame about his neighbours' errors, and never spoke of them willingly; hence he was not likely to divert his mind from the best mode of hardening timber and other ingenious devices in order to preconceive those errors. If he had to blame any one, it was necessary for him to move all the papers within his reach, or describe various diagrams with his stick, or make calculations with the odd money in his pocket, before he could begin; and he would rather do other men's work than find fault with their doing. I fear he was a bad disciplinarian.

Caleb Garth is a touchstone by which most of the other characters in *Middlemarch* may be tested and found wanting. It is noteworthy that George Eliot is careful to record his admiration for Dorothea, whose sincere concern for the problems of rural housing has surprised and delighted him. We may well wonder that George Eliot has succeeded in making of Caleb so genuine a human being rather than a mere symbol of perfection. She has accomplished this, at least partially, by involving him in continual difficulty and embarrassment and by emphasizing the disturbing effect of his honesty upon his family's fortunes.

Viewed in a certain perspective, Lydgate stands in obvious antithesis to Garth. Like Caleb, he is sincerely interested in his work. He is devoted to the new scientific medicine and proud of his profession. But he still feels the necessity of being a fine gentleman, and he resents the limitations upon his career resulting from the fact that he must earn a living, despite his aristocratic connections. He adorns and complicates his existence by marrying the beautiful Rosamond Vincy, a spoiled and wheedling little snob, who soon runs him into debt and alienates the sympathies of his well-to-do family.

> Shallow natures dream of an easy sway over the emotions of others, trusting implicitly in their own petty magic to turn the deepest streams, and confident, by pretty gestures and remarks, of making the thing that is not as though it were.

Despite her selfishness and her stupidity, both of which he recognizes clearly enough, Lydgate remains fond of his wife. The resulting story of domestic difficulty and professional compromise is one of George Eliot's masterpieces. Lydgate is for many readers the most memorable and the most convincing character in *Middlemarch*. George Eliot's estimate of his very real shortcomings is exemplary, a supreme instance of justice and compassion united in a single judgment. We are never allowed to forget the great difference between Lydgate and Casaubon. The latter's learning was never inspired, and his curiosity was dominated by a pseudo-orthodoxy. Lydgate on the other hand might well have been a true scientist. George Eliot comments: "Only those who know the supremacy of the intellectual life . . . can understand the grief of one who falls from that serene activity into the absorbing soul-wasting struggle with worldly annoyances." This, she implies, is equally true of those who have brought such distraction upon themselves.

There is, nonetheless, a coarseness in Lydgate and no effort is made to conceal it. He who in the end is to benefit so largely by the generosity of which Dorothea is capable is at first disturbed by her sincerity.

> He had quitted the party early, and would have thought it altogether tedious but for the novelty of certain introductions, especially the introduction to Miss Brooke, whose youthful bloom, with her approaching marriage to that faded scholar, and her interest in matters socially useful, gave her the piquancy of an unusual combination.
>
> "She is a good creature—that fine girl—but a little too earnest," he thought. "It is troublesome to talk to such women. They are always wanting reasons, yet they are too ignorant to understand the merits of any question, and usually fall back on their moral sense to settle things after their own taste."

And so Lydgate marries Rosamond, a fate that he thoroughly deserves since he has "held it one of the prettiest attributes of the feminine mind to adore a man's pre-

eminence without too precise a knowledge of what it con-
sist[s] in."

Himself half an idealist, Lydgate appears as an excellent foil for Dorothea. It is interesting to notice that
the latter's acceptance of Casaubon reveals motives very
different from those that inspired Lydgate's *mésalliance*.
Again, we may remark that Dorothea profits by her bitter
experience and achieves her freedom in the end. Lydgate
remains throughout very much the same. To the very end
he resents his situation even while he makes a good living
as a specialist in fashionable diseases, and he is inclined,
when in a grumbling mood, to blame his wife for his failure
to have achieved a real distinction.

The leisurely pace of the early chapters is quickened
in the second volume, where the reader may feel a certain
surprise as he is drawn into the melodrama of Raffles and
Bulstrode. Raffles, the sneering blackmailer, is as venomous
a reptile as any to be found in Victorian fiction. With him
we come upon an intricate story of "white-collar crime"
and its exposure. The plot, involving ill-gotten wealth, ugly
and persistent blackmail, and murder or the appearance of
murder, comes to a climax with the death of Raffles.
Bulstrode, the pious hypocrite and mock philanthropist, is,
justly enough, disgraced. But the scandal is soon out of
control. Lydgate's professional reputation is involved in
Raffles' death and the secret, unpalatable enough at this
period, of poor Ladislaw's antecedents becomes known
throughout Middlemarch.

The narrative that carries us swiftly toward this catastrophe is dominated by the unlovely character of Bulstrode,
upon whom George Eliot lavishes her subtlest powers of
analysis. She seems here to be even more fascinated than
she has been previously by Casaubon. The mental machin-

ery of a semi-conscious hypocrisy holds her attention. Her intelligence and her imagination are both aroused to give us a lively and penetrating study. It would seem to be her purpose to make clear that a crooked banker may be, in some sense, a religious person. We are shown how religious sentiment, or its very plausible facsimile, may be incorporated in the personality of an able and intelligent man, greedy for power and, despite a glib show of humility, thoroughly corrupt in his self-deception.

There may be coarse hypocrites, who consciously affect beliefs and emotions for the sake of gulling the world, but Bulstrode was not one of them. He was simply a man whose desires had been stronger than his theoretic beliefs, and who had gradually explained the gratification of his desires into satisfactory agreement with those beliefs. If this be hypocrisy, it is a process which shows itself occasionally in us all, to whatever confession we belong. . . .

This implicit reasoning is essentially no more peculiar to evangelical belief than the use of wide phrases for narrow motives is peculiar to Englishmen. There is no general doctrine which is not capable of eating out our morality if unchecked by the deep-seated habit of direct fellow-feeling with individual fellow-men.

Bulstrode's private deliberations, even while he is cunningly searching some means of extricating himself from a predicament that may bring exposure and disgrace, are couched in terms of a distorted and uneasy piety. It is greatly to George Eliot's credit and owing to her skill, her restraint, and her sense of fairness that Bulstrode appears neither as a monster, like Raffles, nor as a living cliché or caricature but as an unhappy human being, an avaricious hypocrite who, in his incontinence, suffers for his sins both before and after they are exposed. Bulstrode, for all his unloveliness, differs from his fellow men not in kind but only in the degree to which his egotism has counterfeited an apology for his way of life and of business—in short, to the degree in which he has presumed to justify the ways of man to God. George Eliot's analysis has made of such a corrupt consciousness an absorbing object of our curiosity. We would—almost—have more of this hypocrite whose credibility fascinates us. We may feel that an equally re-warding study might well have been devoted to Bulstrode's life after his retreat from Middlemarch. It would be in-teresting to learn whether the presumption that inspired him at the last moment to challenge in Christian terms the motives and overt actions of his accusers would survive the acute humiliation of his exposure. George Eliot describes this humiliation with a delicate sympathy as she makes clear, in a wonderful scene of disclosure between husband and wife, poor Bulstrode's inability to achieve the dignity of confession and repentance.

> He raised his eyes with a little start and looked at her half amazed for a moment: her pale face, her changed, mourning dress, the trembling about her mouth, all said, "I know"; and her hands and eyes rested gently on him. He burst out crying and they cried together, she sitting at his side. They could not yet speak to each other of the shame which she was bearing with him, or of the acts which had brought it down on them. His confession was silent, and her promise of faithfulness was silent. Open-minded as she was, she nevertheless shrank from the words which would have expressed their mutual consciousness as she would have shrunk from flakes of fire. She could not say, "How much is only slander and false suspicion?" and he did not say, "I am innocent."

The fall of Bulstrode and the revelations that go with it put the people of Middlemarch to the test. The ungrounded and uncharitable words of suspicion that follow both Lydgate and Ladislaw only make a dirty business worse. George Eliot's roster of local comment is a masterly report. We hear the gloating of Dill, Crabbe, and Mrs. Dollop and witness the silent aristocratic distaste of the "upright" Sir James, who hopes that the scandal will finally remove Ladislaw from the scene and secure Dorothea from the danger of a second willful alliance. Against this background, Dorothea's generous refusal to think ill of Lydgate, her readiness to help him financially, and her indignation that Ladislaw's origin should be made an object of contempt indicate a courage and maturity rare among the people of Middlemarch and prepare us for her final emancipation. During the two years of her married life she had seen enough of suspicion, and her "intensest experience . . . had set her mind strongly in opposition to any unfavorable construction of others." She was prepared to act on such a conviction. "People," she exclaimed, "glorify all sorts of bravery except the bravery they might show on behalf of their meanest neighbors." In the light of such resolution, the cautious hesitation recommended by Sir James, who advises her to stay out of the "Bulstrode business," seems a very shabby compromise.

This is the end. The authority of Middlemarch and its timid notions of respectability have faded into insignificance. Dorothea is conscious as never before that she must look to herself for the justification of her opinions. In her immature admiration for Casaubon, she had set the blurred image of his superiority above her own judgment. Now, quite without any such external support, she finds herself clearly aware of her own independence and responsibility. The "Bulstrode business" has set her free. It is in this spirit that she resists every effort on the part of her intimates to dissuade her from marrying Will Ladislaw.

> "It is quite true that I might be a wiser person, Celia," said Dorothea, "and that I might have done something better, if I had been better. But this is what I am going to do. I have promised to marry Mr. Ladislaw; and I am going to marry him."

The gentle Celia, sincerely and deeply concerned for her sister's well-being, sees little essential difference between Dorothea's attitude at this time and that of two years earlier. "Dodo" is simply being difficult, making herself and others uncomfortable. Mrs. Cadwallader is certain that Dorothea's interest in Ladislaw is a stubborn and perverse reaction to Casaubon's will. No one, not even Mrs. Cadwallader's kindly and tolerant husband, has the slightest notion of Dorothea's real attitude.

Dorothea is far more clear-headed than any of them, and she knows what she wants. She has felt, to be sure, a reluctant loyalty to the memory of Casaubon, and perhaps some reasonable hesitation to face poverty, or what must have seemed to her very like it, and to have to "learn what things cost"; and she has not been always wholly sure of Ladislaw's devotion. But these hesitations vanish during a swift comedy of errors, and Dorothea, as a last reward of her generosity, learns from Rosamond of Ladislaw's sincerity. True enough, her acceptance of Ladislaw at this time is an act of impulse. But her subsequent decision to abide by this impulse and to seek her happiness with Ladislaw is mature and deliberate. Her family's objections appear at last quite clearly in their true light: they are, although characteristic of their time and place, at best merely frivolous and often something worse. Here George Eliot supports her heroine with genial irony.

"Do you mean that Dodo is going to be married directly, uncle?"

"In three weeks, you know," said Mr. Brooke, helplessly. "I can do nothing to hinder it, Cadwallader," he added, turning for a little countenance towards the Rector, who said—

"*I* should not make any fuss about it. If she likes to be poor, that is her affair. Nobody would have said anything if she had married the young fellow because he was rich. Plenty of beneficed clergy are poorer than they will be. Here is Elinor," continued the provoking husband; "she vexed her friends by marrying me: I had hardly a thousand a-year—I was a lout—nobody could see anything in me— my shoes were not the right cut—all the men wondered how a woman could like me. Upon my word, I must take Ladislaw's part until I hear more harm of him."

"Humphrey, that is all sophistry, and you know it," said his wife. "Everything is all one—that is the beginning and end with you. As if you had not been a Cadwallader! Does any one suppose that I would have taken such a monster as you by any other name?"

"And a clergyman too," observed Lady Chettam with approbation. "Elinor cannot be said to have descended below her rank. It is difficult to say what Mr. Ladislaw is, eh, James?"

Sir James gave a small grunt, which was less respectful than his usual mode of answering his mother. Celia looked up at him like a thoughtful kitten.

"It must be admitted that his blood is a frightful mixture!" said Mrs. Cadwallader. "The Casaubon cuttle-fish fluid to begin with, and then a rebellious Polish fiddler or dancing-master, was it?—and then an old clo—"

"Nonsense, Elinor," said the Rector, rising. "It is time for us to go."

"After all, he is a pretty sprig," said Mrs. Cadwallader,

rising too, and wishing to make amends. "He is like the fine old Crichley portraits before the idiots came in."

Despite the brilliance of this and of other passages, many readers and some of George Eliot's most distinguished critics, Stephen and Leavis among them, have questioned the author's achievement in these last pages. Dorothea herself in her new incarnation is thought to be too hastily drawn, her new virtues suggested rather than fully realized in the text of dialog and incident. Furthermore, Leslie Stephen speaks of Ladislaw as a young man who "appears to have some good feeling" and Mr. Leavis insists that in the life of the novel

. . . he has no independent status of his own—he can't be said to exist; he merely represents, not a dramatically real point of view, but certain of George Eliot's intentions—intentions she has failed to realize creatively. The most important of these is to impose on the reader her own vision and valuation of Dorothea.

Will, of course, is also intended—it is not really a separate matter—to be, in contrast to Casaubon, a fitting soulmate for Dorothea. He is not substantially (everyone agrees) 'there,' but we can see well enough what kind of qualities and attractions are intended, and we can see equally well that we are expected to share a valuation of them extravagantly higher than any we can for a moment countenance. George Eliot's valuation of Will Ladislaw, in short, is Dorothea's, just as Will's of Dorothea is George Eliot's. Dorothea, to put it another way, is a product of George Eliot's own 'soul-hunger'—another day-dream ideal self. . . . We have an alternation between the poised impersonal insight of a finely tempered wisdom and something like the emotional confusions and self-importances of adolescence.

However they may have been intended, these are surely "shooting words." If they are wholly justified, *Mid-*

dlemarch must be classed as a second-rate novel, despite the obvious fact that it contains a brilliant study of life and manners and a number of splendid characterizations. Now, I should like to suggest that in this very matter of superb character study lies our real difficulty. It is certainly true that the character of Ladislaw has been overshadowed by that magnificent rogues' gallery of portraits: Brooke, Casaubon, Lydgate, Mrs. Cadwallader, Bulstrode, and even (God bless him) Fred Vincy. George Eliot has in a way protected Ladislaw, perhaps bowing to Victorian sentiment. Certainly his portrait is not a masterpiece of penetrating irony like those just mentioned. But in almost any other context George Eliot's Ladislaw would, I think, appear substantial enough. Certainly his picture is clearly drawn and his character is consistent. His first appearance, as is true of many young men of his age and position, is that of a dilettante; but once he stands in company with Mr. Brooke, it is obvious that he is made of much firmer stuff. In his relations with Casaubon, he emerges as a sensitive and honorable young man irritated by unreasonable treatment. The touch of vindictiveness occasionally apparent is not out of place. His capacity for the enjoyment of life is attractive and the indignation with which he refuses Bulstrode's hush money is completely convincing. We wish he could have known that his honest scorn had reduced that uneasy scoundrel to tears.

All this is true; yet in the vicinity of Brooke, Bulstrode, and the others Ladislaw remains a dim figure. He seems rather like a good passport snapshot mislaid in a pile of Daumier lithographs, or a Bassanio surrounded by a troupe of Shylocks. As a result the center of gravity of *Middlemarch* is displaced and Dorothea's devotion to Ladislaw may seem to some readers unconvincing. Indeed, I have heard readers ask why Ladislaw is really necessary. After all, they wonder, why could Dorothea not have fallen in love with Lydgate? Such uncertainty can be disastrous and it is certainly a source of real difficulty for all of us, especially on a first reading, when we may well be dazzled by our impressions of other characters.

Even so, I question Mr. Leavis' diagnosis. George Eliot's failure, in so far as she *has* failed, need not be interpreted as a re-emergence of adolescent sentimentalism. Certainly, as Mr. Leavis admits, there would seem to be little that is sentimental or gushing about the author who has followed the fortunes of Lydgate and Rosamond or even of Fred Vincy and Mary Garth. The difficulty is, I am sure, a more superficial one, almost a matter of technique. I suspect that George Eliot was to some degree aware of this inadequacy and included the unfortunate Prelude as a corrective. This she would hardly have done had she been carried away by sentimental enthusiasm. George Eliot remains to the end quite capable of seeing Dorothea in full relief, and her evaluation is a sober one. Thus the reference to St. Theresa is not wholly illegitimate: Dorothea might, under rather different circumstances, have entered a religious house and followed Theresa's path, either before her first marriage or after Casaubon's death. But this comment is far too general to be helpful to the reader either as a warning or as an afterthought. The fault lies in the very structure of the novel whereby Dorothea and Ladislaw are seen in constant conjunction with other characters, relatively speaking, too spectacular in their delineation. After all, we must admit that vice in general, including especially the living paradox of self-deception, offers the novelist a rich material to work with. In the realm of fiction the complexity of consciousness discernible in those souls still, so to speak, in purgatory is the most fascinating subject of all. Thus Dorothea and Will Ladislaw do well to leave Middlemarch. In the end their simple honesty and good sense are out of place there—both from the point of view of the moralist and from that of the story-teller. And yet both have profited by the fact that circumstances have forced them at last to take the measure of their contemporaries, including their friends and relatives. They had found themselves bewildered in a confusion of respectabilities, prejudice, and self-deception, guided only by the abstract idealisms—preconceived and untried—of very young people, Dorothea thinking in terms of duty and responsibility, Ladislaw in those of self-expression.

Unaided, they have withstood the test and mastered the "angry and bewildering current of real experience" [1] far better than most of their contemporaries. As George Eliot hints in her last paragraphs, such achievement, even if obscure and "unhistoric" and lacking in "ideal" beauty, remains as a contribution toward what another great Victorian has described as "that ultimate good sense which we term civilization." [2] We have quoted Virginia Woolf's remark that *Middlemarch* is a book for grown-up people. It is more than that: it is a story about the way in which people grow up.

[1] See Charles Grosvenor Osgood, *The Voice of England* (New York, 1935), Chapter XXXIII. This brief estimate of George Eliot's achievement has seemed to me sober and well-balanced. I should like to see it, instead of Leslie Stephen's note, as a preface to *Middlemarch* in a popular edition.

[2] A. N. Whitehead, *Modes of Thought* (New York, 1938), p. 238.

CHARACTER AND COINCIDENCE IN
THE RETURN OF THE NATIVE

HARDY, 1878

by Charles Child Walcutt

In the opening pages of *The Return of the Native*, Hardy elaborates a theme with a series of symbolic images which he modulates so that, by the time he has got to the end of his first chapter, the theme has been considerably enriched and qualified. At first the bright sky and the dark heath seem to be bold images of two sharply distinguished principles:

> . . . their meeting-line at the horizon was clearly marked.
> . . . the heath wore the appearance of an instalment of night which had taken up its place before its astronomical hour was come . . . while day stood distinct in the sky. . . . The distant rims of the world and of the firmament (at the horizon) seemed to be a division in time no less than a division in matter.

The bright sky and the dark heath seem to be two aspects of life—aspiration contrasted with ability, freedom or will against fate, or intelligence against the dark compulsions of instinct. The glowing sky stands for the potential, the hope, the release—the dark heath for the forces of character and fate that oppress and defeat them. Thus the first statement; but Hardy presently introduces a suggestion of dark power and *life* in the heath which reach up in concord and sympathy toward the darkening sky:

> And so the obscurity in the air and the obscurity in the land closed together in a black fraternization towards which each advanced half-way.

Here are mystery and conspiracy in the unfolding of which the lucid candors of the sky have been superseded by a demonic intent. The sharp line of the horizon, between aspiration and defeat, has vanished. And with such words as "prison," "dignity," and "sublimity" Hardy goes on to suggest that the night time of the heath is indeed the most fitting symbol of the condition of man, ". . . a place perfectly accordant with man's nature—neither ghastly, hateful, nor ugly . . . but, like man, slighted and enduring; and withal singularly colossal and mysterious in its swarthy monotony," and it is beautiful, because

> Men have oftener suffered from the mockery of a place too smiling for their reason than from the oppression of surroundings oversadly tinged.

As soon as these patterns of light and dark have been established, a further change is wrought upon them. The natives appear with their burdens of furze and light a huge bonfire on top of the Rainbarrow, against the skyline. A dozen other fires are in sight, at various places on the heath, each with its particular color and shape. Thus when the light of the bright sky, which I have identified with reason, freedom, and hope, fades, it is replaced by a darker light from human hands. The darker light has the wild character that the author has already attributed to the heath, and it is tempting to see in it a further symbol of the groping dark purposes by which humanity makes its way towards its puzzling ends. They might be the purposes declared by the passions, which certainly make constant use of the intelligence although they use it to irrational and frequently destructive ends. Eustacia, first seen silhouetted against the darkening sky, then by her fire, described as "Queen of Night," with hair that "closed over her forehead like nightfall extinguishing the western glow," is literally and figuratively associated with darkness.

Further attention to human passion—perhaps a suggestion of its isolating, euphoric effect—appears in the strange, illuminated elevation of the natives with their bonfire on the top of the dusky barrow:

> It was as if the bonfire makers were standing in some radiant upper story of the world, detached from and independent of the dark stretches below. The heath down there was now a vast abyss, and no longer a continuation of what they stood on; for their eyes, adapted to the blaze, could see nothing of the deeps beyond its influence.

Is it reading too much into this passage to see an extension of the light and dark imagery to express the illusions by which men temporarily blind themselves to sterner realities —whether the childish exuberance of the natives or the flame of passion lighted and fed by Eustacia?

In the following scene on the barrow, the points of interest are indicated by lights—Eustacia's fire above and the tiny light in the window of the Quiet Woman Inn below—and by the sudden frightening appearance of the reddleman asking the way to Mrs. Yeobright's house. Flames, human flames, in the gathering dusk.

A final passage in chapter I dwells on the permanence of Egdon Heath. It is more stable than the sea; it is unchanged since Roman, since pre-historic times, since the last geological change, in abiding with a steadfastness which is equated with its permanence as a symbol of the nature and condition of man. Now, with these dark symbolic intentions so firmly established in the opening pages, we are led to wonder anew about the status of coincidence in Hardy's cosmos. Is he indeed going to present a tale in which the bright and reasonable visions of men are thwarted by the incompetent, frivolous, or diabolical god described in his poem?

> Has some great imbecility
> Mighty to build and blend
> But impotent to tend
> Framed us in jest and left us
> now to hazardry?
>
> Or come we of an automaton
> Unconscious of our pains?
> Or are we live remains
> Of Godhead dying downward,
> brain and eye now gone?

These possibilities are suggested by what we know of Hardy, but they are not indicated by the symbolism which appears to be so carefully developed in these opening pages of the novel. It would seem that it is time to take a fresh look at the role of coincidence in *The Return of the Native*.

The first coincidence is the fact that the marriage license procured by Wildeve for himself and Thomasin Yeobright was made out for Budmouth instead of for Anglebury. This error causes Thomasin to flee in shame both from the town and from Wildeve (and we recall that she has cause for anxiety in the fact that her aunt had already forbidden the banns, inflicting a mortal insult on Wildeve). She meets Diggory Venn; the event is also the occasion for Wildeve's returning to Eustacia when she lights her signal fire that evening. Very much depends upon this accident. Yet it is not really an accident; it is the purest example of that expression of an unconscious motive that we now call a Freudian error—and at least two characters recognize it as such: "Such things don't happen for nothing," said the aunt. "It is a great slight to me and my family." Diggory Venn has the same reaction: "After what had happened it was impossible that he should not doubt the honesty of Wildeve's intentions" toward Thomasin. Eustacia goes even further, trying to make Wildeve admit that he intentionally delayed the marriage because of his passion for her. Wildeve's attachment to Eustacia and his desire for revenge on Mrs. Yeobright are abundant motivation for his "mistake," and the skillful manner in which he exploits both interpretations of his conduct is further evidence that such use was not entirely unforeseen by him. Although he later rather neutralizes these insights into his subconscious motivation by telling Eustacia plainly that the error with the marriage license was an accident, he does not radically alter the reader's impression of him. Mrs. Yeobright's contribution to the "coincidence," likewise, is a substantial expression of her pride, her character, and her contest with Wildeve for Thomasin. She inflicted the origi-

nal insult; she now carries Thomasin away from the Quiet
Woman by the back window while Wildeve is serving
mead to the singing natives in the front room.

The character of Eustacia Vye is something of a puzzle
because we expect Victorian reticence in a Victorian novel
—and Hardy is so un-reticent that many readers are unable
to believe what is written on the page. Eustacia is not presented in the very act of love, but she is described in quite
unequivocal terms as a sophisticated, promiscuous sensualist
who is willing to take almost any risk to attain new intensi-
ties of passion. Yet she is also beautiful, dignified, intelligent, and noble. Vulgarity, Hardy writes, would be impossible for her. "It would have been as easy for the
heath-ponies, bats, and snakes to be vulgar as for her."
Her dignity and taste are partly natural, partly absorbed by
her from the austerity of the heath country, where the
remembered glitter of Budmouth is transformed by her
romantic imagination into a fairyland instead of transforming her into something tawdry, as it might have done if
she had stayed on there.

Her dignity survives her liaison with Wildeve—and
even the ignobility of being jilted by him. She can still
be imperious in saying, "You may tempt me, but I won't
give myself to you any more," and thus rekindle his desire.
When she has spurned his caress and sent him away,
"Eustacia sighed; it was no fragile maiden sigh, but a sigh
which shook her like a shiver." Physical desire impels her:
"She seemed to long for the abstraction called passionate
love more than for any particular lover." Her sense of the
flight of passion "tended to breed actions of reckless un-
conventionality, framed to snatch a year's, a week's, even
an hour's passion from anywhere while it could be won.
. . . Her loneliness deepened her desire."

Eustacia is innocent and pagan in her sensuality. Hardy seems to attach no moral stigma whatsoever to the simple fact of her eager quest for sexual sensation. We are led to pity her isolation, admire her intelligence and spirit, deprecate her fierce pride, and perhaps contemn her snobbish sense of class (although we cannot be sure that an Englishman would completely agree on this last point). If she is to become implicated in a tragic web, it will be through no simple moral retribution for her physical sins—but perhaps because her life has confused her endowments into a strange mixture of innocence and sophistication:

> As far as social ethics were concerned Eustacia approached the savage state, though in emotion she was all the while an epicure. She had advanced to the secret recesses of sensuousness, yet had hardly crossed the threshold of conventionality.

In this extraordinary summation of her character we see the extent of Hardy's naturalistic rejection of convention, both of character delineation and of personal judgment. His approach to the question of causation does not, to me, appear significantly naturalistic or, to be more specific, *deterministic*. Events have causes, indeed, in the *Oedipus*, even though they are not set forth with the intention of demonstrating scientific laws of causation. The movements of Hardy's characters among circumstance, ignorance, folly, and the compulsions inherent in their natures likewise weave a tragic pattern to which pity and terror rather than blind indignation against fatal coincidence are the proper aesthetic reactions. If the indignation nevertheless appears, is it perhaps because modern man expects more in the way of justice and order from life than the Greeks did? We must return to this question.

Eustacia is offered by Diggory Venn the opportunity to escape to Budmouth, with employment that would not demean her. This she instantly rejects; and with this rejection—carefully placed before the return of the native—she has freely chosen to stay in the lonely country that she detests.

"Accidents" continue to thicken the plot: Mrs. Yeobright in attempting to fan the dying embers of Wildeve's passion for Thomasin sends him straight back to Eustacia. Yet there is more than accident; there is complex irony in the sequence that shows Mrs. Yeobright pridefully rejecting Diggory Venn's renewed suit for Thomasin's hand, thanking "God for the weapon which the reddleman had put into her hands," straightway lying to Wildeve in order to provoke his jealousy—and withal turning the subsequent events in a direction utterly counter to her intentions:

> By far the greatest effect of her simple strategy on that day was, as so often happens, in a quarter quite outside her view when arranging it. In the first place, her visit sent Wildeve the same evening after dark to Eustacia's house at Mistover.

This is not the pitiless meddling of a cruel Fate in human affairs, but the quite probable outcome of human pride, mixed with folly and ignorance, attempting after the most superficial analysis to control a complicated pattern of people, situations, and motives. The inadequacy of Mrs. Yeobright's understanding is at this point abundantly obvious.

There are two plain reasons why Mrs. Yeobright's plan to manipulate Wildeve into marrying Thomasin misfires: She is ignorant of the fact that what Wildeve wants most is to marry Eustacia and leave Egdon Heath. Second, obviously because she is engaged in the symbolic action of enacting the situation which she *wishes* were the fact, she overplays her hand and gives Wildeve the impression that he is being triumphantly rejected in favor of a new suitor:

> "The woman, now she no longer needs me, actually shows off!" Wildeve's vexation had escaped him in spite of himself.

This result of the interview is precisely what Mrs. Yeobright did *not* want. Headstrong pride and miscalculation have achieved it, not malign or blind Fate. Human motives are seldom so expertly laid bare in the novel. If the ensuing interview, in which Eustacia rejects Wildeve because she believes Thomasin has rejected him, is based on an utterly false premise, that is, after all, life. Nor should we forget that Eustacia and Wildeve have been quarreling and at cross purposes for some time, and that her "supersubtle, epicurean heart" is never titillated by certainties. Passion flares brightest when she is uncertain or frustrated. Novelty is her goal, fidelity her abhorrence. The stage is set.

Thus we come to the end of Part I, with all except one of the major characters introduced and their lives tangled by passions and errors which have been fully accounted for. It is not an indifferent or incompetent God who is responsible but human qualities that are almost as old as Egdon Heath. I see the superstitious stupidity of the natives— which Hardy pushes past the grotesque to the verge of the absurd—as his grim background reminder of the frailty of human reason.

As we move into Part II what looks in the accumulation like conicidence appears in the detail to be something else—personal frustration or the reversal of expectations. It strikes Eustacia with painful force that she has set the stage for an attachment between Clym and Thomasin by her part in preventing the latter's marriage to Wildeve. This reversal horrifies her selfish heart:

> "Oh that she had been married to Damon before this," she said. "And she would if it hadn't been for me. If I had only known—if I had only known."

The reader doubtless stands by this time on Thomasin's side, but whatever his reaction to Eustacia's consternation he cannot fail to add a mite to his sense of human purposes gone awry: once again a character has brewed a plot only to discover that there were elements in the mixture which produced a result quite contrary to his taste. Yet the headstrong and selfish plans of Eustacia could hardly be expected to work out along the simple axis of her yearnings, not when her sight is so blinded by passion.

Almost every meeting in the novel seems to involve an element of unexpectedness if not chance. Hardy dwells on the lonely emptiness of the heath, developing an atmosphere of desolation in which the appearance of any person is a surprise and the meeting of two an event. Diggory Venn, who has set up camp and posted himself every night by Rainbarrow to assist at any meetings of Eustacia and Wildeve, knows just where to find the latter with Eustacia's note of rejection and the presents he is to return for her. Yet when they meet, Wildeve jumps as if nipped by the Devil himself, and when they part, after their ironic interview, it would seem as if they had conferred on the outer fringes of Chaos:

> When the reddleman's figure could no longer be seen, Wildeve himself descended and plunged into the rayless hollow of the vale.

A most moving and tender scene builds on these impressions when Thomasin takes her solitary departure for her marriage to Wildeve. She goes like a lamb to the slaughter on an altar built by Folly, Error, and Chance: Mrs. Yeobright's pride of family, which has motivated her various insults to Wildeve, is the prime cause; her failure to inform Clym of the facts is another. Diggory Venn's passion is another; he has carried notes and spied on Wildeve; he has given Mrs. Yeobright the idea for her lie to Wildeve which presently caused the cooling of Eustacia's ardor; he has carried the news which finally caused Wildeve to marry Thomasin in spiteful haste; and he has directly contributed to the growth of these unlovely motives in that worthy's heart. Wildeve likewise has acted in ignorance, rushing into marriage to spite a Eustacia who has virtually forgotten him. In this confusion of ignorance poor Tamsin is victimized by her goodness and strength of character!

Yet something more than convincing details of accident piled on miscalculation must make this event morally and psychologically probable. What is it? It is Thomasin's frailty, which expresses itself in stubbornness, making a virtue of suffering where she has not strength to impose her will on a situation. She is the person made to abase herself and be a victim. We recognize the nobility of such people, yet we feel that their goodness is too willingly bared to the scourge of misfortune. Their very nakedness makes one shrink from them, while they take on the outrages which in this imperfect world one should evade:

> Does he survive whose tongue was slit,
> To slake some envy of a king's?

Sportive silver cried from it
Before the savage cut the strings.

.   .   .   .   .   .

The rack has crumpled up the limb
Stretched immediate to fly;
Never ask the end of him
Stubborn to outstare the sky.

.   .   .   .   .   .

It is no virtue, but a fault
Thus to breathe ignoble air,
Suffering unclean assault
And insult dubious to bear.

Perhaps the fastidiousness of the poet who makes this comment is excessive, but it expresses a feeling which is very common, although often repressed. It is indeed too much that Thomasin should suffer the unclean assault of a Wildeve; and she does consent to it, finally, herself, just as Eustacia has elected to stay on the heath and Clym has elected to return to it.

The character of Clym Yeobright, withheld for 150 pages, destined to be central to the story, demands careful scrutiny. The unhappy force of coincidence seems to mount as we draw into the main action. Could he not have worked out a satisfactory life with Eustacia if it had not been for these misfortunes and accidents he could not control? Hardy writes that Clym is "unfortunate" in being intellectually advanced beyond the readiness of the rural world to respond to his visions:

To argue upon the possibility of culture before luxury to the bucolic world may be to argue truly, but it is an attempt to disturb a sequence to which humanity has been long accustomed. Yeobright preaching to the Egdon eremites that they might rise to a serene comprehensiveness without going through the process of enriching themselves was not unlike arguing to ancient Chaldeans that in ascending from earth to the pure empyrean it was not necessary to pass first into the intervening heaven of ether.

To announce that Clym lives by a high order of idealism and then introduce these considerations in this language would seem to display an ironic attitude toward him; to label the stupid natives "Egdon eremites" passes the ironic, even borders on the derisive; the notion of preaching a "serene comprehensiveness" to such yokels is ridiculed in the telling. Hardy proceeds, somewhat more gently, to explain that Clym's mind is not well-proportioned, that well-proportioned minds do not make heroes and prophets. But he does not say that Clym is the stuff of greatness: here he leaves the reader to look at the facts and judge for himself.

What the facts show is a deep vein of self-destructiveness that runs right through the Yeobright family. We have glanced at it in Thomasin. Repeatedly we see Mrs. Yeobright making things hard for herself. Clym is not to be outdone by his womenfolk. Reading stubbornly on until he has ruined his vision is the act of a man who is subconsciously bent on self-destruction. One may argue against judging too harshly his original venture of making eremites of the yokels, but here the evidence cannot be gainsaid. He is challenged, of course, by the nagging reproach of his disappointed mother, but alas he has inherited a broad stripe of her character. Like Eustacia, he has also a generous share of the endowments which enable mortals to cope with their frailties: namely, intelligence and cultivation, and like her he will not use these unique aids.

An extraordinary bit of evidence to this effect slips in so quietly that one is tempted to see in it a glimpse of

Hardy's unconscious mind as he develops the more obvious motives of his hero. Although arguments do not prevail with his mother, Clym finds that feelings do—that Mrs. Yeobright shares his contempt for mere physical comforts and will, in spite of her ambitions for him to rise through the world of business, intuitively participate in his contempt for the great world. Then comes a strange sentence—

> From every provident point of view his mother was so undoubtedly right, that he was not without a sickness of heart in finding he could shake her—

which seems to reveal that Clym *wants* his mother to disapprove of what he is doing. Could there be a more expressive demonstration of his rebellious and self-destructive motives? His silver cord must vibrate when, finding that he has given an exhumed urn full of bones to Eustacia, his mother only comments, "The urn you had meant for me you gave away." Her disapproval of Eustacia is so fierce, and her expression of it so ominous, that Clym's growing passion is almost matched by the emotional force of his neurotic conflict with his mother. After his evening on the heath with Eustacia's kisses, mother and son glare at each other over tea. This doubles his emotional involvement in the wooing.

It might almost be argued that the glowering contest over Eustacia has allowed Clym to modify the original plan of opening a simple school for the natives. That is, his destructive attachment to his mother is satisfied by the new issue, so that now he can please Eustacia by planning a much more impressive operation which will ultimately put him "at the head of one of the best schools in the county!" Thus easily are his ideals accommodated while the basic destructive drives are kept strong and tense. The images of light and dark, introduced early in the book, are fused in a complex of symbolism by Mrs. Yeobright's flashing reply:

> "You are blinded, Clym," she said warmly. "It was a bad day for you when you first set eyes on her. And your scheme is merely a castle in the air built on purpose to justify this folly which has seized you, and to salve your conscience on the irrational situation you are in."

Seldom has reason been so expertly used in the cause of emotion. In the following scene, when Clym becomes engaged to Eustacia, he sets up a second version—like the subplot in *Lear*—of his destructive relation with his mother: Now he will have two women raging, for Eustacia cannot remain content on Egdon Heath, and Mrs. Yeobright's blazing antipathy for Eustacia is almost completely without basis in observed fact. The fact that she is entirely correct in her estimation of both Eustacia and Wildeve should not be pressed too severely: people respond to others' expectations of them; Mrs. Yeobright gives them no sign of the affection or trust which people commonly repay with good conduct. She expects the worst; they oblige.

The ensuing quarrel with his mother, in which she says words about Eustacia that can never be unsaid, guarantees a permanent hostility between her and the girl. This hostility, which is perhaps the major cause in the tragic action, has grown from deep psychological roots carefully traced by the author. Here is no coincidence, no accident at all. And it will appear that the passions thus generated are strong enough to create all the accidents which follow.

Mrs. Yeobright first offends Wildeve by not entrusting Thomasin's inheritance of golden guineas to him—and then makes the error of choosing a dolt like Christian Cantle to deliver them. Thus she has incited Wildeve and played into his hands. Why should he not take revenge by winning the money from Christian? And in the confusion that follows it is not surprising that Diggory Venn, having won the money back, should give it all (Clym's fifty guineas included) to Thomasin. Hardy says the error "afterwards helped to cause more misfortune than treble the loss in money value could have done."

Well, perhaps, but here Hardy is not letting the facts speak for themselves. The estrangement between Eustacia and Mrs. Yeobright has already been effected, as we have seen. It feeds on incidents that could be explained in a moment between people who did not question each other's good will. But Mrs. Yeobright's tone and phrasing in asking Eustacia whether she has received a gift of money from Wildeve are mortally insulting. They fully account for Eustacia's tearful recriminations. Mrs. Yeobright's question, moreover, is based on pure hostile suspicion which leads her to imagine events that have not occurred—as she has done before. If Hardy had not interpreted this action with the discourse on ill-chance that we have just quoted, the reader might well believe that the quarrel he has witnessed was provoked by Mrs. Yeobright's ungovernable temper and animus. With such a woman, no accident is required. She makes the trouble, prevents the "accident" from being explained away, is determined to quarrel with all of her young kinsfolk, and does.

In this interview (Book IV, Chapter I), a boiling masterpiece of charges and counter-charges, the two women pour out their accumulated grievances. In view of their explosive hostility, it is hard to imagine their maintaining a friendly conversation under any auspices. The guineas are the flimsiest pretext for Mrs. Yeobright to search out

Eustacia and blame her for everything. Without that pretext, she would plainly have soon found another. Near the end of the interview the truth is exactly stated:

> "Don't rage at me, madam! . . . I am only a poor old woman who has lost a son."
> "If you had treated me honorably you would have had him still," Eustacia said, while scalding tears trickled from her eyes. "You have brought yourself to folly; you have caused a division which can never be healed!"

When Clym's eyes fail he deserts Eustacia for sixteen hours of furze-cutting a day. He abases himself to the ranks of the meanest, returning home to fall exhausted on his bed. This is not philosophy; it is—however unconscious—a cruel assault on Eustacia. It is an extravagant neglect, a virtuoso-piece of folly by a man with so luscious and moody a wife. He is tempting her to quarrel with him, so that he can suffer more, and of course she does. And how ironic that while pursuing this course he should add outrage to injury by being aggressively cheerful:

> Eustacia's manner had become of late almost apathetic. There was a forlorn look about her beautiful eyes which . . . would have excited pity in the breast of any one who had known her during the full flush of her love for Clym. . . . Clym, the afflicted man, was cheerful. . . .
> "Come, brighten up, dearest; we shall be all right again. Some day perhaps I shall see as well as ever. And I solemnly promise that I'll leave off cutting furze as soon as I have the power to do anything better. You cannot seriously wish me to stay idling at home all day?"

Idling home, no, but he could be a companion to her and she could read to him. There is wilful neglect in his sixteen hours of exhausting labor. Yet he does not want her to go to a village dance. The speech in which he bids her go is a model of sick martyrdom and self-pity:

> "Go and do whatever you like. Who can forbid your indulgence in any whim? You have all my heart yet, I believe; and because you bear with me, who am in truth a drag upon you, I owe you thanks. Yes, go alone and shine. As for me, I will stick to my doom. At that kind of meeting people would shun me. My hook and gloves are like the St. Lazarus rattle of the leper, warning the world to get out of the way of a sight that would sadden them."

This is touching, but every word of it is false.

Hardy humanizes his heath with a number of similes drawing on more or less unpleasant human physical details: The road crossing it is likened to the part in a Negro's hair. The barrow on the side of the valley appeared "as a wart on an Atlantean brow." The pool by Eustacia's house is "like the white of an eye without its pupil." In a storm, "each stem was wrenched at the root, where it moved like a bone in its socket." And there is "a knot of stunted hollies, which in the general darkness of the scene stood as the pupil in a black eye."

These grotesque images draw human and physical nature together. They give a slightly disagreeable smell of mortality to the heath. They also effect a certain interpenetration, a psychic symbiosis through which each absorbs the qualities of the other. If the heath is a shaggy monster, man is the living image it portrays. His conduct will reflect the icy winds, bleak skies, and tangles of twisted vegetation on harsh soil. The human being to whom these scenes are beautiful must have strong sympathies with them. Stubborn emotion and endurance of mien are qualities that dominate Mrs. Yeobright and Clym—and lead them to tragedy. The heath is thus not a moving force but a symbol of these human qualities; it makes a comment on man's nature rather than giving its qualities to man (as happens in *Wuthering Heights*), and so it seems to detract from the tragic stature that might have been suggested if man had been associated with the setting through nobler images.

The self-destructive impulses, which seem to account for the tragedy far more significantly than coincidence can, make *The Return of the Native* a novel of the greatest insight into character and motivation. The lacerations of the Yeobrights are set forth with such penetration and perspicacity that they reward careful study and repeated perusal. But the question nevertheless reasserts itself: Is this a tragedy or a despairing indictment of Fate?

Coming late into the tragic arena, Hardy has penetrated further into the subconscious than Shakespeare, for example, generally had to do. Hamlet moves on a great stage. The Yeobrights move, really, among their psychological complexities, which Hardy fully accepts as inseparable from the nature and plight of man. They are not "abnormal"; they are not to be eliminated by manipulation of the patient's environment; they are the condition of man. Among them grow aspiration, fortitude, loyalty, and devotion, which Hardy also accepts as realities. Revealing so many destructive flaws among the nobilities of his characters, he makes their contests against error and mischance seem more inevitably doomed to failure than those, say, of Othello. Hardy's tragedy is brought on, perforce, by more ignoble mischances, more petty failings, than those of past heroes. Feelings of bafflement and indignation therefore constantly threaten to divert, replace, or obscure the tragic emotions of pity and fear. Hardy, it appears, participated in such a division of feelings toward his subject—and the confusion may have been nourished by a projection into the novel of insights and experiences with which he was too personally involved to achieve for them the aesthetic distance essential to high tragedy. This is one's judgment as the novel sags, occasionally, among the dreary quarreling or morbid self-pity of the characters. It moves back to a far nobler plane when Eustacia makes her fatal attempt to be a magnificent woman.

A bold reinterpretation is suggested: Perhaps the coincidences are introduced and stressed to make the tragedy seem *less* due to human frailty! Without them, the defects of the Yeobrights and Eustacia would seem to make their defeats inevitable. The coincidences make them appear less due to the qualities inherent in the characters and therefore more due to flaws in the universe. Hardy, in short, is not blaming coincidence but rather using it to take some of the "blame" from his characters. But the trouble is that the flaws in the universe do not remove the flaws in the characters, and so the tension in the novel is sometimes painful rather than tragic.

This shifting of "blame" appears signally in the extraordinary circumstances by which Mrs. Yeobright is left standing before her son's door because he is fast asleep on the floor and Eustacia is talking to Wildeve at the back. The mother has built so strong a case against herself that some such device is essential to reclaim the reader's pity for her. Yet it would not be completely reclaimed—Eustacia's uneasiness and fear of meeting Mrs. Yeobright are too thoroughly justified—if it were not for the older woman's anguish and death. The coincidences and her suffering go a long way toward recalling the tragic emotions; yet they do not, finally. There is too much indignation, too cruel a sense of man's inadequacies, too complete an absence of the tragic recognition and insight by which a suffering character is ennobled. Hardy's universe is ignoble, flawed, almost repulsive—"like the white of an eye without its pupil."

THE UNATTAINABLE SELF: D. H. LAWRENCE'S
SONS AND LOVERS

LAWRENCE, 1913

by Louis Fraiberg

I

Sons and Lovers achieves a large measure of success as a novel despite the fact that the author's vision exceeds his means. In this early book, written during a period of self-discovery, Lawrence was seeing himself and the world afresh and beginning to feel his powers as a literary artist. He discarded two earlier starts which he had made on the book and began it again in the light of newly developing insights. To an impressive degree it demonstrates the capacity to move its readers through an externalization of the author's experience embodied in an appropriate form which, though it is far from technically perfect, is nevertheless very effective.

It is a tragedy of fate, the agent of destiny being the character of the protagonist. Because of the rigid patterns of emotional life imposed upon him during childhood, Paul Morel is never able thereafter to break away from the consequences of a misidentification of two polar opposites, and this determines the future direction of his life. Although he attempts through love and through work to find the meaning of human existence and to place himself in a creative relationship to it, he fails. He manages to experience passion but only fleetingly, and he does not reap the fruits of it, the sense of self, which Lawrence believes to be the reward of submission to and identification with the great life force.

This notion that the psychic imprints of childhood can never be revised—apparently an oversimplification of the Freudian ideas to which Lawrence was introduced during the writing of the book—becomes the key to one level of the action. On another level Lawrence's mystique of sexual experience, for which Paul is the spokesman, serves this purpose, but as a theory it is open to question on some of its own terms, as we shall see. These two frames of reference for behavior, although applied simultaneously to Paul, are not harmoniously interwoven, and their interaction therefore contributes less than it might to the power of the book.

Among the elements that do bind it together structurally, and so enhance its impact upon the reader, are the flower symbolism [1] and the Oedipal relationships.[2] In a letter written shortly after the book's completion, Lawrence himself emphasized the split between physical and spiritual love that brings about Paul's downfall; this conflict provides unity on a third level.[3] All these—and per-

[1] Mark Spilka, *The Love Ethic of D. H. Lawrence* (Bloomington, Indiana, 1955), pp. 37–89.
[2] Daniel Weiss, "Oedipus in Nottinghamshire," *Literature and Psychology*, VII (August, 1957), 33–42.
[3] Aldous Huxley, ed., *The Letters of D. H. Lawrence* (New York, 1932), pp. 78–79.

haps some others in addition—contribute to such success as the novel achieves.

Each of the interpretations is valid within its own limitations. The purpose of this study is to examine the vicissitudes of the hero's career without specific commitment to any of these views and to demonstrate that what happens to Paul Morel is not quite what Lawrence says is happening. It is going too far to say, as some do, that Lawrence is too close to this book, that he is using the writing of it as a form of psychotherapy, or at least as emotional catharsis. There is some truth in this view, as has been shown by Harry T. Moore [4] and Mark Schorer,[5] but it needs to be further defined and documented before we can accurately assess its value.

It seems safe to say, however, that in the portrayal of Paul Morel, Lawrence has not sustained to the point of artistic perfection the keeping of the optimum aesthetic distance from his fictional counterpart and that, consequently, some of Paul's experiences are not wholly integrated into the multi-layered structure to which I have alluded.

Paul is a consistent character—whether his life does or does not approximate Lawrence's own—and his fate is both dramatically believable and emotionally valid. When he fails, by the touchstone of Lawrence's passion-maturity theory, this is also believable and valid. But character and ideology do not always work together in this book. This detracts somewhat from its effect, but to identify their chief discrepancies, as will be done here, is not to imply any derogation of its merits. It is rather to suggest that dur-

[4] *The Life and Works of D. H. Lawrence* (New York, 1951).
[5] "Technique as Discovery," in John W. Aldridge, ed., *Critiques and Essays in Modern Fiction* (New York, 1952).

ing its composition Lawrence was still perfecting his vision
of the world and learning his craft.

II

The self is the product of inborn tendencies, assimilated parental influences and the discoveries made about
both the outer and inner worlds in one's progress toward
adulthood. In *Sons and Lovers*, Paul's heredity is only of
slight consequence, the power of his mother over him is
decisive, and most of his essays in search of an identity are
either ineffectual or so threatening to the emotional status
quo that the maternal influence crushes them. This state
of affairs is the outcome of the "irreversible" emotional
events of his childhood.

Paul's character is shaped by forces to which he merely
responds; he is not the master of his own destiny but a
victim of circumstance. The battle between his mother and
father sets up in him a complementary attraction and repulsion. He is overwhelmed with love by his mother, a
love which he reciprocates to the point where she "absorbs" him; and he is terrorized by his father's violence
toward her, which causes him to reject the elder Morel
both as a father and as a model of masculinity. If there is
originally any possibility of Paul's self-discovery as a boy
and self-determination as a man, it is lost in the interplay
of the powerful primitive forces before which the quiet,
rather passive child is helpless.

When Mrs. Morel is pregnant with Paul she too experiences something of this, which serves as a foreshadow-
ing of her son's fate. "What have I to do with it?" she asks,
and Lawrence adds, "Sometimes life takes hold of one,
carries the body along, accomplishes one's history, and

yet is not real, but leaves oneself as it were slurred over."
This poses a problem for the reader. On the one hand,
"sometimes" the self is not involved in its destiny, but on
the other, it is necessary for life to "take hold of one,"
perhaps for one to submit to life, in order to realize selfhood. It is a paradox which is not resolved in the book.
Both processes take place, but the latter is out of tune with
what happens to Paul and the former with Lawrence's
thesis.

Mrs. Morel, the dominant person in Paul's life, was a
woman with a strong masculine component in her makeup.
Influenced by her father who "was to her the type of all
men . . . puritan, high-minded, and really stern," she
valued intelligence and suffered her first alienation from
her husband when she realized that he was unable to
participate in the discussions of religion, philosophy and
politics that she enjoyed. "The pity was, she was too much
his opposite." In the face of this, the passion which bound
the marriage together in its early days proved to be not
enough. Gertrude Morel was determined to attain an identity of her own, and she partially succeeded, though at a
terrible price.

> She could not be content with the little he might be; she
> would have him the much that he ought to be. So, in seeking
> to make him nobler than he could be, she destroyed him.
> She injured and hurt and scarred herself, but she lost none
> of her worth. She also had the children.

Thereupon, her motherliness took the distorted form of
hatred of her husband and absorption of her sons, first
William, then Paul. It was as though the passion which she
could no longer feel for Morel was split into two streams.
One, transformed into contempt, hostility and loathing, re-

mained in a perverse way the only bond between them. The other, the residue of her love for him, engulfed the sons.

The bitter and explosive family atmosphere, the degradation of the father ("his manhood broke"), the establishment of the mother as the nucleus around whom the children clustered, all these were accomplished facts while Paul was still a small boy. Confronted with this imbalance, he responded in the only way he could—by becoming thoroughly bewildered about his own role. Instead of a father on whom he might model himself there was only a hated, rejected and despised figure who was not altogether a man, whose contribution to the emotional education of his children was chiefly the power to feel only anger and despair intensely. Whatever other feelings he inspired in them from the broken fragments of his manhood were far overshadowed by the strength of this negation. William and Paul, receiving mainly these from him, were thus denied the opportunity to develop a normal aggressiveness which could be utilized and controlled to build a competent and creative character, to find a satisfying self. Instead of a mother whose love could be renounced temporarily in order later to reaffirm it from the base of a growing masculine personality there was only the all-consuming woman whose possession of their souls transformed her sons into her would-be but impotent lovers. Paul's love for his mother, magnified out of all proportion by her demands, and her assumption of the leading role in the family swept him into an identification made up of incompatible masculine and feminine elements. Both it and his hostility against his father were excessive, other emotional avenues were blocked, and Paul was irrevocably deprived of any chance to reach normal maturity.

To be sure, there had been some predisposition for this. "Paul, always rather delicate and quiet . . . trotted after his mother like her shadow. He was usually active and interested but sometimes he would have fits of depression." This was during the period of her preference for William, but even then the fits "caused a shadow in Mrs. Morel's heart, and her treatment of Paul was different from that of the other children." Her special feeling for him brought an eager and effective response. "When she fretted he understood, and could have no peace. His soul seemed always attentive to her." Paul's innate tendencies were thus reinforced and exploited by his mother and his feet placed early on the path he was thereafter to follow.

The first half of the novel is concerned largely with this one-sided picture of Paul's stunted self, though it becomes more complex as the inner conflicts begin to manifest themselves in behavior. In his groping for individuality in the manner of a child, we see some of the difficulties which Lawrence has in being unable to reconcile his emerging artistic vision of the significance of human experience with his artistic compulsion to report that experience naturalistically. As the book goes on, Paul is tormented by a series of ambivalences which he flounderingly tries to resolve. At times he thinks he has done so, but he never really can, and each time he is compelled to admit defeat without knowing what has beaten him and to go his tortured way from one unhappy relationship to another. This failure of his efforts, though necessary to Lawrence's plan, is so rationalized that it mirrors one of the failures of the novel.

It has been said that this book does not have a conventional structure, and this is true on one level. It is built on a number of instances of intensely realized experience each having a thematic significance. But psychologically the series is not a sequence, even though it appears on the surface to be one. The chronological plan of the novel—the essential part of which is Paul's life between childhood and the end of adolescence—does not work because the events do not bring associated changes in character. Paul's responses are fixed. He cannot develop; he can only repeat his suffering. Each attempt to find himself through a relationship with a woman is part of a series which is potentially meaningful (Mother: Miriam: Clara: Mother) but which actually fails. The book is structurally flawed because the failure is always for the same reason and the action is therefore too repetitive for any forward movement to take place. At the end of each episode Paul is back where he started; the situation is different but he is not. His experiences are thus deprived of the meaning they might have had as related parts of a dramatic succession, and while the reader is carried forward on one level, he is held back on the other that ought to accompany it.

The reason for this seems to me to be that Lawrence is still short of the full artistic control of his vision which later—in *Lady Chatterley's Lover,* for example—makes possible the marriage of form and idea and the production of an articulated aesthetic whole. This is entirely outside the question whether one agrees or disagrees with his thesis; it seems to be related to the fact that he has not yet himself fully assimilated it. There is consequently a partial gap between his accurate naturalistic reporting (or invention) of his characters' behavior and its artistic significance. The latter he indicates with more success by the flower symbolism and by other means, which he uses with great skill individually; but the relationships even between them are imperfect. There are thus a number of separate parts of the book which are not pulling together, either for Paul or for the reader.

Once Paul's childhood is past, therefore, the order in which the love incidents occur is not important. His character is set, and he is doomed to repeat himself compulsively, endlessly and tragically. *Sons and Lovers* thus has the outer shape of a picaresque novel, the adventurous travels of the unformed soul among women. Its inner shape is that of the mirror image of a saint's life: it is the equivalent of a search for grace which can never be attained, though at times glimpsed and even touched. In Lawrence's mystique, faith is more efficacious than works, but mystical immersion is better than either.

Paul's childhood, then, produced a boy who was ill-equipped to become a man, either psychologically or in terms of Lawrence's cosmos, although the latter supposedly has no relationship to the former. The experiencing of a moment of spiritual communion either occurs or it does not occur; there is no halfway. On the other hand, once attained, it is never lost. "That is what one *must have*, I think . . . the real, real flame of feeling through another person—once, only once, if it only lasts three months. . . . and once it has happened to you, you can go on with anything and ripen," says Paul to Miriam. But no such ripening takes place in his mother, who has presumably experienced this feeling, and it certainly does not in his father, her partner. In Paul the confusion between his masculine and feminine identifications also makes this impossible.

As a boy he had been withdrawn in significant ways. He retreated into the coziness of the relationship with his mother and suffered greatly when he was forced to emerge from its protection even temporarily, as when he went each

Friday to bring home his father's pay. It was much more to his liking that "Friday was the baking night and market night. It was the rule that Paul should stay home and bake" while he awaited his mother's return from the market. On these occasions there was the acting-out of a partial reversal of roles, as though he were the housewife waiting for her husband. But more important than the act itself was the feeling which accompanied it: "He loved her homecoming." This served further to confirm him in his misidentification.

The end of his childhood was signalized by his successful search for a job—under his mother's guidance, as might be expected. But the necessity of staying away from home during working hours proved even more painful than his trips to the pay office at the mine had been. "Now that he felt he had to go out into life, he went through agonies of shrinking self-consciousness." But he managed to find a tolerable substitute for the lost home atmosphere among the sewing girls in whose department he spent as much time as his duties would allow. "Paul liked the girls best. The men seemed common and rather dull. He liked them all, but they were uninteresting." It was not long before he was established in the factory and getting along quite well. But the reason was not, as would be hoped, that he was beginning to find himself in the responsibilities of growing independence and manhood—quite the contrary. "The factory had a homely feel." There was no growth, no substantive change, only a reaching back for what he had left behind.

At this point in the book there is a glimpse of the role of work in the development of masculine character, but it is only a passing mention, and Lawrence proceeds thereafter to minimize it as a possibly significant part of Paul's experience.

> Paul always enjoyed it when . . . all the men united in labor. He liked to watch his fellow clerks at work. The man was the work and the work was the man, one thing, for the time being. It was different with the girls. The real woman never seemed to be there at the task, but as if left out, waiting.

Although there are later a few hints that Paul's interest in work might contribute positively to his sense of self, Lawrence does not follow them up. Paul is depicted mainly as an observer and commentator rather than as a participant; often, as in this passage, the text abruptly switches to another subject. Here it is the separateness of woman from anything not useful biologically and its obverse, a favorite idea of Lawrence's, the stultifying effect of modern life on normal development. He goes almost so far as to deny any creative possibilities for the individual in society.

This is not altogether explicit in *Sons and Lovers*. Paul rejects the chance of achieving at least a small measure of fulfillment even from his routinized work. He stands aside and adopts an almost feminine passivity. He brings his wages home to his mother, superficially a man's role, but the resemblance ends there, for he uses this merely to add a new link to the unbreakable relationship. "Then he told her the budget of the day. His life-story like an Arabian Nights, was told night after night to his mother. It was almost as if it were her own life." Or as if he had never left home. This excessive sharing—a two-way process—is emphasized again and again. Paul and his mother are one, the corollary to which is that Paul will never be himself.

> His ambition, as far as this world's gear went, was quietly to earn his thirty or thirty-five shillings a week somewhere near his home, and then, when his father died, have a cottage with his mother, paint and go out as he liked, and live

happy ever after. . . . He thought that *perhaps* he might
also make a painter, the real thing. But that he left alone.

In this fantasy he achieves the classical Oedipal goal of
death of the father and possession of the mother, but with a
difference. The father is to die somehow, conveniently, not
through the son's agency, and the mother is to be possessed
not as a lover but as a female companion. One element of
reality intrudes itself: painting, which might *perhaps* lead
to an independent achievement and thereby contribute to a
true masculine self-realization, is rejected and precisely for
this reason.

So Paul reaches the end of childhood with all the major
battles except one already lost. His natural passivity has
been accentuated and exploited by his mother for her own
ends; he has been alienated from his father; the creative
development of his masculinity through work has not begun and will not take place in the remainder of the book.
This contribution to growth appears to be of little interest
to Lawrence, who cares only for Paul's struggle to dis-
entangle himself from his mother and sees that only in
cosmic-biological terms, as though no others were possible.
What matters to him is the relation of man to the natural
forces that brought him into being.

Accordingly, in the attempts of Paul to love Miriam
and Clara there is a reading of love as a sinking—not a
rising—into oneness with nature. But though at moments
Paul attains this apparent spiritual success, it leads him not
to peace but to frustration, and ultimately he is forced to
recognize its equation with death, thus defeating Lawrence's attempt to establish passion as the road to selfhood.
The search for life and its meaning perversely becomes for
Paul the inadvertent but welcome union with death, the

obliteration of self. This is both a logical and fictional contradiction, and it prevents the book from achieving full aesthetic integration. Its power to move the reader, then, depends in part on the fact that the issue is settled (but not closed) in the first half. The second half derives its dramatic value from Paul's inner conflict, from the intensity with which significant moments of experience are depicted, and from the fidelity of many incidents to life.

III

The concluding half of the book describes the failure of Paul's search for a viable self, a failure which stems as much from his over-attachment to his mother as from the inconsistency in Lawrence's theory. If full communion through relationship with another person is the precondition for mature selfhood, then by definition it is irrelevant whether there is a prior attachment to one's mother. But Lawrence has made this attachment crucial for Paul. The psychological, the immediately human, side of the story interferes with the attainment of the mystically human goal that the theory is concerned with. Whether considered novelistically or naturalistically, then, Paul is in an impossible position: he is forever prevented from achieving a satisfactory masculine identification. The problem in *Sons and Lovers*, however, is not identification but identity.

We have already seen that Paul failed to establish the childhood conditions for a healthy development toward an adult selfhood on Freud's terms; his attempts to reach it on Lawrence's terms will also fail. The reason for this is not that there is any weakness in Lawrence's ability to render human nature but that he has not woven the representational into a harmonious pattern with the theoretical.

Miriam is too unfleshly a being to afford Paul the experience of mutual discovery which a first love can bring. She is virginal almost in a saint-like way: although her emotional life is rich, it is split off from sexuality. Paul cannot cope with her since for him strong emotion and physical love ought theoretically to accompany each other. In the early part of their relationship, as his awareness of his need for physical love grows, he suppresses it "into a shame." For her part, she wants only spiritual communion with him, which he rejects because that is all she offers. The paradoxical result of this frustration is to send him in a direction in which salvation might, in part, be attainable. Since their love cannot yet culminate in physical passion, he takes pride in his art and shows her some of his designs. "There was for him the most intense pleasure in talking about his work with Miriam. All his passion, all his wild blood, went into this intercourse with her, when he talked and conceived his work." The sexual imagery in this passage indicates his perversion of work from its normal function to that of a substitute. Sexually thwarted by Miriam, he tries to invest his art with the emotion properly belonging to a physical relationship with her, but this proves futile. Satisfied in neither direction, he is easily drawn back into his mother's orbit by an open act of seduction:

> "And I've never—you know, Paul—I've never had a husband—not really—"
> He stroked his mother's hair, and his mouth was on her throat.

In this newly restored situation, where the love of mother and son can be expressed more overtly than before, Paul is left with only one truly masculine means of expression. But this is in distorted form: he can oppose and hate his father. The elder Morel comes into the room just following the climax of this scene, while Paul and his mother are still embracing each other. " 'At your mischief again?' he said venomously." This is almost an outright recognition of sexual rivalry, and a quarrel follows. Morel is about to strike his wife and Paul is about to defend her by attacking him when she providentially faints. It is the only way the fight could have been prevented. Since Paul's feelings are not discharged in action, no reconciliation takes place, and his relationship with his father remains based on hatred and nourished by it so that it grows more intense than ever. The psychic power in Paul that might have helped to bring him into harmony with himself is once again directed toward destruction, and his unresolvable confusion remains.

Inevitably he breaks with Miriam—although he later returns to her for a short time—since he will not submit himself wholly to her, knowing that passion on such terms cannot benefit him. But he also recognizes that his mother insists on the same bargain, and so he tries once more to find a love which will accept him without absorbing him, which will enable him to achieve passion and so free him. He turns to Clara who seems to promise better things. In some ways she is the very opposite of Miriam. She is worldly, independent, intelligent, socially and politically alive; she does not suffer from Miriam's inhibiting spirituality. Most especially, she is a married woman who is separated from her husband and so an accessible sexual object. If Paul is at last to experience passion, she is an eminently suitable partner.

But first she sends him back to Miriam. His acquiescence in this is a crucial event because now for the first time two conflicting tendencies in Paul are confronted with one another, and the results are important both for his fate and for Lawrence's theory. Paul had entered a period of despondency the serious nature of which his mother recognized. She remonstrated with him, she struggled with him, "she seemed to fight for his very life against his own will to die." To such a pass had his search for the fullness of life brought him. But her efforts were useless. The parting from Miriam, necessary though it had been, had deprived him of vital spirit. "He had that poignant carelessness about himself, his own suffering, his own life, which is a form of slow suicide." But there was still a sufficient remnant of vitality left to make another effort. The trouble now was that Paul would never again be able to press toward life without being haunted by death; never again would he be able to free himself from the confusion between them in his mind.

Heroically overcoming her repugnance and doubt, Miriam finally yielded to him. It was a union of desperate urgency for him and of tragic renunciation for her. She was fully aware that he would not find what he was seeking and so would leave her once more, this time for good. "She relinquished herself to him, but it was a sacrifice in which she felt something of horror. This thick-voiced, oblivious man was a stranger to her." Thus, instead of being united to her in their first act of love, he was parted from her, and her own sense of separateness confirmed the fact that she had lost him. Her feeling of horror was the recognition of his little death, a sample of his dedication, in the very act of love, to ultimate death.

As she had foreseen, there was no satisfaction for him. "He was physically at rest, but no more." What she did not know was the cause of the failure, his association of love with death and the beginning of a positive pleasure in the equation.

> He did not mind if the raindrops came on him; he would have lain and got wet through: he felt as if nothing mattered, as if his living were smeared away into the beyond, near and quite lovable. This strange, gentle reaching-out to death was new to him. . . . To him now, life seemed a shadow, day a white shadow; night, and death, and stillness, and inaction, this seemed like *being*. To be alive, to be urgent and insistent—that was *not-to-be*. The highest of all was to melt out into the darkness and sway there, identified with the great Being.

He had argued with her that "possession was a great moment in life" because of the concentration of strong emotions there, convinced that somehow in the experiencing of these emotions he would become free to discover and ripen his real self. To this she had demurred; her realization was accomplished in different ways. She did not easily accept defeat, however, and had fought to rescue him from the mindlessness of his passion to an awareness of her that would make humanity and love possible. In their love-making she had been vigilant never to permit him

> any relaxing, never any leaving himself to the great hunger and impersonality of passion; he must be brought back to a deliberate, reflective creature. As if from a swoon of passion she called him back to the littleness, the personal relationship. . . . His eyes, full of the dark, impersonal fire of desire, did not belong to her.

And after their virginal carnality, in which was forged the terrible bond that kept them superficially linked while in-

Louis Fraiberg

wardly each rejected the other, Paul gave voice to its
meaning for him.

> "To be rid of our individuality, which is our will, which
> is our effort—to live effortless, a kind of conscious sleep—
> that is very beautiful, I think; that is our after-life—our im-
> mortality."

In his very first experience of passion, therefore, he was on
the road to losing, not finding, himself, and he had begun to
ascribe to not-being, to death, the value properly belonging
to life. Imagining that he was on the threshold of obtaining
his desire, he arranged a course of sterile lovemaking with
Miriam to which she was able to lend only her body. Again
and again during their week together he returned hoping to
experience the depth of feeling whose meaning he had so
misinterpreted, but each repetition of the act only dimin-
ished the intensity felt during the climax and forced on him
an awareness of its true quality. The futility of his attempt
became more and more obvious, although he did not give
up easily. "For a second he wished he were sexless or dead.
Then he shut his eyes again to her, and his blood beat back
again." He exhausted himself to no purpose.

Full love was not possible for him; "there remained
afterwards always the sense of failure and of death. If he
were really with her, he had to put aside himself and his
desire. If he would have her, he had to put her aside."
The test on Miriam had failed. Paul's quest for life and the
meaning of self had taken the downward path toward death
and the obliteration of self. But it was a long and tortuous
path. He was left tantalizingly unfulfilled, each time with
a tiny taste of what fulfillment could mean. Unfortunately
for him, the obstacle to complete fulfillment was at the
same time the agent of destruction, and so each new attempt

only confirmed his failure. He had taken what seemed like a decisive step, but it had not brought the results he had hoped for.

> As he rode home [from his week with Miriam] he felt that he was finally initiated. He was a youth no longer. But why had he the dull pain in his soul? Why did the thought of death, the after life, seem so sweet and consoling?

The solution would be attempted again, this time with Clara, and again it would fail.

IV

It began auspiciously enough. Their first lovemaking was easy and natural, like a true marriage—and yet he was not wholly free from concern. " 'Not sinners, are we?' he said, with an uneasy little frown." Clara's reassurance sent him home temporarily appeased, but he was still groping for an understanding of the prize which now seemed to be within his grasp.

He had reason to feel unsure of it; the same canker that had corroded his relationship with Miriam affected the apparent success with Clara, and he was at last compelled to acknowledge it.

> "You know, mother, I think there must be something the matter with me, that I *can't* love. When she's there, as a rule, I *do* love her. Sometimes, when I see her just as *the woman*, I love her, mother; but then, when she talks and criticizes, I often don't listen to her.

Just as before, he could not accept Clara as a person with her own valuable qualities—valuable to him as well—but only as a convenient vehicle for his spurious passion. And he could not love her because passion was not enough. It did not provide a union with her; she remained only a catalyst for his self-destruction. Even worse than this, by committing himself to the search for realization solely through this impersonal means, he had cut himself off from other ways that promised better chances of success. In communion with the vital center of life, which should have brought clarity of purpose, he found paradox and confusion. No, this was not the road to the self.

Part of the difficulty lay in Lawrence's view of the communion to be obtained through passionate sexuality. As described in *Sons and Lovers* it consists of a surrender to the experience, the "little death" of sexual intercourse, which then leads to a kind of nirvana.

> As a rule, when he started lovemaking, the emotion was strong enough to carry with it everything—reason, soul, blood—in a great sweep. . . . Gradually the little criticisms, the little sensations, were lost, thought also went, everything borne along in one flood. He became, not a man with a mind, but a great instinct. . . . everything was still, perfect. . . . This wonderful stillness in each thing in itself, while it was being borne along in a very ecstasy of living, seemed the highest point of bliss.

This describes the physical experience and its aftermath, but it attempts to give it significance on too primitive a level. Paul reaches "the highest point of bliss" through two negations of what is necessary for the achieving of true self-realization. First, mind is swallowed up by instinct; the human is thus degraded into the merely biological, which Lawrence then tries to give a value of the highest rank. Man's powers of mind become "the little criticisms," and they are simply lost in the torrent of all-devouring instinct, which is here equated with the greatest good. Second, at the peak of the experience, what gives the ecstasy its meaning, according to Lawrence, is not the surge of life but its opposite, stasis, which can only be interpreted as the immediate apprehension of death. These are not presented as balanced forces complementing each other; the sub-human triumphs.

In Paul, too, negation has long been dominant, and it has taken the form of the very preference for instinctual experience that Lawrence here regards as success in life. He never resolves this contradiction in *Sons and Lovers*.

Paul's position is now impossible, as is demonstrated once more, this time in his fight with Dawes, Clara's estranged husband. In this struggle Paul is pure "instinct without reason or feeling." He is on the point of choking Dawes to death when he stops himself and limply allows his antagonist to kick him into unconsciousness. Having failed in the search for himself through love and through passion, Paul is left with the ability to express himself only through hostile, aggressive, destructive acts. In the fight with Dawes he halts at the brink of murder and turns his desire to kill against himself by the expedient of submitting to the other's attack. The Oedipal pattern is, of course, obvious here, but it is not our present concern, which is the warping of Paul's personality. He now enters a period of estrangement from his mother, and the deterioration of his relations with Clara proceeds unchecked. In the sullen grip of destructive passion, he nevertheless tries again to find the joy he had momentarily felt in sexual union, but his sporadic couplings with Clara only succeed in driving them farther apart.

. . . she grew to dread him. He was so quiet, yet so strange. . . . She began to have a kind of horror of him. . . . He wanted her—he had her—and it made her feel as if death itself had her in its grip. She lay in horror. . . .

Clara, like Miriam before her, sensed the perversion of his values and recoiled from his commitment to death, feeling the same loathing as her predecessor. It was hopeless, and he finally cut his ties with Clara altogether, going so far as to give her back to Dawes, his conqueror. Then, in a perverse way, the hostility he had felt for his sexual partner was transferred to his mother, who was now dying of cancer. Its clash with his excessive love for her gave rise to an irrepressible and insoluble final conflict.

The act which sealed his fate, however, and made it forever impossible to break his childhood bonds was the mercy-killing of his mother. It was the final tragedy, worked out with the inevitability of fate, which gave death the victory over love and completed the destruction of Paul's character. Mrs. Morel was growing steadily worse. Her pain was so great that her children could not bear to watch.

> "She'll live over Christmas," said Annie. They were both full of horror.
> "She won't," he replied grimly. "I s'll give her morphia. . . ."
> That evening he got all the morphia pills there were, and took them downstairs. Carefully he crushed them to powder.
> "What are you doing?" said Annie.
> "I s'll put them in her night milk."
> Then they both laughed together like two conspiring children. On top of all their horror flickered this little sanity.

Miriam and Clara had felt horror at the chill of his embraces. Now he himself was feeling it in an act of love and murder. Perhaps its merciful aspect woke him for a moment to its impact.

He had been most tender, even erotic, with his mother in her illness; when she died he embraced and kissed her like a lover, but he was revolted by the coldness of her mouth. "He bit his lip with horror. Looking at her, he felt he could never, never let her go." Nevertheless, a moment later he turned away and matter-of-factly began making the necessary arrangements.

Unable to mourn normally and freely to express a healing grief, he was prevented by his knowledge that in killing her he had killed something of himself. To his guilt was added a feeling of self-loss. The deed had sprung not simply from the wish to spare her further pain but likewise from his all-but-conscious recognition that he was governed forever by the impulse to deny the rights of others in him, to sever the connections which might bind him and them to life, and to seek instead a false union in the greater-than-human universality which he felt fleetingly in moments of surrender to strong emotion. Even this, as we have seen, could be attained only at the cost of isolating himself from his partner and thus separating rather than uniting, denying rather than fulfilling. Both Miriam and Clara had seen what he was not fully able to see, that his apparent grasping of life was actually its rejection.

Committed to the cult of transcendent experience, Paul was condemned to the Faustian penalty, the loss of his soul. He was caught in the fatal contradictions of Lawrence's theory as well as those of his own personality. The highest experience had turned out to be the negation of experience, and an inner war was launched in which polar opposites were equated without their contradictions being reconciled. The possibility that Paul might attain recognition of a viable self and develop it in a creative masculine direction succumbed to the converging assaults of the contending forces. All that was left for him was the decline into death.

The tone of the final passage of the book is somber, as befits a tragedy. Paul's struggle has come to nothing. He is apathetic, and he recognizes the meaning of his despondency. "What am I doing? . . . Destroying myself." But though the battle is lost, the defeated side is not wholly exterminated. Something indefinable in him, "a stroke of hot stubbornness inside his chest resisted his own annihilation." A few remaining flickers signal his automatic but hopeless resistance, never strong enough to overcome the long-prepared defeat. And so the book ends with Paul refusing to surrender but overwhelmed because the means of victory have been denied him from the beginning.

He looks up at the night sky and sees his own minuteness and insignificance. Life itself has no permanent place here.

> Everywhere the vastness and terror of the immense night which is roused and stirred for a brief while by the day, but which returns, and will remain at last eternal, holding everything in its silence and its living gloom. . . . On every side the immense dark silence seemed pressing him, so tiny a spark into extinction. . . .

His desire to live is now no more than a feeble, reflexive gesture against fate. For a moment the memory of his mother returns to him, and he briefly thinks of saving himself through identification with her. But this would mean a self-annihilating identification with death. He is thwarted everywhere. No other choice is left.

The last paragraph of the book, which has seemed to some an affirmation of victory for life and for Paul, can yield this meaning only if the plain tendency of all that has gone before is ignored or if the book is regarded as leading to a sequel in which all will be reversed. It reads, in part:

> But no, he would not give in. Turning sharply, he walked towards the city's gold phosphorescence. His fists were shut, his mouth set fast. He would not take that direction, to the darkness. . . . He walked towards the faintly humming, glowing town, quickly.

This certainly reads like an affirmation, but it contradicts everything that has happened to Paul up to now. It is probable that it reflects what has happened to Lawrence himself, his attainment of a satisfying sexual relationship and the finding of his artistic powers, which however, lapse here long enough to let him write an incongruous conclusion to Paul's story. As Mark Schorer says in "Technique as Discovery," Paul here does what "nothing in his previous history persuades us that he could unfalteringly do."

What appears to have taken place is a split between Lawrence the man and Lawrence the writer. As has often been suggested, he could not always sufficiently separate himself from his material. Paradoxically, one of his strengths as a writer is this very capacity to derive artistic truth from a fictionalization of the events of his own life. Fictional success depends on the achieving of a proper distance from the personal emotion so that the work may acquire a certain autonomy, an artistic harmony and wholeness largely independent of its author. Put another way, it depends on a fusion of the experiences depicted in the book with the author's novelistic intentions so that theme, symbols, characters and action become parts of an integrated whole.

In *Sons and Lovers* Lawrence has not been altogether successful in this. True, the theme provides one kind of unity; the symbolism of nature underlying and accompanying the action helps fix it into one kind of novelistic pattern; the Oedipal conflicts help bring the book into correspondence with one kind of observed experience. But in this book—only his third—the theme is imperfectly worked out. Lawrence's vision of a larger significance for man's existence is not yet fully formed, and it contains inner contradictions.

As a character in a novel Paul is somewhat lacking in interest. His childhood mis-identification has caused him to acquire too simple a perception of himself: instead of a balance of love and hate he suffers an imperfect fusion of them which can be overtly expressed only intermittently as one momentarily displaces the other. His is the ambivalence of dissociation, not of integration or of the kind of internal conflict which holds the reader by the resolution of tensions. The psychological truth about Paul has not been transmuted into adequate fictional terms. The book is not even a study of disintegration, for Paul's character was not a properly functioning one to begin with. The trouble is that the characterization is too flat and that the contest is over too soon. As a consequence, no changes—either developmental or disintegrative—can take place. The entire second half of the book is devoted to the reiteration of this fact by showing the compulsive, repetitive nature of Paul's relationship with three different women none of whom succeeds in altering the sameness of his response to love.

The Unattainable Self: D. H. Lawrence's *Sons and Lovers*

If salvation, in Lawrence's view, comes from the attainment of a separate, mature self through shared passion, then it is made impossible for Paul because of his almost Pavlovian conditioning. If the experience of passion is supposed to lead to the greatest good, then the book confuses the issue by equating the outcome of passion with death. If the dramatic impact of a novel depends on the significant choices made by the characters, then this is weakened here since Paul's psychological fate is imposed upon him from without and he is rendered incapable of choosing. If a tragedy ought to rise progressively from climax to climax until the final resolution is reached, then in *Sons and Lovers* there is a flattening-out of this effect because the issue is settled before we are halfway through, and the remainder is merely a confirmation, thrice repeated, of what we already know. Lawrence has provided the inevitability, but he has failed to provide the equally necessary surprise.

This is not a finished book. Paul's oscillation between life and death is not permitted to stop, as we have seen, even at the very end. This can make sense only if the book is regarded as a kind of prologue to the rest of the Lawrence canon, a position which is difficult to defend. The key to its understanding seems rather to lie in the changes for the better which took place in Lawrence's own life during its composition. Genius though we may call him, during this time he was not yet a finished—or mature—artist. His achievement in *Sons and Lovers* is a partial triumph of his own passion and developing skill over the intransigence of his materials.

THE CURRENT OF CONRAD'S *VICTORY*

CONRAD, 1915

by R. W. B. Lewis

The opening sentences of *Victory* introduce us half-playfully to a number of "close relations," the surprising similarities between seeming contrasts—coal and diamonds, the practical and the mystical, the diffused and the concentrated, an island and a mountain. All of them have their literal and thematic importance in the story, which describes a profound conflict rooted in opposition and likeness, and which has to do with coal, diamonds and an island; but the first effect of such dialectical teasing is the imparted sense of enlargement and creativity, of some idea or insight being made to grow. The last sentences of *Victory*, and especially its last word, are something else again:

"And then, your Excellency [says good Captain Davidson], I went away. There was nothing to be done there."
"Clearly," assented the Excellency.
Davidson, thoughtful, seemed to weigh the matter in his mind, and then murmured with placid sadness:
"Nothing!"

Between that initial sense of conceptual growth, with its cautious jocularity, and the thoughtful sadness of the closing negation there lies the truth of *Victory*, and its reality.

Victory is, in fact, a novel intimately concerned with questions of truth and reality, as it is with lies and illusion. Those big considerations force themselves on the imagination of the characters, and hence upon that of the reader; for it is that kind of novel, the kind Conrad normally attempted to write. In his preface to *The Nigger of the Narcissus*, Conrad defined art as the effort to render the highest justice "to the visible universe, by bringing to light the truth, manifold and one, underlying its every aspect." That creative ambition found an exact analog in the experience narrated in *The Nigger of the Narcissus* itself, in the story's movement from the emphasized darkness of the ship's nighttime departure to the sunlit morning that greets its arrival in the English channel—after a voyage featured by the crew's effort to bring to light the truth and reality incarnate in the dying dark man, James Wait. And measured by Conrad's own standard, *Victory* achieves the conditions of art; for the manifold *and* unitary truth of things is just what Conrad succeeds in making real and visible, and what the persons of his island drama are most vitally concerned with. How the process is managed in this particular instance is the subject of present examination. But we have first to take a hard pull on our intellectual reins.

Revisiting *Victory* today, one cannot help being struck by its "existentialist" qualities—by how much it shares the intellectual preoccupations and postures notable in continental literature during recent decades. Here, for instance, is an elaborated image of human isolation: the isolation not only of man from man, but even more of man from his metaphysical environment—Axel Heyst, the rootless drifter, who has settled alone upon a singularly remote little island, near an abandoned coal mine, there to meditate in silence his late father's reflections upon "the universal nothingness" and "the unknown force of negation." Here, too, is the familiar counter-attack upon metaphysical isolation, the unsteady impulse towards human fellowship—those compassionate gestures towards Morrison and the girl called Lena which belie Heyst's habitual detachment and are the source of his misfortunes and maybe of his redemption. Here is the articulated obsession with the feeling of existence and of non-existence, as clues both to character and action. "If you were to stop thinking of me, I shouldn't be in the world at all," Lena says to Heyst; and, "I am he who is—" announces plain Mr. Jones, in a breath-taking moment which, in context, has an overpowering propriety. Here are modes of nihilism yielding to modes of self-annihilation, in the oddly similar catastrophes of both hero and villain. Here, in short, is a tale of violence that oscillates richly between the fundamental mysteries of being and nothing. Conrad, we are inclined to say, is the still insufficiently acknowledged grandfather of the most recent literary generation.

To say so is not necessarily to praise Conrad; and it is more likely, indeed, to impose upon him a false identity. *Victory* is not—and it cannot be discussed as—a novel of ideas, for example, in the manner of Malraux's *Les Noyers de L'Altenburg*. Nor is it a calculated work of metaphysical revolt, like Camus's *The Plague*. Conrad did of course display attitudes, and he had a stiff little set of convictions. But E. M. Forster has rightly, if unsympathetically, made the point that Conrad had no "creed"—no coherent order of intellectual principles; and no more than other novelists

writing on English soil did Conrad possess that occasional
French and German talent for making the war of thought
itself exciting. He wanted to exploit the power of words,
as he said, in order "to make you hear, to make you feel—
before all to make you *see*"; and the end of each of his best
novels was simply its own composition. He did not believe
with Malraux that art is "a rectification of the universe, a
way of escaping from the human condition"; and he would
scarcely have understood Camus's parallel and derivative
contention that "the novel is born simultaneously with the
spirit of rebellion and expresses, on the aesthetic plane, the
same ambition." *Victory* dramatizes basic aspects of truth
and being; but as regards the human condition, its main
aim is only to observe it in the way of art—with that idle
but no less intense and sustained attention for which
Conrad accurately thought he had a natural ability, and
with which he recalled observing the living model for
Victory's heroine.

The novel's final word—"Nothing!"—is, accordingly,
less a cry of appalled metaphysical recognition than the
quiet acknowledgement that the adventure is over and the
art that described it has peacefully exhausted itself. It is in
the mood less of Camus's Caligula than of Shakespeare's
Hamlet: "The rest is silence." The drama is done, and
everybody who had a significant part in it is dead. Lena
is dead, accidentally shot by Mr. Jones. Heyst has died by
fire; Jones has died by water; and both deliberately, as it
seems. Ricardo has been killed by Jones's second try at him;
and Pedro has been dispatched by Wang, the houseboy.
"There are more dead in this affair," Davidson remarks to
the Excellency, "than have been killed in many of the
battles of the last Achin war." The bungalow and the other
two houses are burned to ashes; the boat has drifted out to

sea; a corpse lies rotting on the scorched earth. To close
the account, only the word "nothing" needs to be uttered.

And yet. If there is no metaphysical vision or purpose at work in the novel, there can nevertheless be felt
running through it something like a metaphysical tide. Or
better, perhaps, one senses the active presence, the dangerous undertow, of a metaphysical current giving the story
its energy and its direction. In the same way, if the tale
is not plainly intended as an allegory, one feels in it nevertheless something like an allegorical swelling, as though
everything were about to become bigger than itself. That
very impression affects the nerves of the persons in the
book. "I have a peculiar feeling about this," says Mr. Jones.
"It's a different thing. It's a sort of test." In the long list
of Conrad's writings, *Victory* also comes to us as a different thing and a sort of test. It is Conrad's test of the nature
of fiction: in general, of the ability of drama to move
towards allegory while retaining intact its dramatic form
and essence; and in particular, the ability of fiction to move
towards drama while retaining its identity as fictional narrative. It is a test of the way truth and reality can become
the subject-matter of a novel which hangs on to its novelistic nature. And the result, in my judgment, is indicated by
the last word Conrad actually did write to this book, as
he tells us: the single word of the title.

Victory (1915) is itself the last of those works both
Conrad and his critics have agreed to call major; and it
ranked with *Nostromo* (1904) as Conrad's personal favorite. Conrad's appraisal of his writings was, I think, both
sound and suggestive. He always had a special fondness
for *The Nigger of the Narcissus* (1897), recognizing it for
what it was, his first genuine artistic accomplishment; and
his satisfaction with *The Secret Agent* (1907) was

grounded correctly in his belief that he had succeeded, in that novel, in treating "a melodramatic subject ironically," as he wrote in the copy he gave his friend Richard Curle. But he disagreed with readers and critics who thought that *Lord Jim* (1900) was his best book; he felt the tale did not justify the great length of the novel, and suspected that he should have stuck to his original idea, which was to restrict the narrative to the pilgrim ship episode. The most he could say for *Under Western Eyes* (1910) was "rather good." We should probably speak more warmly, but the pain of composition clings to the pages of *Under Western Eyes;* and the congealing of the action (for example, in Part III) is for long stretches greater than all the interpolated reflections on the art of fiction can overcome. About *Chance* (1913), in a manner not uncommon with authors, he began to talk deprecatingly the moment it became so huge a success. But he remained steadfast in his conviction that his two supreme efforts were the vast tale of the South American seaboard and the tight little story of Axel Heyst.

Surely he was right. *Nostromo* was, as Conrad knew, his largest canvas and his "most anxiously meditated work." It is also one of the greatest novels in English, with a greatness so complex and extensive that only belatedly and partially has it become appreciated. *Victory* is a triumph of a different kind, of a nearly opposite kind. Here Conrad has presented almost all the themes that interested him, but he has refracted those themes through the closely observed conduct of a tiny group of people in a tiny and absolutely isolated setting. *Nostromo* and *Victory* thus stand in a relation similar to the relation between *King Lear* and *Othello* (or perhaps like that between *The Possessed* and *Crime and Punishment*). Both *Nostromo* and *King Lear* comprehend more of the world and of human experience than the mind can comfortably contemplate; both are made up of a variety of parallel plots and involve several different groups of persons; in each we discover what Francis Fergusson calls "action by analogy," and the action so richly exposed in its multiplicity of modes reveals something not only about the individuals concerned but about the hidden drift of history, the secret and tragic movement of the universe. Both works engage the artist's most disturbing power—the prophetic power, which is of course not the ability to read the particular and immediate future, but the ability to read the future implicit in every grave and serious time, the future man is perennially prone to. In *Victory*, on the other hand, as in *Othello*, the action emerges directly from the peculiar temperaments of a few eccentric individuals. What happens, both artistically and psychologically, happens as a result of the impact of one unique personality upon another. This is not to deny any largeness to *Victory;* it is only to identify the source of the special largeness it does reveal. It is to say that the novel shows an allegorical swelling rather than an allegory, and that the creative force is less a pre-existent design the characters are re-enacting (for example, the myth of Eden, of the man and the woman in the garden and the invasion by the serpent) than the jarring effect of the human encounters.

The germ of *Nostromo* was an anecdote, the theft of a lighter-full of silver. But the germ of *Victory* seems to have been the remembered look of several unrelated persons glimpsed at sundry times and in sundry places. *Nostromo* houses characters enough for half a dozen novels; but it says something about Conrad's attitude towards them that he took most of their names from an old book of memoirs

(G. F. Masterman's *Seven Eventful Years in Paraguay*, published in 1869) which gossiped about people called Carlos Gould, Monygham, Decoud, Fidanza, Barrios and Mitchell (*sic*). Conrad's inventive power in *Nostromo*, I am suggesting, was mainly or at least primarily directed to the exposure of action through plot. In *Victory*, however, we remark a thinness, almost a casualness, of plot invention; for Conrad's attention here was directed initially towards people—towards the exposure of action through character. The distinction is exaggerated, and with luck we can make it collapse; but for the moment it can be helpful. It is intended, in any case, as a slight revision of the wonderfully fertile distinction offered by Jacques Maritain, in *Creative Intuition in Art and Poetry*—the distinction between "the poetry of the novel" and "the poetry of the theater." The latter, Maritain argues, is essentially the poetry of the action; action comes first in the dramatic composition, and other elements—character, especially— are subordinated to and controlled by the shape of the action, which it is their chief function to illuminate. The poetry of the novel, Maritain continues, is the poetry of the agent, for the aim of fiction is not so much to present an action as to shed light upon the human heart. The incidents in a novel are accordingly selected in order to illuminate the peculiar and representative nature of individual human beings. M. Maritain's remarks and my respectful revision of them help explain the sense in which *Victory* is a test of the nature of fiction. For the "agents" of the book did come first in Conrad's planning and in his writing. But by his manipulation of his characters, Conrad brought into being an action virtually invulnerable in its design.

"Conrad was fond of discussing characters in *Victory*," Curle reports; and in his author's note, Conrad discusses little else. He shares with us the memories that went into the making of the novel: a professional card-sharper he had seen once in the West Indies in 1875; the silent wide-eyed girl in a café orchestra in the South of France; the wandering Swedish gentleman who became "the physical and moral foundation of my Heyst." "It seems to me but natural," Conrad says, "that those three buried in the corner of my memory should suddenly get out into the light of the world." The reference was actually to the three bad men, Mr. Jones and Martin Ricardo and Pedro; but it applies equally to the three key figures in the story. They gathered together irresistibly in Conrad's imagination, just as they gather together for the culminating experience of each of their lives on Heyst's island. They are made known to us exactly through the process of gathering. And indeed the first and most obvious way to chart the unfolding scheme of the book is to point to the important moments in that process.

We meet Axel Heyst on the first page. We hear of Lena thirty-six pages later in Mrs. Schomberg's reluctant mutter to Davidson: "There was even one English girl." Mr. Jones makes his appearance fifty-five pages later yet: "a guest who arrived one fine morning by mail-boat . . . a wanderer, clearly, even as Heyst was." Conrad then devotes nearly seventy pages to acquainting us with the three desperadoes, and with the critical differences between them. But even before he begins that section, the gathering process has been at work in the meeting and the drawing together of Heyst and Lena, and their flight to the island refuge. The entire group of major characters (the Schombergs, of course, excluded) is not assembled in a single place until a little more than half-way through the book: when Wang interrupts the moment of deepest intimacy between Heyst and Lena to announce that a boat (containing, as we learn, Mr. Jones and his henchmen) is approaching the jetty. From that instant, the whole of the novel is caught up in the collision of personalities—in what Henry James (speaking about one of Ibsen's plays) called the lunging of ego against ego, the passionate rocking of soul against soul; every ego against every ego, in Conrad's masterful treatment of it, and every soul against every soul. From the instant the boat is sighted—or more accurately, from the instant Heyst goes down to the jetty to stare in amazement at the spectacle of the three white men drifting in from nowhere, seemingly more dead than alive —Conrad's complex artistic purpose becomes clear and begins to fulfill itself. The individual characters, explored individually or in small combinations, now meet and join in an adventure which becomes an action larger and more significant than any of them. The novel, that is, begins to assume the defining quality of drama.

Throughout the course of it, however, Conrad continues to exploit the peculiar resources of the novel, for the traditional aims of the novelist; but he does so, at the same time, as a way of heightening and solidifying the dramatic design. In elaborating the distinction I have mentioned, Jacques Maritain observes that since the shape of the action is determining in a drama, contingencies and coincidences and simple accidents have no place there; but that these devices are proper to fiction, since they can be exactly the occasion for some special insight into character. During the latter half of *Victory*, the plot is heavily dependent upon a series of "evitable" incidents, of which two may be cited as typical: the theft of Heyst's gun by Wang, and the shooting of Lena by Mr. Jones. The latter is pure accident: Jones had intended to kill Martin Ricardo.

The former is a contingency—Wang might have had a gun of his own, or Heyst another revolver hidden away somewhere. Each incident is important to the plot as plotted. But alternatives can easily be imagined, and neither incident seems indispensable to the larger purpose. Yet both incidents serve to shed light on the characters involved and are insofar novelistically justified; and in the light they shed, a truth and a reality begin to appear, as elements towards which an action is steadily in motion.

These incidents, in short, are literally accidental, but they are symbolically inevitable and dramatically appropriate. The theft of the gun tells us a good deal about the curiously hidden nature of the houseboy, his swift and agile selfishness with its portion of quiet cruelty; and it reinforces the sense pervading the world of the book, that in it the distance between men is nearly absolute. At the same time, by rendering Heyst physically defenseless, it provides an "objective correlative" for his more fundamental defenselessness, that of a man of thought like himself in the hour of necessary action. The time spent in puzzling and worrying over the absence of the gun is time artistically well spent. The death of Lena has a still higher degree of propriety. Mr. Jones's bullet, though aimed at Ricardo, only grazed Ricardo's temple before burying itself in Lena's heart, just "under the swelling breast of dazzling and sacred whiteness"—the accident is compounded by the terrible chance that the bullet should strike her exactiy there. Yet we need little instruction from the Freudians to perceive that the accident probably masked an act of deepest deliberation. Towards Ricardo, Mr. Jones felt only fury mixed with a lively sense of danger; but towards Lena, towards any woman, he felt the much more destructive emotion of radical disgust. The shooting of Lena is one of the last and most meaningful of the gestures by which we take the full measure of plain Mr. Jones—the evil ascetic, the satanic figure whose satanism springs from a loathing of women and a horror of sex. (Graham Greene, who has writen a short essay called "Plain Mr. Jones," and who is indebted to Conrad on many counts, has provided a comparable image in Pinkie Brown, the inflamed ascetic of *Brighton Rock*.) And in the mode of her death, we have the final revelation and indeed the vindication of Lena's character. Hers is the touching figure of the young woman of smudged virtue who prays she may lose everything for the sake of the man she loves (again, a figure we encounter in Graham Greene). She has drawn upon herself the death that threatened Axel Heyst. To do so is not only a part of her character. It is a part of her plan.

Each of the main figures in *Victory* has his or her private plan; and in this respect, *Victory* too, like *Nostromo*, has a number of plots—as many as the number of central characters; the plot in each case being what happens at last to the individual plan. As each plan is lit up for us, so much more of the action comes into view. In human terms, the separate plans are catastrophically irreconcilable, and in their difference they provide the "manifold" truth —to use Conrad's word—that the novel brings to light. But artistically, they form a living pattern of parallels and contrasts, and so provide the unitary truth Conrad equally envisaged.

Each of these secret programs of conduct is rooted in the mystery of one or two absolute characteristics. Schomberg's malice, for example, is an absolute trait of character, as unmotivated as the malice of Iago. Like Iago's hatred of Othello, Schomberg's hatred of Axel Heyst can pretend to a specific reason: Heyst's snatching away of the girl, which

led to the funny Faulknerian madhouse involving Schomberg and the orchestra leader Zangiacomo, over which
Conrad used to laugh reminiscently. But the hatred existed
already, existed even before the episode, which Schomberg
so evilly misrepresented, of Heyst and poor Morrison.
Schomberg's private plot, rooted in his malice, is the business of his so-called revenge upon Heyst, along with the
business of diverting the outlaws from his own hotel to the
safe distance of Heyst's island. In its vicious way, it is successful, but not because it has anything to do with the
facts about Heyst and Lena. Schomberg's plot is strictly
his own creation; it is not nourished to any real extent by
external circumstances. The same is true of his malignancy.
It is a key factor in releasing the terrible events of the
book; but it is not developed by outside pressures, it is
revealed by them. Thus it is with the determining features
of the other people in *Victory*. For here, as is customary in
Conrad's work, the characters do not grow, they only grow
more visible. That is the precise effect of their mutual
impact.

Mr. Jones is perhaps the most fascinating instance
in the novel of the motion towards visibility, if only because it is the most paradoxical. What becomes fully and
finally visible about him is a kind of absence, a nothingness.
His plan is the least reconcilable of all the plans, and hence
the most irreducible symptom of the "manifold" aspect of
Victory: because Mr. Jones's plan opposes not only the
substance of all the others but the very terms of their
existence. Ricardo, we remember, has his own particular
reasons—reasons he cannot disclose to Mr. Jones—for urging the invasion of Heyst's island; and no doubt some dumb
dream of conquest occupies the primitive skull of Pedro.
But the mission of Mr. Jones undercuts all that. It has to do

with the condition of his being, which is as it were a mockery of being itself. Heyst reports to Lena on his conversation with Jones:

> " 'I suppose you would like to know who I am?' he asked me.
>
> "I told him I would leave it to him, in a tone which, between gentlemen, could have left no doubt in his mind. He raised himself on his elbow—he was lying down on the campbed—and said:
>
> " 'I am he who is—.' "

"No use asking me what he meant, Lena," Heyst adds. "I don't know." What Jones meant was probably a theatrical blasphemy. In very similar words, according to the Old Testament, God announced his name and his nature to his chosen people: "I am," or "I am that I am." Jones, of course, is not god-like, and especially not god-like in the sense of representing the source of being itself. He is devil-like—his character bulges in the direction of the devil (he is not *the* devil, any more than *Victory* is an allegory); and exactly because he represents the source of non-being.

The association with Satan gratifies Mr. Jones immensely. He describes, in an echo from the Book of Job, his habit of "coming and going up and down the earth"; and Heyst replies that he has "heard that sort of story about someone else before." Jones at once gives Heyst a ghastly grin, claiming that "I have neither more nor less determination" than "the gentleman you are thinking of." But the nature and end of his determination emerge from a later allusion to the devil. Jones speculates for Heyst's benefit that a man living alone, as Heyst had been living, would "take care to conceal [his] property so well that the devil himself—." Heyst interrupts with a murmured "Certainly."

Again, with his left hand, Mr. Jones mopped his frontal bone, his stalk-like neck, his razor jaws, his fleshless chin. Again, his voice faltered and his aspect became still more gruesomely malevolent, as of a wicked and pitiless corpse.

Those last four words summarize the character of Mr. Jones and point to his unswerving purpose: he is not only deathly, he is the cause that death is in others. To Schomberg, too, Jones had seemed "to imply some sort of menace from beyond the grave"; and in Heyst's first view of him, Jones is "sitting up [in the boat], silent, rigid and very much like a corpse." At the outset of their duel, Jones seems to exert a greater force of sheer existence than Heyst; for Heyst, as he confesses mournfully in language highly reminiscent of one of Hawthorne's isolated men, has lived too long among shadows. But Heyst's determining quality has only been lying dormant; he is like the indolent volcano, to which he is lightly compared on the second page of the book; he is moving—though moving too late and too slowly—towards existence and reality. Jones's characteristic movement is all in the other direction.

The force in Jones is all negative, though not the less emphatic for being so. That is why he hates and fears women, for they are fertility incarnate and the literal source of life. Jones's particular and personal plot is not really to seize Heyst's alleged treasures, but to inflict his deathiness upon others. He comes as an envoy of death, disguised as an envoy of the living: of death not in the sense of murder, but in the sense of a fundamental hostility to existence. He is the champion of the anti-real, and he arrives at just the moment when Heyst, because of the presence and love of Lena, is feeling "a greater sense of reality than he had ever known in his life." Jones's plan, too, is superficially successful: everyone he has brushed against on the island is dead. Jones is dead also; but he has not been killed, he has simply shrunk, collapsed, disintegrated. He has reached the limit of his true condition. And what is visible of him at the end is exactly the outward signs of that condition. "The water's very clear there," Davidson tells the Excellency; "and I could see him huddled up on the bottom between two piles, like a heap of bones in a blue silk bag, with only the head and feet sticking out."

Mr. Jones's most astute enemy in the book is not Heyst but the girl Lena, though Jones and Lena never in fact confront one another. But Lena is the one person able to understand not only the threat represented by the invaders, but the very threat of the threat; and she understands it so well that, as things develop, she can formulate her own plot and purpose to herself with exactness—to "capture death—savage, sudden, irresponsible death, prowling round the man who possessed her." Lena stands for a possibility of life. Yet curiously enough, her role as the actual source of Heyst's sense of being is rendered less visible—rendered, that is, with less apparent success—than are the deadly negations of Mr. Jones. Lena is the one member of the cast who remains in partial darkness. Many critics have remarked upon this, and some have gone on to say that Conrad rarely had much luck with his women. But his achievement elsewhere is not always unimpressive: Winnie Verloc, in *The Secret Agent*, seems to me one of the most compelling females in modern literature; and one has little difficulty making out the attractive features of Emily Gould and Flora de Barral, in *Nostromo* and *Chance* respectively. It may even be that a kind of haziness, a fragility of substance was intended in the portrayal of Lena. She *is* like that, and the frailty of her being determines the nature of her plot. For her aim is precisely to win for herself a greater measure of reality, by forcing upon the man she loves a greater recognition of her. She lives in his acknowledgement of her: "If you were to stop thinking about me I shouldn't be in the world at all. . . . I can only be what you think I am." This is a trifle unfortunate, since Heyst, the only human being who could have seen Lena, can never manage to see quite enough. Richard Curle observes nicely about Lena that she is "the supreme example of a 'one-man' woman, so supreme that even the reader is kept out of the secret." Heyst peers at her in the half-light, and we peer over his shoulder, dimly discerning a creature of considerable but only guessed-at bodily appeal and intense but only partially communicated spiritual desire.

Her desire is stated plainly enough for us, as it takes form after Ricardo's attempt to rape her. From that moment onward, "all her energy was concentrated on the struggle she wanted to take upon herself, in a great exaltation of love and self-sacrifice." And we know enough about her history to find that exaltation plausible. We have heard of her mother's desertion of her father, of her father's career as a small-time musician and of his removal to a home for incurables; we have heard of her bleak childhood and adolescence, her blurred unhappy life with a travelling orchestra; we can easily imagine what Heyst's compassion must have meant to her. "I am not what they call a good girl," she has said; and through Heyst's impression of her, we are struck by her mixture of misery and audacity. She alone fully understands that it is Schomberg who has put the outlaws on Heyst's trail, and she can comprehend the hotel-keeper's motiveless motive. Lena's plot, accordingly, is the most coherent of all the plots, and the most important. It is also the most private, since it requires of her that she lie both to the man she hates and the man she loves. She is altogether successful, at least as successful as Schomberg or Mr. Jones. She does disarm Ricardo, literally and psychologically; the dagger she takes from him is indeed "the spoil of vanquished death" and "the symbol of her victory." By dividing Ricardo from Jones, she creates a situation in which, as the demonically brilliant Jones instantly realizes, Ricardo must be killed; and through a chain-reaction, she is responsible also for the death of Pedro and Jones himself. All this we know, understand and can rehearse. But Conrad has nonetheless not finally managed to fulfill his ambition with respect to Lena. He has not made us see Lena completely. Between her and ourselves, there falls a shadow. It is, of course, the shadow of Axel Heyst.

If the victory is Lena's—if her end, as Conrad insisted, is triumphant—the major defeat recorded in the novel is that of Heyst. His is the ultimate failure, and for the reason he gives in almost the last words we hear him speak: "Ah, Davidson, woe to the man whose heart has not learned while young to hope, to love—and to put its trust in life." But that very statement demonstrates that Heyst, by acknowledging his failure and perceiving its cause, has in the literary manner of speaking been saved. He is, at the last, completely in touch with truth. And similarly, if Heyst's personal plan—which is not only to rid the island of its invaders and to protect Lena, but also to join with Lena in an experience of full reality—if that plan is the least successful plan in the book, Heyst is nonetheless the true and steady center of the novel from its beginning to its end. So central is Heyst within the rich composition of *Victory*, that neither his character nor his conduct may be

clearly seen apart from that composition. They are identified only through a series of analogies and contrasts, and
as the vital center of the book's design.

As analysis moves to the figure of Axel Heyst, it moves
of necessity from the Many to the One—from the many
separated individuals with their irreconcilable differences of
purpose to the pattern in which they seem to echo and
reflect and repeat one another. It is the felt flow of the
Many into the One that accounts for the feeling one has of
a strong metaphysical current running deep through the
novel, of very real human beings and events gathering
together in a way that suggests an allegory of universal
proportions. Let it be emphasized again that we have to
do with a process, not with an imposition. And as it develops, we begin to detect parallels between contrasting
and inimical elements, continuities between divisions—and
by the power of the book's current, more radical contrasts
between newly observed parallels. At the center is Axel
Heyst, whose entire being—*artistically*, within the actual
pages of the book—is created by the play of likeness and
difference.

We must, accordingly, approach Heyst by way of
those relationships—which is to reconsider some of the
persons already inspected, but to consider them now not
in their enormous differences, but in their unexpected
similarities: an undertaking the first page of *Victory* (with
its references to the similarities between coal and diamonds,
an island and a mountain) has warned us would be the key
to the novel's meaning. Between Lena and Ricardo, for
example, between the mystically devoted young woman
and the thick-headed roughneck who plunges headlong
through the blue serge curtain to assault her, an unexpected
likeness is uncovered. It is a fatality in Ricardo's crude

imagination that he should exaggerate it. "You and I are made to understand each other," he mumbles, after a stupor of surprise and admiration at the vigor of Lena's resistance. "Born alike, bred alike, I guess. You are not tame. Same here! You have been chucked out into this rotten world of 'ypocrits. Same here!" Because of his conviction of their likeness, Ricardo trusts Lena more simply and unquestioningly than Heyst trusts her; Ricardo trusts what there is in Lena of his own animal and prehensile nature, and he dies of that trust, as Heyst dies of mistrust. But within disastrous limits, Ricardo is right—he and Lena do have a good deal in common. "Perhaps because of the similarity of their miserable origin in the dregs of mankind," Lena realizes, "she had understood Ricardo perfectly." Even her physical strength and tenacity match his: "You have fingers like steel! Jiminy! You have muscles like a giant." That is scarcely the pathetic child seen through Heyst's impression of her, the child suffering helplessly the venomous pinchings of Mrs. Zangiacomo; and the ferocity of her response to Ricardo's attempted rape correctly suggests a ready perception, based on experience, of that kind of jungle behavior. It also suggests the strength in Lena which has been brought to the surface since the Zangiacomo days: brought to the surface and focussed as a powerful instrument, through the effect upon her of Heyst.

An important ingredient in her strength is a talent for lying, exercised for the sake of truth. Ricardo is quite justified in attributing to Lena a duplicity equal to his own; he knows that both of them have had to become skilled in duplicity as the one indispensable resource in the world's hypocritical "game of grab." "Give the chuck to all this blamed 'ypocrisy," urges Ricardo. Lena seems to agree, and she embarks deceptively upon a plot to deceive

Heyst—"her gentleman," as Ricardo calls him—which notably parallels Ricardo's systematic deception of *his* gentleman, Mr. Jones. It seems to Ricardo natural that Lena should lie to the man who has befriended her; such is the norm of behavior in the world he inhabits: that is, the world of *Victory*. It is what people do to each other in that world: witness Mrs. Schomberg's trickery of her own gentleman, her fat braggart of a husband. The cluster of duplicities has, up to a point, a common element, for each aims initially at the salvation of the man deceived. Mrs. Schomberg, when she helps frustrate her husband's plans (his "insane and odious passion") by helping Lena to escape, imagines she is keeping Schomberg out of serious trouble and preserving their wretched marriage. Ricardo's organization of the invasion of Heyst's island is a contrivance to rescue his chief from the habitual state of sloth into which Jones had fallen. To do so, Ricardo must cunningly keep silent about the presence on the island of a young woman; since, were Jones to hear about it, he would instantly abandon the adventure. Only later does Ricardo's helpful deceit deepen into betrayal. And as to Lena, "she was not ashamed of her duplicity," because "nothing stood between the enchanted dream of her existence and a cruel catastrophe but her duplicity." She will deceive every one, and she will especially deceive Heyst; she will wear the mask of infidelity to save the life of the man towards whom her fidelity is the very assurance of her existence.

The relationship between Lena and Ricardo thus illuminates one of the major themes of the novel—the theme of truth-telling, and the significance of truth-telling, as a value, in the scheme of human behavior. By the same token, Lena and Ricardo illuminate the character of Axel

Heyst; for it is almost a weakness in Heyst that—at the opposite extreme from Mr. Jones and his self-association with the Father of Lies—he has an absolute regard for truth. He is so obsessed with truth that he becomes literally disempowered when confronted with lies; and he is so inflexible towards truth that only lies can save him. Even more than the theft of his gun, as it seems, it is the lies Schomberg has spread about Heyst's treatment of Morrison that, when they belatedly reach Heyst's ears, succeed finally in rendering him defenseless by provoking in him the emotion of paralyzing disgust. His only defense thereafter is the multiple duplicity of Lena.

It is not inappropriate that such should be the case, for between Morrison and Lena, too, there is a revealing similarity. Lena shares with Ricardo a certain seamy background and a certain practical toughness; but with Morrison, the unfortunate master of the trading brig *Capricorn*, she has shared the magnanimity of Axel Heyst. The story of Morrison is a sort of rehearsal for the story of Lena; for like Lena, Morrison is not only the object; he is in a sense the victim of Heyst's compassion. Morrison is miraculously rescued by Heyst in a way that, as events work out, both leads to and makes plausible the rescue, not long after, of Lena; and the consequence in both cases is a fresh involvement, a chance for life, that results in fact in their death. Both look upon Heyst as a kind of god, especially because to both Heyst's conduct appears purely gratuitous, like the undeserved and disinterested mercy of God. It is not merely pity; Heyst's father had advised him to "cultivate that form of contempt which is called pity," but the salvaging of Morrison and the benevolent theft of Lena are due to no such calculated attitude. They reflect rather a temperament which, as we are told, was incapable of scorning any decent emotion—a temperament so fine and rare as to seem literally godlike to the bedevilled of the book's world. When Heyst offers Morrison the money to save the latter's boat, Morrison gazes at him as though "he expected Heyst's usual white suit of the tropics to change into a shining garment down to his toes . . . and didn't want to miss a single detail of the transformation." In the procedure typical of *Victory*, a reaction which will later become serious, complex and tragic is presented in the early pages in simple and partly comic tonalities. Lena's reaction to Heyst's rescue of her is less extravagant and open-mouthed; but it partakes of a still deeper awe and of a genuinely self-sacrificial reverence.

In the same way, it is Morrison who first strikes the note, in his droll and touching way, which will develop into a theme close to the tragic heart of the book. Morrison wonders in panic if Heyst is joking about the money. Heyst asks austerely what he means, and Morrison is abashed.

> "Forgive me, Heyst. You must have been sent by God in answer to my prayer. But I have been nearly off my chump for three days with worry; and it suddenly struck me: 'What if it's the Devil who has sent him?' "
>
> "I have no connection with the supernatural," said Heyst graciously, moving on. "Nobody sent me. I just happened along."
>
> "I know better," contradicted Morrison.

That moment has its louder and more serious echo a couple of hundred pages later, when Heyst catches sight of Jones and his henchmen approaching the jetty. He stares at them in disbelief: "[He] had never been so much astonished in his life."

The civilisation of the tropics could have nothing to do with it. It was more like those myths, current in Polynesia, of amazing strangers, who arrive at an island, gods or demons, bringing good or evil to the innocence of the inhabitants—gifts of unknown things, words never heard before.

"Gods or demons, bringing good or evil. . . ." Those ambiguous phrases greet the first glimpse Heyst and Jones have of each other; and they frame and give shape to the most telling of the patterns of similarity and contrast that *Victory* has to offer—the one that says most about Heyst himself, and the one that best reveals the drama of which he is the protagonist. Between Heyst and Jones, the differences are of radical dimensions. Heyst is a bringer of good (though the recipients of his gifts suffer evil by consequence). Jones is a bringer of evil (though his gift is the occasion of greatest good for Lena, and her victory). Heyst has some godlike element in his nature; but the insinuation makes him highly uncomfortable. Jones has a kind of private understanding with the Devil, and that insinuation never fails to excite him. But between Axel Heyst and plain Mr. Jones, there is a vibrant flow of analogies, a movement back and forth like electrical currents.

A likeness is registered at the instant Jones first turns up in the novel; a guest at Schomberg's hotel arriving from Celebes, "but generally, Schomberg understood, from up China Sea way; a wanderer clearly, even as Heyst was." Both men are drifters by profession—"I'll drift," Heyst had decided as a young man; both have occupied themselves for many years by "coming and going up and down the earth." Both men are gentlemen, in the conventional meaning of the word and within the book's definition as pronounced by Martin Ricardo: "That's another thing you can tell a gentlemen by, his freakishness. A gentleman ain't accountable to nobody, any more than a tramp on the roads." Heyst invokes a comparable notion: "I, Axel Heyst, the most detached of creatures in this earthly captivity, the veriest tramp on this earth. . . ." As gentlemen and as tramps, both Jones and Heyst are products of highly civilized society who have chosen the career of the rootless outsider. Both are well-born, perhaps aristocratic; they are elegant, sophisticated, mannerly; both have an excessive vein of fastidiousness, a too easily outraged austerity. And both are outcasts who in different ways are outside the law: Heyst by being in some manner beyond and above it, Jones by being several degrees beneath it. With one of his ghastly grins, during their first interview, Mr. Jones confesses to Heyst that the latter was not the man he had expected to meet. For he sees or thinks he sees, startlingly, *son semblable, son frère.*

Jones misjudges Heyst just as Ricardo misjudges Lena, and with the same limited warrant. "We pursue the same ends," Jones remarks; and he argues that his presence on the island is neither more nor less "morally reprehensible" than Heyst's. Jones assumes that, like himself, Heyst is simply a gentlemanly scoundrel, sharing with him the impulse common to gifted men—the criminal impulse. About this mistake there is something as ridiculous as it is fatal; but Jones has intuited a fragment of the truth. Heyst does share with Jones a basic indifference to the habitual practices of society and to its moral verdicts. He appraises the world in terms nearly identical to those of Jones: "The world's a mad dog," Heyst tells Davidson. "It will bite you if you give it a chance." These two lean and handsome gentlemen, these radical drifters, have an extraordinary amount in common, and Jones's contention is justified—

"Ah, Mr. Heyst . . . you and I have much more in common than you think." Jones and Heyst reflect each other with a sort of perfection, the way an object is reflected in a mirror. Each is the other seen wrong way round.

That is why they are dramatically indispensable one to the other—the visibility of each is dependent upon the presence of the other. They come from opposite ends of the universe, and they meet where opposites are made to meet: in a work of art. The strength of each often appears as an extension of the other's weakness and vice-versa; which is one reason why the conflict between them, as it assumes its form, seems to extend endlessly, to enlarge almost beyond the reach of human reckoning. It brushes the edge of allegory, and touches briefly on the outskirts of myth—one of "those myths, current in Polynesia, of amazing strangers . . . gods or demons." But the drama hangs on to its human vitality and its immediacy and continues to draw its force from the peculiar nature of the two men involved—the man of intellectual sensibility with an inadequate but incipient trust in life; and the man of occasional action with a strenuous but insufficiently examined faith in the power of death. Mr. Jones's tendency to sloth, which leaves him spread motionless over three chairs for hours at a time, is reflected in Heyst's long periods of meditation on the hostility of thought to action, while he lounges on the verandah and smokes his cheroot. But Jones's condition has the terrible and explosive power of an ancient sin; and Heyst's skepticism is marred by a vein of tenderness. If Heyst had mistrusted life more completely, he would perhaps have been a better match for Jones from the outset. As it is, the novel catches him at the moment when mistrust is giving way to an urge toward reality and communion.

He had long since, so he tells Jones during their last conversation, divorced himself from the love of life; but then he adds, with painful accuracy, "not sufficiently perhaps." So he acts and reacts without "distinctness." His conception of the world, taken from his father, had for too many years been of something "not worth touching, and perhaps not substantial enough to grasp." The experience of Lena was beginning to put substance into the world; but Heyst can neither participate fully in that experience nor resist it, for he has absorbed either too much or too little of his father's doctrine that "the consolation of love" is the cruelest of all the stratagems of life. He can still insist that "he who forms a tie is lost," but his actual feeling is that he is about to find himself, that Lena is giving him "a greater sense of his own reality than he had ever known in his life."

Greater: but still inadequate to fit him for the challenge that arises. For that challenge is exactly the embodiment of the challenge his father had honorably faced. "With what strange serenity, mingled with terrors," Heyst thinks about his father, "had that man considered the universal nothingness! He had plunged into it headlong, perhaps to render death, the answer that faced one at every inquiry, more supportable." It is only four pages later that Wang arrives to announce the approach of a strange boat. And Mr. Jones, the corpse-like figure at the tiller of the boat, is himself the harbinger and representative of that "universal nothingness." He is the body of that death "that faced one at every inquiry." Trapped between a waning skepticism and an undernourished sense of reality, Heyst cannot emulate his father; cannot make the plunge or launch the assault. All he can do, at the end, is to take death upon himself, purgatorially, by fire.

But, if Heyst is unable to plunge, Jones (like Ricardo on his lower level) plunges too incautiously. The sinister mission he engages on is unsupported by the necessary amount of cold intelligence—of just that kind of intelligence that Heyst possesses supremely. Heyst begins finally to exercise it at Jones's expense during their climactic interview, after Heyst has learned the reason for the invasion of the island—Schomberg's preposterous falsehood about treasures hidden on it. At this instant, a reversal is effected, and Heyst takes command of their relationship; it is his strength now which becomes visible because of the revelation of Jones's weakness. "You seem a morbid, senseless sort of bandit," Heyst says with weary contempt. "There were never in the world two more deluded bandits —never! . . . Fooled by a silly rascally innkeeper," he goes on remorselessly. "Talked over like a pair of children with a promise of sweets." It is the logical weakness of Jones's asserted belief in universal fraudulence that it must contain in itself an element of the fraudulent. If he had been wholly convinced of the depravity of all the inhabitants of a wholly vicious world, Jones would have trusted less in the strength of his authority—his graveyard power—over Martin Ricardo; and he would not have overlooked the possibility of mere vulgar vindictiveness in Schomberg. He leapt too swiftly from sloth into action, in a way that, in retrospect, invests one of Heyst's casual pronouncements, made early in the book, with prophetic implications: "Action is the devil."

Heyst and Jones need each other for artistic visibility; but both of them need Lena, as she needs them, to make clear the full shape of the drama they have begotten between them, when the current of the novel carries them (this is one's impression) into a dimension beyond the dimension occupied by all the other persons in the book. The action disclosed by the effect of those three upon each other is the gradual location of that dimension, of the very domain of reality and truth. The domain lies somewhere between the dialectical stirrings of the book's first page and the observation of nothingness on its last—somewhere, as it turns out, between the intellectualism of Heyst and the deathiness of Jones. Between the two kinds of failure, Lena's victory is squeezed out in a way that is a victory both for her and for the novel in which she has her being. As against Jones, Lena has dedicated herself to the actual cause of living; and as against Heyst, she has seized with fingers of steel upon the immediate and necessary facts of behavior. Her practicality (again the book's first page is recalled) derives from a mystical exaltation that transcends the particular situation and attains to universal value while remaining sharply and intently focussed upon the single figure of Axel Heyst. Lena's accomplishment reflects the accomplishment of the novel. *Victory* is, in a sense, a reproach to the fascination with death of so much modern fiction. But even more, perhaps, it is an admonition about the tendency of both fiction and criticism to intellectualize the art—to lose the drama in the allegory; or to deform the art—to lose the novel in the drama. The form of *Victory* grows dramatic, and it gives forth intimations of allegory. But it remains faithful to its own nature, for it never makes the mistake of Mr. Jones—it never fails to take account of the variable and highly unpredictable character of individual human beings.

ULYSSES, THE DIVINE NOBODY [1]

JOYCE, 1922

by Richard Ellmann

In the languorous close of Joyce's *Ulysses,* Molly Bloom recalls how she and her husband embraced among the rhododendrons on Howth Head, and how she gave him a bit of seedcake out of her mouth. Even if *Finnegans Wake* did not represent the fruit of the Tree of Eden as the "seedfruit," we would suspect that Joyce was holding before us an image of young love as the Garden of Eden. The young Bloom and Molly will do well enough as Adam and Eve, but one character is singularly absent from the idyllic scene. There is no serpent in this garden, and without the serpent, there is no sin. The fall of man, instead of being bitter, is the sweetest memory we have. Molly and her husband live in a world where the devil has no place; and in the famous peroration of her monolog she says, "Yes," to her husband, to the flesh, and to all this neo-pagan world.

[1] Much of this essay is included, in somewhat different form, in the author's biography, *James Joyce* (Oxford University Press, 1959), copyright by Richard Ellmann.

Joyce was nearly forty years old when he wrote this passage at the end of *Ulysses,* and in many ways it is the culmination of his intellectual development up to that time. The history of the serpent in his work is curious enough; through two witnesses we can trace it back almost to the beginning of his consciousness. His brother Stanislaus begins his memoir of James Joyce with his earliest recollection, of James assuming the role of serpent in a family playlet about Adam and Eve. Joyce must have been about six years old at the time. Another witness of these early years is Eileen Vance, the girl mentioned under her own name in *A Portrait of the Artist as a Young Man.* She informs me that James, at the age of six or seven, had a favorite way of punishing a brother or sister who offended him. He would put him face down on the ground, set a red wheelbarrow over him, don a red stocking cap, and then utter sounds to indicate that he, as devil, was making the miscreant crackle and sizzle in the flames of hell. It is extraordinary to find James taking the satanic role in this childlike way.

Extraordinary, because much of the excitement of *A Portrait of the Artist as a Young Man* centers on Stephen's gradual assumption of the role of Lucifer, but a Lucifer of a special sort. For just as the Garden of Eden is purged of sin at the end of *Ulysses,* so Stephen's enactment of the role of Lucifer is deprived of evil intent. The book develops a complicated tension between a waning and waxing process: Stephen's Catholicism wanes away, to be replaced by what he considers a higher faith in art. He is not anti-Catholic: it is rather that Catholicism no longer attracts him. That is, the thrilling, appalling words of the devil, *non serviam,* awaken his consciousness of sin in the middle of the book, but eventually the same words express his consciousness of the virtue in his proud rejection. So when he says to his friend Cranly, at the end of the *Portrait*, "*Non serviam*," he no longer means, I will not serve God, for God does not enter in; he means rather, I will not serve priest or king, or anything less than my art. To be Lucifer is perilous, but that is the world's fault, not Lucifer's.

The whole development of Stephen Dedalus is mirrored in this kind of revaluation of his vocabulary. Catholicism furnishes him with the words; and he furnishes them with the meanings. The fall of man, at first so damnable, becomes at last a necessary part of life, like growing up, with which it is virtually synonymous. It is a fortunate fall not because, as St. Augustine says, it makes possible our redemption by Christ, but because it releases the life that has been coiled up within us. Not to fall is too hard, Stephen thinks, but it is also too dull and unrewarding. He could say with Heraclitus that the way down and the way up are the same.

Similarly the word *call*, which for a time is the call to the priestly vocation, gradually becomes the call to life. Joyce accomplishes Stephen's maturity by changing the meaning of his vocabulary; the verbal panoply of the Church becomes, in its new form, a means of liberating him from the Church. Christ's act of casting off his cerements and rising from the tomb is turned into Stephen's soul rising from the grave of boyhood in order to create a new beauty. The resurrection occurs within us. The word is made flesh, Stephen thinks, in the virgin womb of the imagination, and thus the birth of Christ becomes a metaphor for the birth of a work of art. Of the two chief methods of defecting from religion, denial and transmutation, Stephen pursues the second. His brother notes that James Joyce had no conflict over leaving the Church; he shed his religion like an old skin. Instead of serving the Church, he made it serve him. He moves thereby into a neo-pagan world; I say neo-pagan rather than pagan because Joyce's world is not pre-Christian, nor anti-Christian, but post-Christian. We can distinguish between the attitudes of Stephen Dedalus and Buck Mulligan, for Mulligan is anti-Christian, seeing Christianity as gibberish, while Stephen is post-Christian, in that he finds new secular meanings to fill the husks of religious words he regards as dead.

In *Ulysses* Joyce represents Stephen Dedalus as still preoccupied with the reinterpretation of Christianity. In the Proteus episode Stephen argues in great and complex detail the relationship of Christ to his mother's husband and to his true father, God. There is no reason to suppose that he believes in either manifestation of the godhead, but the imagery helps him to phrase his alienation from his own father, who is a mere Joseph, and his longing for kinship with some greater self. This interest in spiritual parenthood is not new in Stephen; in the *Portrait* it emerged in another aspect, the spiritual parenthood of a work of art. Stephen's aesthetic metaphors were physical in origin: he referred in *A Portrait* to writing as a process of "artistic conception, artistic gestation, and artistic reproduction," and when he came to explain the dramatic form of art, which he considered the highest, he described it as the creation of independent beings.

This quest for creation remains vital for him, but in *Ulysses* he seems younger, more son-like, more anxious to overcome his isolation. He wishes to anastomose with the world through finding a true father in Bloom. Bloom has achieved effortlessly what Stephen has worked so hard to find. He is a born skeptic where Stephen is a made one. He is fully committed to worldly experience, where

Stephen is only diffidently committed. To suggest their kinship Joyce, as is well known, establishes many secret affinities between them: each is without his front door key, each thinks of the same subjects and walks in the same places, each wears mourning, each lacks a focus for his affections. Each finds his truth outside the Church.

It has been suggested that Joyce has no sympathy, really, for either Stephen Dedalus or Bloom, and considers their shared skepticism an unfortunate part of modern vulgarity. Some critics have even begun to reclaim Joyce for the Church. No one will deny that he was profoundly affected by his Catholic upbringing, but it is equally certain that he gave up his religion. I have suggested some of the internal marks of Joyce's disbelief: his revaluation of the fall of man by making it human rather than diabolic, beneficent rather than pernicious, his revaluation of the call and of the resurrection into secular terms, and his adoption of a benevolent Lucifer as model for his hero. In letters Joyce said that he thought himself to be incapable of any belief, and his conduct bears out this statement. After about his seventeenth year he refused to take the sacraments: he was never married in a church, and not married at all until twenty-seven years of living voluntarily with the same woman in his irreligious equivalent of marriage; that he submitted at last to a civil ceremony was due to his wish that his children should inherit his property without complications. It is true that he attended church during Holy Week, but he did not kneel at the altar; instead he remained standing at the back of the church and enjoyed the music. He attended services of the Eastern Church and of Danish Lutheran churches for the same or like reasons. He did not allow his children to be baptized, although not doing so entailed difficulties for them and for him.

He opposed the baptism of his grandson. He did not ask
for extreme unction, nor did he cry out in his last moments for pardon, being, as his son wryly commented, too
busy thinking about his pains in this world to be concerned
over his pains in the next. In later life, the recent edition
of his *Letters* confirms, he looked back at his early religious
belief with amusement, and sent Ezra Pound a limerick
about the hero of the *Portrait:*

> There once was a lounger named Stephen
> Whose youth was most odd and uneven;
> He throve on the smell
> Of a horrible hell
> That a Hottentot wouldn't believe in.

But if Joyce was skeptical toward religion, he was not
skeptical toward the medley of hope and failure which he
was romantic enough to call "life." His temperament re-
tained a faculty of adoration, but it was turned not toward
God but toward all creation, what he calls in the *Portrait*
"the fair courts of life." "Welcome, O Life," cries Stephen
Dedalus at the end of the *Portrait* in a conclusion as decisive as Molly Bloom's "yes" at the end of *Ulysses.* I do
not mean to suggest that Joyce's attitude toward life was in
any easy sense optimistic; instead of saying that things
usually work out well, he would probably say that they
usually work out badly. There was no sin on Howth Head,
but the joy of that moment is a joy recalled, and recalled
from beneath years of diminution and trouble.

But even if life tends to be dissatisfying, it contains
moments which redeem it. Joyce describes these as eucharistic, and the word "eucharistic" is another to which he
attaches a neo-pagan significance. So in *Stephen Hero*
Joyce has Stephen say, "I must wait until the Eucharist

come to me," and then set about "translating the phrase into common sense." The eucharistic occasions are moments of fullness and of passion, and the moment of love that Molly remembers at the end of *Ulysses*, and that her husband recalls earlier, is such an occasion. The eucharist brings not God but what Yeats calls "profane perfection of mankind" instead. Another such occasion in Joyce is the young love of Gretta Conroy and Michael Furey in "The Dead," and still another is Anna Livia Plurabelle's memory of submission to her husband-father at the end of *Finnegans Wake*. These memories exist; they push up from among dead things to heal our thirst, like the moment in Eliot's Hyacinth Garden in "The Waste Land." But where Eliot sees human love as only a stepping-stone to higher love, and therefore as a brief ecstasy which is mostly agony, for Joyce the memory is not agonizing, and human love, if not ideal, is the best we have.

Besides the eucharistic occasions which are ecstatic, there are also in Joyce less ecstatic moments which again he describes by a religious word, "epiphanies." The epiphany did not mean for him the manifestation of godhead to the Gentiles, the showing forth of Christ to the Magi, although that is a useful metaphor for what he had in mind. The epiphany is the sudden revelation of the whatness of a thing, the moment in which, he says, "the soul of the commonest object . . . seems to us radiant." The artist is charged with such revelations, and he must look for them not among gods but among men, and often in casual, unostentatious, even unpleasant moments. That Dublin is small and life in it uneventful does not in the least prevent moments of insight and elevation from occurring there. It is because of Joyce's recognition of the potentialities implicit in day-to-day reality that he attaches so much importance, even a talismanic importance, to portraying that reality accurately. In one of his letters he denounces George Moore for not knowing that a railroad train runs between two small places on the Irish coast. But a more brilliant illustration is given by Frank Budgen in his book on the making of *Ulysses;* Joyce, he says, once told him this story:

> "A German lady called to see me today. She is a writer and wanted me to give an opinion on her work, but she told me she had already shown it to the porter of the hotel where she stays. So I said to her: 'What did your hotel porter think of your work?' She said: 'He objected to a scene in my novel where my hero goes out into the forest, finds a locket of the girl he loves, picks it up and kisses it passionately.' 'But,' I said, 'that seems to me to be a very pleasing and touching incident. What did your hotel porter find wrong with it?' And then she tells me he said: 'It's all right for the hero to find the locket and to pick it up and kiss it, but before he kissed it you should have made him wipe the dirt off it with his coat sleeve.'"

> "And what did you tell her?" Budgen asked Joyce.

> "I told her," said Joyce, "(and I meant it too) to go back to that hotel porter, and always to take his advice. 'That man,' I said, 'is a critical genius. There is nothing I can tell you that he can't tell you.'"

The heavy moral I would find in this lighthearted tale is that the illuminations of life exist within life, not above it, and are inseparable from the dirt in which they are imbedded. If we try to alembicate them into pure gold we lose them. The poetry of rubbish-heaps cannot survive the removal of the rubbish. It is essential to understand Joyce's position if we are to understand the meaning of *Ulysses,* for we must not suppose that he, like T. S. Eliot, finds nothing in rubbish but rubbish. He used to say, "Birth and death are violent enough for me," and he remarked to Djuna Barnes, "Never write about the extraordinary. That is for the journalist." He likes small moments, small cities, small people, and delights in discovering the crystallizations of little lives into epiphanies. "Don't make a hero out of me," he said to a French admirer; "I'm only a simple middle-class man."

The fact that Eliot uses the same technique of paralleling contemporaneity and antiquity that is implicit in the title of *Ulysses* has made it difficult to read Joyce without reading into his books something of Eliot's scorn of the modern world and of the world in general. There is no evidence that Joyce scorned either. If you mentioned to him the atrocities of the Nazis, he would remind you of the atrocities of the Inquisition in Holland. The essence of Eliot's charge against the modern world is that it has no religious faith, but to Joyce it has, if anything, too much. We might well expect, then, that in taking up the *Odyssey* his object would not be to display a contrast between ancient grandeur and modern ignobility. In an essay he wrote before he was eighteen, he declared that it was a sinful foolishness to sigh back for the good old times. He chooses a pagan hero because he is a neo-pagan himself. What he looks for in the ancient epic is what he looks for in the modern world, moments of epiphany, revelations of the souls of men and incidents. The same impulse which made him call his young man in the *Portrait* "Dedalus" makes him call his next hero "Ulysses." Joyce searches the epic past, as he searches the present, for its humanity, not its supernaturalism. As a boy he liked the supernaturalism, but in maturity he came to insist that the *Odyssey* was to be understood as in large part a naturalistic epic, that all its places, for example, such as Circe's island and Scylla and Charybdis, were actual places on the map. This view, which Joyce began to develop on his own, has received confirmation in the researches of the French scholar Victor Bérard.

Putting aside for a moment the question of the book's total meaning, we can instructively survey the history of its composition. Joyce thought about writing *Ulysses* for eight years before he began to write it, and he then spent eight years more in executing his design. When he was in Rome in 1906, he wrote his brother that he would soon start on a story to be called *Ulysses*, which would deal with a Mr. Hunter in Dublin, a man who was supposed to be Jewish and was rumored also to have an unfaithful wife. He failed, however, to write the story, and about two years later decided he would expand it into an Irish *Peer Gynt* and make a short book of it. He had already decided that it would take place in one day, and he appears to have thought of it at first as a tragedy.

After 1908 he did not speak of the book, but the material for it was gathering in his mind. He was able to work out its infidelity theme not only from the example of Hunter but from some unfounded suspicions of his own wife. He took to reading Thomas Aquinas, a page a day, and found in Thomas's mind, which he described as a sharp sword, the material he needed for much of the Proteus episode. In 1913 he worked out a theory of *Hamlet*, substantially the same as that of Stephen in *Ulysses*, and presented it in two lectures to a Triestine audience. His design gradually expanded so that the short book became a very long one. Someone has suggested that a defect of *Ulysses* is that it is a bloated short story: I think this is not true; the book's theme requires its length. As a matter of fact, Joyce conceived of all of his books at first as smaller than they eventually became. The *Portrait,* for example, was originally a sixteen-page essay, and *Finnegans Wake* swelled in composition in the same way.

In constructing a modern Ulysses, Joyce applied himself to amateur scholarship. If his theories were sometimes as wide of the mark as Schliemann's, they ended in the creation of *Ulysses* as Schliemann's ended in the discovery of Troy. As W. B. Stanford has pointed out, Joyce read and studied the principal works written since Homer in which Ulysses or Telemachus figures, including works by Virgil, Ovid, Dante, Shakespeare, Racine, Fénelon, Tennyson, Stephen Phillips, D'Annunzio, and Hauptmann, as well as secondary material such as Bérard's books and Samuel Butler's *The Authoress of the Odyssey.* At the end of July, 1917, he talked with his friend Georges Borach in Zurich about the *Odyssey* in a way which suggests how present to him Homer's hero was:

"The most beautiful, all-embracing theme," he told Borach, whose German notes Joseph Prescott has translated,

is that of the Odyssey. It is greater, more human than that of Hamlet, Don Quixote, Dante, Faust. The rejuvenation of old Faust has an unpleasant effect upon me. Dante tires one quickly; it is as if one were to look at the sun. The most beautiful, most human traits are contained in the Odyssey. . . . Now *in mezzo del cammin* I find the subject of Ulysses the most human in world literature. Ulysses didn't want to go off to Troy; he knew that the official reason for the war, the dissemination of the culture of Hellas, was only a pretext for the Greek merchants, who were seeking new markets. When the recruiting officers arrived he happened to be plowing. He pretended to be mad. Then they placed his little two-year-old son in the furrow. Observe the beauty of the motifs: the only man in Hellas who is against the war, and the father. Before Troy the heroes shed their life-blood in vain. They want to raise the siege. Ulysses opposes the idea. The stratagem of the wooden horse. After Troy there is no further talk of Achilles, Menelaus, Agamemnon. Only one man is not done with; his heroic career has hardly begun: Ulysses.

To Frank Budgen, Joyce commented that Ulysses was the only complete, all-round character in literature: he "is son to Laertes, . . . father to Telemachus, husband to Penelope, lover of Calypso, companion in arms of the Greek warriors around Troy and King of Ithaca." When Budgen asked what he meant by a complete man, he said he meant a good man as well as one known from all sides. By good, he explained to Paul Suter, another friend, he did not mean saintlike, *gut*, but *gutmütig*, goodnatured or decent. "If he does something mean or ignoble," Joyce said, "he knows it, and says, 'I have been a perfect pig.' "

These remarks suggest that Joyce was primarily interested in the resemblance between Ulysses and Bloom rather than in the difference. Certainly he endows Bloom with great good will toward human beings and toward animals. Bloom starts off the day by feeding his cat, then some seagulls, and in the Circe episode feeds a dog. He remembers his dead son and dead father; he is also concerned about his living daughter. And he never forgets his wife for a moment. He contributes very generously, beyond his means, to the fund for the children of his friend Dignam who has just died. He helps a blind man cross a street. When he begins to see Stephen Dedalus as a kind of son, he follows him, tries to stop his drinking, prevents his being robbed, risks arrest to defend him from the police, feeds him, and takes him home in what Joyce calls, half humorously, "orthodox Samaritan fashion."

Another aspect of Bloom's character Joyce borrowed as much from Dante as from Homer. In Dante Ulysses makes a voyage which Homer does not mention, a voyage which expresses his lust for knowledge. In the wonderful twenty-sixth canto of *The Inferno*, Ulysses says: "Neither fondness for my son, nor reverence for my aged father, nor the due love that should have cheered Penelope, could conquer in me the ardor that I had to gain experience of the world, and of human vice and worth." This longing for experience, for the whole of life, is like that of Stephen crying at the end of the *Portrait*, "Welcome, O Life," but Bloom is able to cover even more of life and the world in his thoughts than Stephen is. He does so, too, without the element of ruthlessness that Dante criticizes in Ulysses, which is also prominent in the Stephen of the *Portrait*.

Critics have sometimes found the relationship of Bloom and Ulysses to be more tenuous than I have suggested; and Ezra Pound, for example, insists that the purpose of using the *Odyssey* is merely structural, to give solidity to a relatively plotless work. This view does not seem just. For Joyce the counterpoint was important because it revealed something about Bloom, about Homer, and about existence. For Bloom *is* Ulysses in an important sense. He is by no means a Babbitt. Our contemporary notion of the average man, *l'homme moyen sensuel*, is a notion conditioned by Sinclair Lewis and not by Joyce. I may add that it is not a notion which is congenial in Ireland. Irishmen are gifted with more eccentricities than Americans and Englishmen. To be average in Ireland is to be eccentric. Joyce knew this, and moreover he believed that every human soul was unique. Bloom is unusual in his tastes in food, in his sexual conduct, in most of his interests. A critic has complained that Bloom has no normal tastes, but Joyce would undoubtedly reply that no one has. The range of Bloom's peculiarities is not greater than that of other men.

At the same time, Bloom maintains his rare individuality. His responses to experience are like other people's, but they are wider and cleverer. Like Ulysses, though without his acknowledged fame, he is a worthy man. Joyce does not exalt him, but he makes him special. Aldous Huxley says that Joyce used to insist upon a "medieval" etymology for the Greek form of Ulysses' name, *Odysseus;* he said it was a combination of *Outis*—nobody, and *Zeus*— God. The etymology is merely fanciful, but it is a controlled fancy which helps to reinforce Joyce's picture of the modern Ulysses. For Bloom is a nobody—an advertisement canvasser who, apart from his family, has virtually no effect upon the life around him—yet there is God in him. (Babbitt would be simply a nobody.) By God Joyce does not intend Christianity; although Bloom has been generously baptized into both the Protestant church and the Catholic church, he is obviously not a Christian. Nor is he concerned with the conception of a personal god. The divine part of Bloom is, simply, his humanity—his assumption of a bond between himself and other created beings. What Gabriel Conroy has to learn so painfully at the end of "The Dead," that we all—dead and living—belong to the same community, is accepted by Bloom from the start, and painlessly. The very name "Bloom" is chosen to support this view of Bloom's double nature. Bloom is, like Wallace Stevens' Rosenbloom, an ordinary Jewish name, but the name also means flower, and Bloom rises from the earth with the same spontaneity and naturalness that a flower does. Lenehan in the book comments about him, "He's a cultured allroundman, Bloom is, . . . He's not one of your common or garden, . . ." He exceeds other men not by transcending their interests but by being more deeply and widely human than they are. He achieves this state in part by not belonging in a narrow sense, by ignoring the limits of national life; he is not so much an Irishman as a man.

If we accept Bloom as a modern personification of the Ulyssean spirit, and not as a parody of Ulysses, we can better appreciate what the relation is between *Ulysses* and the *Odyssey*. Or rather, what the relations are, for there are two. One is comic and mock-heroic; in the Cyclops episode, as Stuart Gilbert notices, there is a parallel between the sharp, hot spear that Ulysses uses to blind the Cyclops, and the hot cigar that Bloom keeps brandishing in front of the citizen. And there are many more of these parallels. For example, in the *Odyssey* a stratagem of Ulysses is the invention of the Trojan horse; in Joyce's book Bloom gives an involuntary and unconscious tip about the prospects of a dark horse in the races. In the Homeric legend, too, Ulysses steals the statue of Pallas Athena, and in Joyce's book Bloom goes to take an erotic, profane look at the statues of the goddesses in the National Museum. The many humorous cross-references of this kind have lent support to the idea that *Ulysses* is a great joke on Homer; but jokes are not necessarily so simple, and these have a double aim. The first is the mock-heroic, the mighty spear juxtaposed with the two-penny cigar. The second, a more subtle one, is what might be called the ennoblement of the mock-heroic. This demonstrates that the world of cigars is devoid of heroism only to those who don't understand that Ulysses' spear was merely a sharpened stick, as homely an instrument in its way, and that Bloom can demonstrate the finer qualities of man by word of mouth as effectively as Ulysses by thrust of spear.

Joyce's version of the epic story is a pacifist version. He developed an aspect of the Greek epic which Homer had emphasized less exclusively, namely, that Ulysses was the only good *mind* among the Greek warriors. The brawny men, Achilles and Ajax and the rest, relied on their physical strength, while Ulysses was brighter, a man never at a loss. But of course Homer represents Ulysses as a good warrior too. Joyce makes his modern Ulysses a man who is not physically a fighter, but whose mind is unvanquishable. The victories of Bloom are won in the spirit, not the body. This is not a Homeric concept, except in embryo; it is compatible with Christianity, but it is not Christian either, for Bloom is a member of a secular world. It is post-Christian. Homer's Ulysses has been spiritualized, but he retains the primary qualities of prudence, intelligence, sensitivity, and good will. Consequently, Joyce, as we would expect, found the murder of the suitors at the end of the book to be too bloody, so he has Bloom defeat Boylan in Molly Bloom's mind by being the first and the last in her thoughts as she falls off to sleep. In the same way, in the play "Exiles" Richard Rowan defeats Robert Hand in Bertha's mind.

The ultimate proof of Joyce's sympathy with Bloom, and of Bloom's possessing a *Zeus*-quality as well as an *outis*-quality, is Bloom's interior monolog. Joyce's use of the monolog has not been fully understood. V. S. Pritchett accuses him of fathering innumerable dull monologs by other writers, but the imitators never succeed in imitating the one quality which is all-important, the poetic quality. It must be said that Joyce rarely allows Bloom to talk the

way he thinks and usually prefers to caricature his conversation, as in this passage from the Eumaeus episode:

> I'm as good an Irishman as that rude person I told you
> about at the outset and I want to see everyone, all creeds
> and classes pro rata having a comfortable tidy-sized income,
> in no niggard fashion either, something in the neighbour-
> hood of £300 per annum. That's the vital issue at stake and
> it's feasible and would be provocative of friendlier inter-
> course between man and man. At least that's my idea for
> what it's worth.

But when Bloom thinks, he uses phrases of extraordinary intensity. In the first chapter in which he appears his
mind wanders to thoughts of the East; he imagines himself
walking by mosques and bazaars, and says to himself, "A
mother watches from her doorway. She calls her children
home in their dark language." Passing Larry O'Rourke's
public house, he says, "There he is, sure enough, my bold
Larry, leaning against the sugarbin in his shirtsleeves watching the aproned curate swab up with mop and bucket."
Or, when he considers the cattlemarket where he once
worked, he says to himself, "Those mornings in the cattlemarket the beasts lowing in their pens, branded sheep,
flop and fall of dung, the breeders in hobnailed boots
trudging through the litter, slapping a palm on a ripe-
meated hindquarter, there's a prime one, unpeeled switches
in their hands." Or when he thinks of modern Palestine:

> A barren land, bare waste. Volcanic lake, the dead sea: no
> fish, weedless, sunk deep in the earth. No wind could lift
> those waves, grey metal, poisonous foggy water. Brimstone
> they called it raining down: the cities of the plain: Sodom,
> Gomorrah, Edom. All dead names. A dead sea in a dead
> land, grey and old. Old now. It bore the oldest, the first
> race. A bent hag crossed from Cassidy's clutching a naggin

bottle by the neck. The oldest people. Wandered far away over all the earth, captivity to captivity, multiplying, dying, being born everywhere.

It might be supposed that this is Joyce talking for Bloom, and not Bloom's way of thinking at all, that just as even the lackeys in Shakespeare speak like poets, so does everyone in Joyce. But this is not so. Stephen and Molly, it is true, have their own particular forms of eloquence, although Molly's is limited in scope and Stephen's is hyperconscious; Bloom's surpasses theirs. But there are other examples of interior monolog in *Ulysses* which show none of this disparity between conversation and inward thought. In the Wandering Rocks episode, Father Conmee is on his way to the Artane orphanage to arrange to have one of Dignam's children admitted there, and Joyce writes:

> The Superior, the Very Reverend John Conmee S. J. reset his smooth watch in his interior pocket as he came down the presbytery steps. Five to three. Just nice time to walk to Artane. What was that boy's name? Dignam, yes. *Vere dignum et iustum est.* Brother Swan was the person to see. Mr Cunningham's letter. Yes. Oblige him, if possible. Good practical catholic: useful at mission time.

And here is another example, of the Dignam boy himself:

> Master Dignam walked along Nassau street, shifted the porksteaks to his other hand. His collar sprang up again and he tugged it down. The blooming stud was too small for the buttonhole of the shirt, blooming end to it. He met schoolboys with satchels. I'm not going tomorrow either, stay away till Monday. He met other schoolboys. Do they notice I'm in mourning? Uncle Barney said he'd get it into the paper tonight. Then they'll all see it in the paper and read my name printed and pa's name.

These examples confirm that Bloom differs from lesser Dubliners in that his internal poetry is continual, even in the most unpromising situations. It is one of the primary indications of the value Joyce attaches to him.

The theme of *Ulysses* is simple, and Joyce achieves it through the characters of Bloom and to a lesser extent of Stephen and Molly. It is the triumph of kindness and decency over cruelty and brutality. In the first episode at the Martello tower, it is Mulligan who is brutal, who has said of Stephen, "It's only Dedalus whose mother is beastly dead," who torments him by referring to his mother and by keeping the uncongenial Haines as a guest in the tower. Later in the day Mulligan reveals his cruelty once more by leaving Stephen in the lurch, and Lynch does the same. As Stephen is opposed to Mulligan, Bloom is opposed to Boylan, the embodiment of merely animal sensuality, but his kindness and decency emerge throughout the book. When he goes to dine at the Burton, he finds the men there slurping up their food like animals, and decides to go elsewhere. In the Cyclops episode he defends love, which he defines, meekly but deftly, as "the opposite of hatred," against force, hatred, anti-Semitism, chauvinism. In the Oxen of the Sun episode Bloom alone tries to keep the medical students from profaning birth, conception, and death while Mrs. Purefoy is undergoing her dreadful three-day labor. In the Circe episode, Stephen and Bloom are saved from becoming brutes by their filial and paternal devotion. Finally, in the Penelope episode, Molly ends the day by yielding once more to her husband and forgetting Boylan. Sensitivity and decency triumph over force and brutality. Joyce is one of the last secular writers to use the word "soul," and in his work the soul carries off the victory.

VISION AND DISCOVERY IN E. M. FORSTER'S
A PASSAGE TO INDIA

FORSTER, 1924

by Richard M. Kain

On the shelf of twentieth-century fiction stand those literary mastodons, the encyclopedic novels of Thomas Mann, Marcel Proust, and James Joyce, in which modern civilization is exhaustively evoked and analyzed. Beside them the seemingly slight *A Passage to India* has unobtrusively taken its place. F. R. Leavis, a critic certainly not given to superlatives, has termed it "a classic: not only a most significant document of our age, but a truly memorable work of literature."

The action itself is simple enough, merely an episode in the complex of Anglo-Indian suspicion and prejudice. One readily recalls the trial of the Mohammedan doctor, Aziz, for a presumed attack upon a young Englishwoman, Adela Quested. Adela had come to India anticipating marriage to a British civil servant, Ronny Heaslop. Though the factions reach a feverish height at the time of the trial, the novel maintains the tone of the comedy of manners, the author frequently intruding genial and whimsical remarks in the style of Meredith or Trollope. Yet above this comic level rise notes of poetry and prophecy.

It is easy to miss the higher reaches of E. M. Forster's vision, or to feel uncomfortable in the presence of a humorist who unexpectedly tumbles one into a state of mystic contemplation, and just as unpredictably bounces him back to the absurdities of reality. In his engaging lectures on fiction (*Aspects of the Novel*) E. M. Forster has warned that the prophetic note demands suspension of the sense of humor, for "one cannot help laughing at a prophet." But reality itself is absurd when viewed under the aspect of eternity. And what if one may laugh *with* the prophet instead of *at* him?

Of traditional English humor, examples readily spring to mind. There is Chaucerian whimsicality in Forster's observation that as dawn breaks "the stationmaster's hens began to dream of kites instead of owls." The comedy of humors is well exemplified by the conduct of the natives in the presence of their foreign rulers, the eternal comic situation of the servant outwitting his social superior, as when the kitchen staff shouted that dinner was ready, meaning merely that they wished it were ready. This comedy of situation takes a metaphysical twist when the novelist's remarks about tipping reach beyond the area of social relationships:

> One can tip too much as well as too little, indeed the coin that buys the exact truth has not yet been minted.

There is the more blatant satire of the English at the club who felt "strengthened to resist another day" when hearing the national anthem, with its "meagre tune" and its "curt series of demands on Jehovah."

But the author's humor can go deeper than this and

become disquieting to the serious-minded. At the climax of the fantastic religious carnival, the celebrants break forth into foolery, Forster tells us, for their faith does not preclude humor:

> All laughed exultantly at discovering that the divine sense of humour coincided with their own. "God is love!" There is fun in heaven. God can play practical jokes upon Himself.

Since both matter and spirit share in the divine plan, "if practical jokes are banned, the circle is incomplete." Forster, who prefers the humane skepticism of Montaigne to the iron dogma of a Moses or St. Paul, has asserted that "I do not believe in Belief." His claims for tolerance and sympathy may have even fewer advocates now than in 1939 when he contributed an essay to the symposium *What I Believe*. We are in an age of iron and not one of irony, unfortunate as the fact may be.

Forster's attitude accounts for the mixture of amusement and respect with which he views, not merely Indian customs, but life itself. In his fiction there is a constant urbanity, both piquant and penetrating. The vicissitudes of his reputation have been appropriately ironical. He is a man who refuses to be pigeonholed. He has been admired for his graciousness and condemned as irresponsible, hailed as the voice of liberalism and denounced for his affiliations with the Bloomsbury intelligentsia. One might have thought that an artist should be judged by his work and not by his personal associations; yet Forster has received much of the same irrelevant and vituperative comment as that aroused by the personalities of Bloomsbury— Roger Fry, Clive Bell, Lytton Strachey, Virginia Woolf.

F. R. Leavis, one of England's most important literary

critics despite the fact that he sometimes forgets the fun in heaven, ascribes Forster's shortcomings to Bloomsbury, giving as an instance of superficiality a passage from this novel. In one of his characteristic asides to the reader, Forster has speculated on the impossibility of complete human sympathy with all suffering:

> How indeed is it possible for one human being to be sorry for all the sadness that meets him on the face of the earth, for the pain that is endured not only by men, but by animals and plants, and perhaps by the stones?

The reference to the stones is what worries Leavis, suggesting to him an intolerable facetiousness. He exclaims at "how extraordinary it is that so fine a writer should be able, in such a place, to be so little certain just how serious he is." Yet, in an excellent study of the novel, Gertrude M. White has recently noted that the very phrase which aroused this objection is integral to the thematic pattern of religious images that so enrich the novel. Far from being a lapse in taste, it is actually "one more echo in a book of echoes," related to the theme and mood as well as to the structure.

Nevertheless, one may detect a trace of condescension, or at least of dramatic irony in Forster's remarks on religion. Yet for sympathetic readers such a tone is a preservative against pompousness or pretension. With the thunder of a Leavis or a Swinnerton ringing in one's ears, it is indeed difficult to attend to the peculiar quality of Forster's art. The reader who comes armed with the heavy weapons of pedantry, puritanism, or class consciousness will surely take the lightest whimsies with the earnestness of Malvolio. Even the sympathetic may overlook the wisdom that underlies the humor. One is therefore refreshed in hearing William Plomer denominate the novelist (in a recent review of *The Hill of Devi*) as "a man with a forceful, complex, and altogether fresh comment to make about human beings."

About human beings, yes; and about the relationships of groups—Hindu, Muslim, British—in the trouble-spot of Asia. But above all, about the place of man, with his snobberies and his ideals, in a universe dramatically evoked by the primeval tropical jungle. Image of the mystery and vastness which surrounds mankind, the Indian plains, caves, hills, and desolate sky provide a cosmic background for a journey toward understanding and vision.

Throughout his career as a novelist, Forster's dominant theme has been that of the attainment of harmonious union, whether between personalities, social groups, or contrasting ideas and attitudes. Such a happy achievement was his at the university, where

> Body and spirit, reason and emotion, work and play, architecture and scenery, laughter and seriousness, life and art—these pairs which are elsewhere contrasted were there fused into one. People and books reinforced one another, intelligence joined hands with affection, speculation became a passion, and discussion was made profound by love.

So Forster wrote in the biography of his Cambridge friend, the humanist G. Lowes Dickinson. In 1912 they had visited India together, and, to complete the network of interconnections, it was Walt Whitman's rhapsodic prophecy of the union of mankind that provided Forster's title. Whitman envisaged a time when "All these separations and gaps shall be taken up and hook'd and link'd together," even that of nature and man.

The separations of man and man as well as those of

man and nature become symbolized in the opening description of Chandrapore. Situated on the Ganges (but at a spot not considered holy!) the city lies abased at the river edge, long abandoned by the shift of the imperial road, its inhabitants resembling the protozoic slime. Inland and on a higher level are the appurtenances of white domination—hospital, railway—and above them the civil station. Surmounting all is the sky of changing hues and changing seasons, the source of fertility. Beyond the sky the stars, and beyond the stars the infinity of space.

On the primary level the problem of interconnection is that of social groups, and here Forster displays such awareness that the novel has long been considered the best exposition of the Anglo-Indian situation.

Authoritative evaluation of the political and ethnic aspects has been beyond the competence of the novelist's commentators. I am no exception. It is natural that Forster be charged with exaggerating the insolence of the English. Yet, as Rose Macaulay pointed out in her pioneer book on Forster (1938), it was one of his convictions that "never in history did ill-breeding contribute so much towards the dissolution of an Empire," as he concluded his essay "Too Late" (1922).

Modern criticism has wisely emphasized the impersonality of art. E. M. Forster, in a pamphlet on anonymity (1925), concurs with T. S. Eliot's dictum that artistic success is dependent upon the transforming power of the imagination. The distinction between experience and art is well defined in Mark Schorer's essay, "Technique as Discovery." The critic, therefore, has little concern with content, in the sense of source material; "it is only when we speak of the *achieved* content, the form, the work of art as a work of art, that we speak as critics." Forster's recently published letters from India, vivid and charming as they are, reveal this immense distance between the raw material of experience and art. Indeed, the novelist found that his manuscript, begun in England, "seemed to wilt and go dead" on the actual scene, because "the gap between India remembered and India experienced was too wide." Yet by the very publication of the letters and his notes to the Everyman edition of the novel, he gives tacit assent to the value of biographical detail. To compare source and finished work is to gauge the scope of the creative process.

It is interesting to reconstruct from the notes the handling of locale. Forster seems to have chosen widely separated areas of the vast sub-continent in order to create a microcosm of India. Chandrapore's location on the Ganges is suggested by Bankipore in Bihar (eastern India, near Bengal); Fielding's house is in the south, at Aurangabad, province of Hyderabad; in the extreme north, the scenery of Kashmir is drawn upon for the description of the caves, while the festival at Mau with which the novel concludes is developed from the two places Forster visited extensively in 1921, Dewas and Chhatarpur in Central India.

His first visit in 1912 was followed by a longer stay as private secretary to the maharajah of the tiny province, Dewas Senior. The state had been divided by two brothers in the eighteenth century. Each area held scarcely 80,000, and in some places the division between the twin states ran down a village street!

To read the letters, published in 1953 as *The Hill of Devi*, is to find, at far remove, models for Aziz, for Ronny and his mother, even the mysterious collision. Dewas itself was a shabby, inefficient outpost. It was not even anti-British. The romantic scenery of the novel derives from nearby Chhatarpur. Deep in the jungle, with the spires of Hindu and Jain temples rising through the morning mist, the *"magical"* city contrasted with ugly, wretched Dewas, where so much seemed ridiculous and inept. Though he apologizes, he does admit that to him Hindu observances combined the fatuous and the philosophic. Despite the inanities of the festival, the rajah had genuinely religious and ethical impulses. How could one reconcile his admirable asceticism, his humanitarianism, and a classic ideal of balanced self-development with his mindless swaying before shrines of rubbish?

Islam was different, with its rational vision, its stark and clear architecture: *"After all the mess and profusion and confusion . . . it was like standing on a mountain."*

Yet there was something important in Dewas beyond the petty treacheries, the baffling insolence and servility, the inedible meals, and the amusing inefficiency of the idle water-pumping machinery. As a neighboring ruler expressed it, there was only one solution for anxiety. Personal worries occupy the mind, he said, "unless I can meditate on love." And upon his return to England, his former employer sent him a message "to follow his heart and his mind will see everything clear." Was the advice profound or naive? It seemed superficial, for "doors open into silliness at once," and yet, Forster wondered, to follow such an ideal—"to remember and respect and prefer the heart"— was there any better guide? In regard to the crucial political question, Forster had some misgivings as to whether *"good manners can avert a political upheaval."* He concluded, however, that, though they might come nearer to averting one in the East than anywhere else, *"it's too late."*

Throughout his stay Forster saw little of Anglo-Indian friction. He was the only European in Dewas, and his companions were without exception sympathetic to the English. Such is the transforming power of the imagination that the commonplaces of a tourist's outlook can be deepened into the prophetic insights of the novel. India provided Forster with more than this scanty source material. It became a symbol of human awareness and of the human condition. In the novel, curiosity about seeing India parallels the problem of friendship between races. Shortly these themes lead to the larger question of man's place in the universe.

Adela and Mrs. Moore arrive, eager to see the real India, much to the amusement of the provincial English at the club, who have never troubled to see anything but each other. There are a hundred Indias, we are told; in infinitely interlocking circles mankind and the scale of nature seem to be ranked:

> All invitations must proceed from heaven perhaps; perhaps it is futile for men to initiate their own unity, they do but widen the gulfs between them by the attempt.

Only in heaven, Forster continues, are the many mansions wherein difference and harmony can be reconciled. Beyond that, even the missionaries disagree:

> Consider, with all reverence, the monkeys. May there not be a mansion for the monkeys also? Old Mr. Graysford said No, but young Mr. Sorley, who was advanced, said Yes; he saw no reason why monkeys should not have their collateral share of bliss, and he had sympathetic discussions about them with his Hindu friends.

At the point of wasps, however, even he became uneasy, while to mention the bacteria within Mr. Sorley himself was "going too far," since "We must exclude someone from our gathering, or we shall be left with nothing."

Thus does Forster expand the social comedy into areas of wider and more perplexing application. Circles are constantly before our minds, those of the echoing caves, those of the sky and infinite space beyond, those of social classes. As for the most immediate, the reader shares with the English visitors their discovery of the many Indias, and with Mrs. Moore the more profound query as to whether beyond the redoubled echoes of space there is muddle or mystery. The major racial groups—Muslim, Hindu, and English—are imaged by the mosque, the temple, and the civil station, but each segment is further differentiated by classes. The missionaries, we learn, live "out beyond the slaughterhouses" and never come to the club. The important division in this novel is that based upon the degree of tolerance and sympathy possessed by members of each group. Mr. Fielding, Dr. Aziz, and Professor Godbole attain the most sympathetic attitudes in their respective groups, yet they are transcended by the intuitive insight of Mrs. Moore, who feels the presence of God in the mosque and awakens an immediate response from Dr. Aziz. She scolds her son Ronny for his lack of sympathy for the natives, and approaches Hindu reverence for life in murmuring "Pretty dear" to the long-legged yellow wasp on the cloak peg in her room. One recalls this at the time of Mr. Sorley's puzzlement over wasps in heaven, and even later when Professor Godbole's Brahman meditations turn to Mrs. Moore:

"One old Englishwoman and one little, little wasp," he thought, as he stepped out of the temple into the grey of a pouring wet morning. "It does not seem much, still it is more than I am myself."

In relation to the other characters, Mrs. Moore, through her human sympathy, takes her place at the center of a circle, segments of which might represent the major religious and racial groupings in the novel. In developing the theme of relationships Forster thus uses a radial pattern of characters. The theme itself, familiar to readers of his earlier fiction, is here given a more concretely convincing embodiment in the actualities of British India.

From the outset the reader senses a firm but not rigidly inflexible structure. The three books into which the novel is divided are denominated "Mosque," "Caves," and "Temple," terms which apply to characteristic parts of the locale, and which represent also, according to the novelist's introduction to the Everyman Library edition, the Indian seasons of cold, heat, and rain. On a further level, the three terms represent aspects of India—Muslim, Brahman, and cosmic—which Forster and his characters are to explore. In the first part the many Indias are surveyed and an attempt to connect them is projected through the excursion to the Marabar Caves; the second part is concerned with the shattering disaster in the cave and the subsequent scandal and trial; the conclusion, an epilogue, years later, deals with memories and hopes. Though union cannot take place here and now, the grounds for it are at least understood. Thus do the three parts of the story comprehend real phases of the argument. *A Passage to India* is a work of art with a true beginning, middle, and end.

Yet at no point does the reader feel that the fable has become simplified into a mere skeleton of allegory. Perhaps the major reason that Forster has succeeded so well is that his themes are so sensitively orchestrated. One is inevitably led to cite the author's discussion of rhythm in his *Aspects of the Novel*. The secret of Proust's art,

Forster explained, is that a repeated phrase never becomes a fixed tag with a single symbolic meaning, but develops as the narrative proceeds, and contributes to "the establishment of beauty and the ravishing of the reader's memory." Sometimes almost unnoticed, sometimes prominent— Forster's example is the well known musical phrase by the composer Vinteuil—the motif fulfills the true place of rhythm, "not to be there all the time like a pattern, but by its lovely waxing and waning to fill us with surprise and freshness and hope."

Here one can note the true contemporaneousness of the arts, for Proust was exploiting a technique which was simultaneously making its appearance in the work of Mann and Joyce, as well as Forster, what the novelist Philip Quarles in Huxley's *Point Counterpoint* called the "musicalization" of fiction. For music was providing a technical model to artists who wished to convey the multi-leveled nature of human consciousness and the many dimensions of reality. Yet even among the masters of the evocative image, Forster stands a peer. The themes of the caves, echoes, and circles interweave a web of meaning. Indeed, musical technique is so much a part of Forster's art that Peter Burra's emphasis on this phase won the novelist's commendation and inclusion in the Everyman edition of the novel.

More than mere method, music is integral with meaning. Peter Burra even suggested that Forster might have become a novelist only by accident, and that of his works *A Passage to India* is one "whose thought, like music's, cannot be fixed, nor its meaning defined." Critics have been tempted to diagram the novel in terms of separation, crisis, and union through Hinduism (Gertrude M. White), or as a projection of the way of works as represented by Aziz, the way of knowledge as in Fielding, and the final way of love as in Professor Godbole, with no single way completely satisfactory (Glen O. Allen). But Forster's traditional irony, the richness and complexity of his outlook, and his preference for mankind's "shy crablike sideways movement" to "the great tedious onrush known as history" (phrases from the conclusion of *Aspects of the Novel*)— these temperamental considerations should deter us from seeking any specific thesis.

One treads with caution in an area where the slightest footfall reverberates. Rarely has a harmony of setting, themes, and repeated motifs been better achieved. To recognize the associations which arise in the three or more Indias of the work is necessary, but to label them too precisely is to make of images "banners" (as Forster put it in his discussion of rhythm) and hence to deprive them of many imaginative reaches.

As an instance of Forster's art one may examine the symphonic development of the theme of nature, or of man's awareness of the perplexing vastness and impersonality of the universe. Aldous Huxley once wrote satirically of what he felt to be the inadequacies of romantic nature-worship. He entitled the essay "Wordsworth in the Tropics" and meditated ironically as to how well the transcendentalism of the milder Lake District could survive such a change of climate. Forster became a Wordsworth in the tropics, seeking in such a terrifying environment the ultimate existential answer to the problem. Graham Greene later felt a similar compulsion when he travelled to Liberia to study the starting point of civilization, and to retrace the path it had followed, perchance to discover where it has gone astray.

The note of cosmic mystery is sounded in the first words—"Except for the Marabar Caves" there is nothing extraordinary in the region. The brief opening chapter evokes more than it describes, for beneath the wide expanse of sky there stretches the prostrate earth, punctuated by the "fists and fingers" of the Marabar Hills. Here is the scene of social frictions, petty even though they involve the fate of empires, dwarfed as they are by the immense background before which they are played.

As the Mohammedan friends chant their poems, "India —a hundred Indias—whispered outside beneath the indifferent moon." Later they are specified—Hindus drumming, owls, the Punjab mail—and the moon looks down upon all, even on the English club, but especially on the intuitive Mrs. Moore, who feels "a sudden sense of unity, of kinship with the heavenly bodies," and who looks with Brahman kindliness on the wasp, a silent, sleeping ambassador from the fecund jungle outside. Social conflict and cosmic mystery become inextricably intertwined as the novel proceeds. Thus, as the attempts at sociability between the English and the Indians fail at the reception, the novelist intrudes an unexpectedly eloquent meditation:

> Some kites hovered overhead, impartial, over the kites passed the mass of a vulture, and with an impartiality exceeding all, the sky, not deeply coloured but translucent, poured light from its whole circumference. It seemed unlikely that the series stopped here. Beyond the sky must not there be something that overarches all the skies, more impartial even than they? Beyond which again. . . .

Perspective upon perspective unfolds. The native society has its circles of exclusion too—pleaders, then clients, then lower levels, "humanity grading and drifting beyond the educated vision, until no earthly invitation can embrace it." All unities are spurious—the nothingness of the night; a nationalist committee comprising Hindus, Muslims, Sikhs, Parsis, and a Jain; above all, the fateful expedition to the Marabar Caves, doomed to failure because Aziz "had challenged the spirit of the Indian earth, which tries to keep men in compartments."

Philosophy itself seems to demand limits, else the presumed order of the universe degenerates into a muddle. The Brahman Professor Godbole sings a hymn to Shri Krishna, begging him to come, but he fails to come, either in this or in any other song. In India identities are lost. No one recognizes the mysterious beast hit by an automobile; a bird cannot be named; bells of various temples jangle rather than sound in unison, and the inevitable monsoon comes to appear the only reality. Surely, as Fielding reflected, "There seemed to be no reserve of tranquillity to draw upon in India." But even this generalization becomes false in a land of false clues and hidden mysteries, for either there is no tranquillity, "or else tranquillity swallowed up everything, as it appeared to do for Professor Godbole." What sense can one make of a land which, like Godbole, "calls 'Come' through her hundred mouths, through objects ridiculous and august," but never defines what it is that one is to reach? The Hindu comes closest to explaining. The appearance of good as well as that of evil involves the whole universe:

> "Good and evil are different, as their names imply. But, in my own humble opinion, they are both of them aspects of my Lord. He is present in the one, absent in the other, and the difference between presence and absence is great, as great as my feeble mind can grasp. Yet absence implies presence, absence is not non-existence, and we are therefore entitled to repeat, 'Come, come, come, come.' "

Time has its mysteries as well as space. The Ganges itself, "though flowing from the foot of Vishnu," is not old in geological terms. The Marabar Hills present a scene of prehistoric desolation, yet as a kite again wings overhead, Forster breaks off with another suggestion of beginninglessness: "Before birds, perhaps. . . ."

Even the benevolence of Mrs. Moore quails before the terrifying reality of India. Her plight can actually be equated with that of E. M. Forster's earlier philosophy of good will and tolerance when faced with stark violence in man and nature. She begins to fear a loss of faith in the existence of God: "Outside the arch there seemed always an arch, beyond the remotest echo a silence." She is disillusioned over the pother made about marriage:

> She felt increasingly (vision or nightmare?) that, though people are important, the relations between them are not, and that in particular too much fuss has been made over marriage; centuries of carnal embracement, yet man is no nearer to understanding man.

On the expedition to the caves the sunrise was disappointingly dull, the landscape seemed to lack vitality, yet at the same time to be "infected with illusion." In such an environment, how remote is the loveliness of Grasmere! The allusion to Wordsworth was intentional, the novelist has informed a recent critic, Mr. James McConkey. The onrushing force of nihilism rises in a hysterical crescendo as the caves are approached. The train wheels emit a meaningless, monotonous rhythm. In the caves themselves there is not only a convolution of sound in the famous echo, but a labyrinth of optical reflection, until the mind reels before an intimation of chaos:

> The echo in a Marabar cave is . . . entirely devoid of distinction. Whatever is said, the same monotonous noise replies, and quivers up and down the walls until it is absorbed into the roof. "Boum" is the sound as far as the human alphabet can express it, or "bou-oum," or "ou-boum,"—utterly dull. Hope, politeness, the blowing of a nose, the squeak of a boot, all produce "boum."

And, recollecting an earlier description of the highly reflecting walls, wherein a lighted match gives birth to another flame which "rises in the depths of the rock and moves towards the surface like an imprisoned spirit," Forster concludes the passage:

> Even the striking of a match starts a little worm coiling, which is too small to complete a circle but is eternally watchful. And if several people talk at once, an overlapping howling noise begins, echoes generate echoes, and the cave is stuffed with a snake composed of small snakes, which writhe independently.

Thus are combined in one narrative symbol of the cave, many of the motifs of the novel—echo, arch, muddle—as well as those of the *Upanishads* (Glen O. Allen's essay is most helpful here). The sound suggests the mystic syllable A U M, representative of the three-fold godhead: creator, preserver, and destroyer (Brahma, Vishnu, Siva). Atman and Brahman, or Self and Not-Self, reside traditionally in a cave. The snake in a completed circle represented eternity to the Egyptians; here, uncompleted, it is "eternally watchful" instead.

No wonder that Mrs. Moore reaches a point of infinite contradictions, in which "the universe, never comprehensible to her intellect, offered no repose to her soul."

She becomes indifferent to her family, even to life itself. Her mood is eloquently rendered:

> She had come to that state where the horror of the universe and its smallness are both visible at the same time—the twilight of the double vision in which so many elderly people are involved.

Just as practical affairs assume that the world is basic, so do "heroic endeavour, and all that is known as art" assume a background of eternity. In Mrs. Moore's state of mind, "the twilight of the double vision,"

> a spiritual muddledom is set up for which no high-sounding words can be found: we can neither act nor refrain from action, we can neither ignore nor respect Infinity.

One recalls the mindless cancellation of all values in the cave: "If one had spoken vileness in that place, or quoted lofty poetry, the comment would have been the same—'ou-boum.'"

A comparable state of the soul pervades the parting of Adela and Fielding. Though they spoke cordially, "the words were followed by a curious backwash as though the universe had displaced itself," and though they lacked heroic aspirations, "wistfulness descended on them," and they saw ordinary life with something of Mrs. Moore's renunciation—"the shadow of the shadow of a dream fell over their clear-cut interests, and objects never seen again seemed messages from another world."

But Mrs. Moore's departure from India suggests the possibility that negation is not the final answer. For as the boat leaves the harbor at Bombay the hillside of Asirgarh, with its mosque and fortress, seems somehow persistent and challenging. Mrs. Moore dies on shipboard, never learning what the reader discovers as her son returns to India two years later, that she is gazing in the direction of the shrines at Mau, where the survivors reach their closest possible reconciliation. And though she closed her life with an almost petulant indifference, it was her spirit that healed the wounds of misunderstanding between Aziz and Fielding. Her goodness cannot be defined, or measured, Forster reflects as he describes the Mohammedan's gratitude:

> What did this eternal goodness of Mrs. Moore amount to? To nothing, if brought to the test of thought. She had not borne witness in his favour, nor visited him in the prison, yet she had stolen to the depths of his heart, and he always adored her.

Thus, in language reminiscent of the Beatitudes, the novelist once again suggests the profound yet seldom-heeded injunction concerning those who have not charity and are nothing. It is "kindness, more kindness" that India needs, according to Dr. Aziz, a phrase which Fielding recalls when he senses the emptiness of Adela's recantation, resting as it did on "cold justice and honesty." And here the Biblical overtones are even more apparent:

> Truth is not truth in that exacting land unless there go with it kindness and more kindness and kindness again, unless the Word that was with God also is God.

Fielding can realize Adela's shortcomings, her lack of real affection for Indians and her desire to see India rather than Indians (Aziz notes that for the British seeing India is equivalent to ruling it). But Fielding himself can become trapped by his sense of proportion; when he declares that the emotions of Aziz are disproportionate to their causes, he lays himself open to the retort: " 'Is emotion a sack of potatoes, so much the pound, to be measured out?' " Perhaps this is the answer to the much vaunted classic ethic of proportion, once shared by Forster, and expressed in this novel by Fielding's relief as he comes into contact with Mediterranean civilization on his return to England after the trial. In light of the wisdom that comes from mosque, caves, temple, is there not something "public school" in Fielding's praise of "the civilization that has escaped muddle, the spirit in a reasonable form"?

In this attitude of quiescent tolerance we sense the reality behind the natives' myth of "Esmiss Esmoor" which rises as a chant at the trial, in their deification of her character, in Professor Godbole's sense of her presence at the Temple services, and in the echo of her name in the song to Radhakrishna. Mrs. Moore expressed a liking for mysteries, and rebuked Fielding for calling India a muddle; her awareness is described in similar terms—"Perhaps life is a mystery, not a muddle." Perhaps, Fielding reflected, we may "exist not in ourselves, but in terms of each other's minds." Perhaps the English view that "There is no God but God" is merely "a religious pun, not a religious truth."

Thus do the echoes reverberate through the book, the questions unanswered, even uncomprehended by most. With unconscious irony Dr. Aziz had said that there would be no muddle on his party (to the Caves); but Aziz is "public school" in a way too, his "comparatively simple mind" confronting "Ancient Night" in discussing the caves with Professor Godbole. Fielding's mind is also too simple to get beyond the notion of the echoing of evil: "It belonged to the universe that he had missed or rejected." Only in the Hindu atmosphere at Mau is the religious pun dissipated; only there, one is tempted to add, do the echoes lead to the greater truism, "God is love!"

It is not surprising that Professor E. K. Brown has selected the theme of the echo as an example of what he calls an expanding symbol, for it embraces these queries about the universe, it is dramatized in the return to India of the English group at the end, and it even occurs in the recall of the mysterious road accident at the time of the disaster in the caves. Above all, the theme of awareness connects the political and racial theme with the religious, and it differentiates the character groups from each other and within each group. For the lack of intuition gives rise to inescapable tangles between cultures—"A pause in the wrong place, an intonation misunderstood, and a whole conversation went awry."

Delight in these thematic harmonies must not obscure appreciation of Forster's narrative gifts. His insight into character ranges from the whimsical to the satiric. One recalls his contempt for the complacent English sahib, arrogant and provincial, to whom race-relations are an unimportant side-issue to the main job of governing! On the more serious level, Dr. Aziz is Forster's triumph. Mrs. Moore's spirit almost defies successful embodiment, but Aziz is always convincing, no matter which direction his volatile personality takes. In mellow and meditative moods he turns instinctively towards poetry, especially the grandeur of the Mogul past. The joys of friendship and love are tangible to him, as is the religious experience. It is in following the reactions of Aziz that Forster displays his second great narrative gift, his command of dramatic tension.

As the doctor becomes contentious under the strain of false accusation, Forster demonstrates the corrupting effects of prejudice. There is a steadily mounting hysteria of misunderstanding. The slightest incident is misunderstood. Even petty matters such as social amenities arouse mass hatred. The narrow-minded, the "Turtons and Burtons," succumb first, but before the end even the level-headed Fielding becomes distrustful and Aziz truculent. The crisis nears. Political interests replace human sympathies. The herd-instinct, enemy of understanding, becomes awakened. The English close the gap of individual differences, prating of protecting the women and children, "that phrase that exempts the male from sanity." The native barrister is cowed. Mrs. Moore becomes disaffected, as we have seen, and Fielding, Dr. Aziz, and Professor Godbole fall into conflict with and misunderstanding of one another. At the club Fielding vainly advises moderation, only to have the mass of English opinion drive him to the breaking point of tears and rage. It is officialdom, it is snobbery, it is possessiveness—Forster's diagnosis varies, but the brutal truth remains.

The story subjects the novelist's former liberal faith to a crucial test. Virginia Woolf saw in it "signs of fatigue and disillusionment," and others have suggested that the breakdown of this faith explains Forster's long silence as a novelist. Humanity withers before the forces of bigotry just as it reaches the verge of nihilism in the caves. In view of his courage in facing the test, some of the charges made against Forster seem impertinent, particularly the one of superficiality. Reuben Brower rightly analyzes our dissatisfaction with the conclusion. His essay, in *The Fields of Light* (1951), attributes the incompleteness of the novel's resolution to the fact that Forster longs for a religious emotion which his earlier irony had undermined. Certainly it has been the experience of many readers that the Hindu ceremony has seemed undramatic and unconvincing, and the telepathic influence of Mrs. Moore far from adequate to resolve earlier tensions. Yet if no satisfactory answer is given, the questions are raised. Indeed, is any answer possible in the human quest for truth?

We may reasonably doubt the effectiveness of the contemplative virtues in facing those who are by hate and power possessed. But impatience with one who so resolutely avoids the grand gesture has lessened. The desire for comforting dogmas shows no sign of abating in these uncertain times, yet our experience with recent crusades has led to a deeper respect for the author's defense of the civilized virtues. Greater awareness of Forster's subtle handling of themes has also contributed to his reputation, and the application of textual analysis to his work has brought forth sensitive explications. Among the most useful are those of his long-time admirer E. K. Brown in his *Rhythm in the Novel* (1950), Brower's essay in *The Fields of Light* (1951), and the articles in *PMLA* by Gertrude M. White (1953) and Glen O. Allen (1955). His reputation, never in doubt, has grown steadily in the years since his rediscovery in 1943, when the reprinting of the early novels coincided with Lionel Trilling's excellent survey of his career. For the future, there seems no ground for doubt. The discerning will always return with gratitude to one who, as the *Times Literary Supplement* has recently stated, seems to delight us in an indefinable fashion:

> We fall back into the pleasing bewilderment of paying Mr. Forster the highest honours for representing we know not precisely what, for writing beautifully we cannot see precisely how, for being major in a manner so beguilingly characteristic of minor.

NOTES ON THE CONTRIBUTORS

IRVIN EHRENPREIS' latest book is *The Personality of Jonathan Swift* (1958), and he is currently working on a detailed biography of Swift. Mr. Ehrenpreis has contributed to many scholarly periodicals both in this country and abroad, writing on English literature of the eighteenth century and on recent American literature. He is the author of *The "Types Approach" to Literature* (1945), editor of Swift's *Enquiry into the Behavior of the Queen's Last Ministry* (1956), and co-editor (with Herbert Davis) of Swift's *Political Tracts 1713–1719* (1953). An associate professor of English at Indiana University, he has been awarded a Fulbright research fellowship, a Guggenheim fellowship, and a fellowship of the American Council of Learned Societies.

RICHARD ELLMANN was Briggs-Copeland assistant professor of English at Harvard from 1948–1951 and has been a professor of English at Northwestern University since that time. He has received Rockefeller, Guggenheim, and Kenyon Review fellowships. His chief publications include: *Yeats: The Man and the Masks* (1948, reissued as paperback, 1958), *The Identity of Yeats* (1954), and *James Joyce*, a biography (1959). Mr. Ellmann edited and translated the *Selected Writings* of Henri Michaux (1951) and edited Stanislaus Joyce's *My Brother's Keeper* (1958). He has contributed to *The Kenyon Critics* (1951),

The Achievement of D. H. Lawrence (1953), and English Institute *Essays* (1955). He co-edited (with Ellsworth Mason) a volume of critical writings by Joyce (1959).

LOUIS FRAIBERG, who has taught at Wayne State University, the University of Michigan, and Louisiana State University at New Orleans, specializes in the fields of psychology and literature. He has published studies of Freud and the psychology of art in such periodicals as *American Imago, American Literature, Literature and Psychology,* and *International Journal of Psychoanalysis.* His first book, *Psychoanalysis and American Literary Criticism* (1959), was published by the Wayne State University Press.

RICHARD M. KAIN, professor of English at the University of Louisville, is currently working on a lengthy study of E. M. Forster. He has published extensively on James Joyce and is the author of *Fabulous Voyager: James Joyce's "Ulysses"* (1947, paper cover edition, 1959). He edited, with Marvin Magalaner, *Joyce, the Man, the Work, the Reputation* (1956).

LEO KIRSCHBAUM, professor of English at Wayne State University, has lectured all the way from Liverpool University to Hebrew University, Jerusalem. He is the author of *The True Text of "King Lear"* (1945), *Clear Writing* (1950), *Shakespeare and the Stationers* (1955), and edited *Edmund Spenser: Selected Poetry* (1956).

R. W. B. LEWIS has taught at Bennington College, Rutgers University, and Princeton and has served as dean of the Salzburg Seminar in American Studies. He was Kenyon Fellow in Criticism in 1953 and received a grant from the National Institute of Arts and Letters. His articles and reviews have appeared in such periodicals as *The Yale Review, Furioso,* and *The Hudson Review.* Mr. Lewis' *The American Adam* was published in 1955 and *The Picaresque Saint* in 1959.

JOSEPH PRESCOTT has taught at Harvard University, Boston University, University of Alabama, Yale University, the University of Connecticut, and Wayne State University. He has served as an examiner at Oxford and lectured for the U. S. Information Service in France. He is a contributor to learned journals in various countries (America, Japan, Ireland, England, Italy, Argentina, and Australia) and to the *Encyclopaedia Britannica.* He was guest editor of a special James Joyce issue of *La Revue des Lettres Modernes* and has been honored with a Ford fellowship and a grant from the Modern Language Association.

MARK SPILKA's essay on Hemingway's *The Sun Also Rises* appeared in *Twelve Original Essays on Great American Novels.* Other studies, on such writers as Lawrence, Kafka, Fielding, and Dostoevsky have been published in various literary journals. His study of the novels of D. H. Lawrence, *The Love Ethic of D. H. Lawrence,* appeared in 1955 and has been reprinted as a paperback. Mr. Spilka wrote the introduction to the Indiana University Press edition of Dostoevsky's *The Double.* His essay on *Great Expectations* will form a chapter in the comparative study of Dickens and Kafka on which he is now working. Mr. Spilka is on the staff of the English Department of the University of Michigan.

NEWTON P. STALLKNECHT, professor of Philosophy and chairman of the Philosophy Department at Indiana University, is a fellow and director of the School of Letters. He is the author of *Studies in the Philosophy of Creation* (1934), *Strange Seas of Thought, Studies in William Wordsworth's Philosophy of Man and Nature* (1945), and many essays and reviews in philosophical and literary journals. He has collaborated with R. S. Brumbaugh on two textbooks, *The Spirit of Western Philosophy* (1950) and *The Compass of Philosophy* (1954). Mr. Stallknecht was honored with the presidency of the Metaphysical Society of America in 1955.

HARVEY SWADOS, teacher, journalist, and critic, is perhaps best known as a creative writer. His short stories, many of which have been anthologized, have appeared in such magazines as *The Antioch Review* and *New World Writing*. He is the author of three novels: *Out Went the Candle* (1955), *On the Line* (1957), and *False Coin* (1960). Mr. Swados was awarded a Sidney Hillman prize in 1959 for his article, "Myth of the Powerful Worker," which first appeared in *The Nation*.

CHARLES C. WALCUTT, professor of English at Queens College, New York, has taught at Washington and Jefferson College and the University of Oklahoma. He was director of the American Institute at the University of Oslo, Norway, during 1958 and lectured in other Scandinavian capitals. He is chairman of the Literature and Society Section of the Modern Language Association and is on the Executive Committee of the National Council of Teachers of English. His writings include a monograph on the American novelist Winston Churchill, and two books: *American Literary Naturalism* (1956) and (with Sibyl W. Terman as co-author) *Reading: Chaos and Cure* (1958). His essays have appeared in such publications as *American Literature, PMLA,* and *The Sewanee Review,* and he was the recipient of the *Arizona Quarterly* award for 1958.

GERALD WEALES has written on the theatre, the movies, and literature for many publications including *Hudson Review, American Scholar, New World Writing,* and *The Reporter.* His short stories and poetry have been featured in *Prairie Schooner, Atlantic,* and *Ellery Queen's Mystery Magazine;* and his novel for children, *Miss Grimsbee is a Witch,* was published in 1957. His forthcoming novel for adult readers is entitled *The Bluebird Caper.* His recently completed study of religious drama, *Religion in Modern English Drama,* will be published by the University of Pennsylvania Press. Mr. Weales is currently an assistant professor of English at the University of Pennsylvania, having taught at Georgia Tech, Newark College of Engineering, Brown, and Wayne State.

Manuscript edited by Barbara C. Woodward
Designed by S. R. Tenenbaum
Set in Linotype Janson and Spartan type faces
Printed on Warren's Olde Style Antique Wove
Bound in Joanna Mills Natulin
Manufactured in the United States of America